# TOEFL® MAP

# ACTUAL TEST

New TOEFL® Edition

Reading 1

DARAKWON

# TOEFL® MAP
# ACTUAL TEST

**Reading 1**

**Publisher** Chung Kyudo
**Editors** Cho Sangik, Zong Ziin
**Authors** Michael A. Putlack, Stephen Poirier, Allen C. Jacobs
**Designers** Park Narae, Chung Kyuok

First published in April 2022
By Darakwon, Inc.
Darakwon Bldg., 211, Munbal-ro, Paju-si, Gyeonggi-do 10881
Republic of Korea
Tel: 82-2-736-2031 (Ext. 250)
Fax: 82-2-732-2037

**ISBN** 978-89-277-8008-3 14740
978-89-277-8007-6 14740 (set)

**www.darakwon.co.kr**

**Photo Credits**
Shutterstock.com

**Components** Main Book / Translation Book
9 8 7 6 5 4 3      24 25 26 27 28

# TOEFL® MAP
# ACTUAL TEST

**New TOEFL® Edition**

**Reading 1**

# INTRODUCTION

Studying for the TOEFL® iBT is no easy task and is not one that is to be undertaken lightly. It requires a great deal of effort as well as dedication on the part of the student. It is our hope that, by using *TOEFL Map Actual Test Reading* as either a textbook or a study guide, the task of studying for the TOEFL® iBT will become somewhat easier for the student and less of a burden.

Students who wish to excel on the TOEFL® iBT must attain a solid grasp of the four important skills in the English language: reading, listening, speaking, and writing. The Darakwon *TOEFL Map* series covers all four of these skills in separate books. There are three different levels in all four topics. In addition, there are *TOEFL Map Actual Test* books that contain a number of actual tests that students can use to prepare themselves for the TOEFL® iBT. This book, *TOEFL Map Actual Test Reading*, covers the reading aspect of the test by providing reading passages in the TOEFL® iBT actual test format.

*TOEFL Map Actual Test Reading* has been designed for use both in a classroom setting and as a study guide for individual learners. It contains a total of seven full-length reading actual tests. Each test contains a varying number of reading passages. Every passage is the same length as those found on the TOEFL® iBT. The passages also have the same numbers and types of questions that appear on actual TOEFL® iBT reading section passages. In addition, the changes that were made to the TOEFL® iBT in August 2019 have been incorporated into this book. By studying these passages, learners should be able to prepare themselves to take and, more importantly, to excel on the TOEFL® iBT.

*TOEFL Map Actual Test Reading* has a great amount of information and should prove to be invaluable as a study guide for learners who are preparing for the TOEFL® iBT. However, while this book is comprehensive, it is up to each person to do the actual work. In order for *TOEFL Map Actual Test Reading* to be of any use, the individual learner must dedicate him or herself to studying the information found within its pages. While we have strived to make this book as user friendly and as full of crucial information as possible, ultimately, it is up to each person to make the best of the material in the book. We wish you luck in your study of both English and the TOEFL® iBT, and we hope that you are able to use *TOEFL Map Actual Test Reading* to improve your abilities in both of them.

Michael A. Putlack
Stephen Poirier
Allen C. Jacobs

# TABLE OF CONTENTS

# HOW IS THIS BOOK DIFFERENT

### CONTAINS PASSAGES MOST RECENTLY PRESENTED

- Has 24 passages in total
- Reconstructs the most frequently asked questions after analyzing real TOEFL® iBT questions
- Reflects the changes made to the TOEFL® iBT in August 2019

### CONSISTS OF VARIOUS TOPICS

- Deals with academic topics such as the humanities, sciences, and arts

### PROVIDES AN EXPLANATION FOR EVERY QUESTION

- Shows the question types and provides detailed explanations
- Presents tips for getting a higher score

### PRESENTS TRANSLATIONS OF THE READING PASSAGES

- Contains translations for all passages

### OFFERS FREE MP3 FILES

- Provides MP3 files for free at www.darakwon.co.kr
- Includes QR codes for listening to the MP3 files instantly

# HOW TO USE THIS BOOK

## QUESTION

This book contains every type of question that appears on the TOEFL® iBT. The difficulty level of the questions is the same as those on the actual TOEFL® iBT.

## EXPLANATION

Every question has its own detailed explanation, so readers can learn why some answer choices are correct while others are not.

## TRANSLATION

In case some Korean readers cannot fully understand the script, a translation section has been attached to the book. This section can help readers grasp the meanings of certain passages.

## WORD REMINDER

Words and expressions that frequently appear on the actual TOEFL® iBT are listed in this section. In addition, readers can learn key words related to specific topics.

# ABOUT THE TOEFL® iBT

## TOEFL® iBT Test Sections

| Section | Tasks | Time Limit | Questions |
|---------|-------|------------|-----------|
| **Reading** | Read 3-4 passages from academic texts and answer questions. | 54 – 72 minutes | 30 – 40 questions |
| **Listening** | Listen to lectures, classroom discussions, and conversations and then answer questions. | 41 – 57 minutes | 28 – 39 questions |
| **Break** 10 minutes | | | |
| **Speaking** | Express an opinion on a familiar topic and also speak based on reading and listening tasks. | 17 minutes | 4 tasks |
| **Writing** | Write essay responses based on reading and listening tasks and support an opinion in writing. | 50 minutes | 2 tasks |

## TOEFL® iBT Test Contents

The TOEFL® iBT test is a test given in English on an Internet-based format. The TOEFL® iBT has four sections: reading, listening, speaking, and writing. The test requires approximately three and a half hours to take.

## Combining All Four Skills: Reading, Listening, Speaking, and Writing

During the test, learners must use more than one of the four basic skills at the same time. For instance, learners may have to:

• listen to a question and then speak a response

• read and listen and then speak a response to a question

• read and listen and then write a response to a question

## What Is the TOEFL® iBT Test?

The TOEFL® iBT test measures how well learners understand university-level English. The test requires students to use a combination of their reading, listening, speaking, and writing skills to do various academic tasks.

## Which Learners Take the TOEFL® iBT Test?

Around one million people take the TOEFL® iBT test every year. The English abilities of most people taking the test are anywhere from intermediate to advanced. The following types of people most commonly take the TOEFL® iBT test:

• students who will study at institutes of higher learning

• students who wish to gain admission to English education programs

• individuals who are applying for scholarships or certificates

• learners who want to determine the level of their English ability

• students and other individuals who are applying for visas

## Who Accepts TOEFL® iBT Test Scores?

In more than 130 countries around the world, over 8,000 colleges, universities, agencies, and other institutions accept TOEFL® iBT scores. In addition, the following places utilize TOEFL® iBT scores:

• immigration departments that use the scores when issuing visas

• medical and licensing agencies that award various certificates

• individuals who are trying to determine the level of their English ability

# ABOUT THE READING QUESTION TYPES

## Type 1  Vocabulary Questions

Vocabulary questions require the test taker to understand specific words or phrases that are used in the passage. These questions ask the test taker to choose another word or phrase that is the most similar in meaning to the highlighted text. The vocabulary words that are highlighted are often important words, so knowing their meanings is often critical for understanding the entire passage. The highlighted words typically have several meanings, so test takers need to be careful to avoid selecting an answer choice simply because it is the word's or phrase's most common meaning.

## Type 2  Reference Questions

Reference questions require the test taker to understand the relationship between words and their referents in the passage. These questions most frequently ask the test taker to identify the antecedent of a pronoun. In many cases, the pronouns are words like *he*, *she*, or *they* or *its*, *his*, *hers*, or *theirs*. However, in other cases, relative pronouns like *which* or demonstrative pronouns like *this* or *that* may be asked about instead. This type of question seldom appears on the test anymore.

## Type 3  Factual Information Questions

Factual Information questions require the test taker to understand and to be able to recognize facts that are mentioned in the passage. These questions may cover any facts or information that is explicitly covered in the passage. These may appear in the form of details, definitions, explanations, or other kinds of data. The facts which the questions ask about are typically found only in one part of the passage—perhaps in a sentence or two—and do not require a comprehensive understanding of the passage as a whole.

## Type 4  Negative Factual Information Questions

Negative Factual Information questions require the test taker to understand and to be able to recognize facts that are mentioned in the passage. These questions may be about any facts or information that is explicitly covered in the passage. However, these questions ask the test taker to identify the incorrect information in the answer choices. Three of the four answer choices will therefore have correct information that can be found in the passage. The answer the test taker must choose will either have incorrect information or information that is not found in the passage.

## Type 5    Sentence Simplification Questions

Sentence Simplification questions require the test taker to select a sentence that best restates one that has been highlighted in the passage. These questions ask the test taker to note the main points in the sentence and to make sure that they are mentioned in the rewritten sentence. These sentences use words, phrases, and grammar that are different from the highlighted sentence. They also sometimes do not appear in a passage. When they are asked, there is only one Sentence Simplification question per passage.

## Type 6    Inference Questions

Inference questions require the test taker to understand the argument that the passage is attempting to make. These questions ask the test taker to consider the information that is presented and then to come to a logical conclusion about it. The answers to these questions are never explicitly stated in the passage. Instead, the test taker is asked to infer what the author means. These questions often deal with cause and effect or comparisons between two different things, ideas, events, or people.

## Type 7    Rhetorical Purpose Questions

Rhetorical Purpose questions require the test taker to understand why the author mentioned or wrote about something in the passage. These questions ask the test taker to consider the reasoning behind the information that is being presented in the passage. For these questions, the function—not the meaning—of the material is the most important aspect to be aware of. The questions often focus on the relationship between the information mentioned or covered either in paragraphs or individual sentences in the passage and the purpose or intention of the information that is given.

## Type 8   Insert Text Questions

Insert Text questions require the test taker to determine where in the passage another sentence should be placed. These questions ask the test taker to consider various aspects, including grammar, logic, connecting words, and flow, when deciding where the new sentence best belongs. Recently, there is almost always one Insert Text question per passage. This question always appears just before the last question.

## Type 9   Prose Summary Questions

Prose Summary questions require the test taker to understand the main point of the passage and then to select sentences which emphasize the main point. These questions present a sentence which is essentially a thesis statement for the entire passage. The sentence synthesizes the main points of the passage. The test taker must then choose three out of six sentences which most closely describe points mentioned in the introductory sentence. This means that three of the choices are minor points, have incorrect information, or contain information that does not appear in the passage, so they are all therefore incorrect. These are always the last question asked about a Reading passage. Recently, they appear on the test very frequently.

## Type 10   Fill in a Table Questions

Fill in a Table questions require the test taker to have a comprehensive understanding of the entire passage. These questions typically break the passage down into two—or sometimes three—main points or themes. The test taker must then read a number of sentences or phrases and determine which of the points or themes the sentences or phrases refer to. These questions often ask the test taker to consider cause and effect, to compare and contrast, or to understand various theories or ideas covered. These are always the last question asked about a Reading passage, but they have become less common recently.

# TOEFL® MAP
## ACTUAL TEST
### TEST Reading 1

01

# Reading Section Directions

This section measures your ability to understand academic passages in English. You will have **54 minutes** to read and answer questions about **3 passages**. A clock at the top of the screen will show you how much time is remaining.

Most questions are worth 1 point but the last question for each passage is worth more than 1 point. The directions for the last question indicate how many points you may receive.

Some passages include a word or phrase that is <u>underlined</u> in blue. Click on the word or phrase to see a definition or an explanation.

When you want to move to the next question, click on **Next**. You may skip questions and go back to them later. If you want to return to previous questions, click on **Back**. You can click on **Review** at any time, and the review screen will show you which questions you have answered and which you have not answered. From this review screen, you may go directly to any question you have already seen in the Reading section.

Click on **Continue** to go on.

ACTUAL TEST **01**

# The Evolution of the Whale

An ancient whale skeleton found in Wadi Hitan, Egypt

The whale is the world's largest animal and is well suited to its underwater environment, yet there is evidence it was not originally a water creature but instead evolved from a land species approximately fifty million years ago. This comes from fossils paleontologists have uncovered in places such as Egypt and Pakistan, which were previously underwater. A close examination of these fossils has proven that an ancient species of whales once had both legs and numerous similarities to the modern-day hippopotamus. As a result, scientists today accept that a hippopotamus-like creature moved into the ocean around fifty million years ago and, over the course of millions of years, evolved into the modern whale.

The notion that whales evolved from land animals was regarded as ludicrous ever since Charles Darwin proposed his theory of evolution in the mid-1800s. Although Darwin himself believed whales had evolved in some manner, he could not prove it. In fact, no evidence came to light until the late twentieth century. In the 1980s, American paleontologists working in Pakistan and Egypt found some fossils of whales with legs. They unearthed these fossils on ancient sea beds. Previously in the past, the area that is Pakistan and Egypt today was covered by a body of water called the Tethys Ocean. The ocean encompassed much of the Middle East as well as the Mediterranean Sea. Paleontologists digging in Egypt unearthed more than 1,000 whale fossils in Wadi Hitan. It was there in 1989 that they discovered an ancient species of whale with rear legs, ankles, feet, and toes.

The discovery of legs on a whale led the investigating paleontologists to assume that whales had once walked on land. The particular species that was discovered, however, had never done that. They concluded that its legs were too small and weak to have enabled it to have walked.

Additionally, some other features found on the fossils led the paleontologists to believe that the whale had only lived in the water. After their discovery, the team began searching the fossil record for an ancestor of that whale with feet—an animal that had once lived on land but had eventually moved to the sea. Interestingly, years earlier in the 1950s, some scientists learned that whale blood possesses similar properties to the blood of animals in the mammalian order that includes pigs, deer, camels, and hippopotamuses. Then, in the 1990s, a team of molecular biologists determined that the whale's closest living relative is the hippopotamus. Finally, in 2000, some paleontologists noticed that the ankle bones of the fossilized whale were practically identical to those of animals in the family of mammals which hippopotamuses belong to.

Nevertheless, experts remain uncertain as to which species was the whale's original ancestor. Thus far, the oldest whale-like fossils found date back fifty million years, so any ancestors of the modern whale must have lived and evolved after that time. Some scientists theorize that a hippopotamus-like ancestor of the whale dwelled in the shallow coastal waters of the Tethys Ocean. There, it found abundant food sources and protection from land predators. Gradually, it started staying in the water more often than on land. Its body shape likely changed to help it adapt to aquatic life. For instance, its nostrils moved back toward the top of its head and became a blowhole while its legs gradually evolved into webbed fins, and its tail transformed into a fluke. This new species might have occasionally returned to land to drink fresh water or to mate and bear young, but after a few more million years, it came to live in the water permanently.

The final stage of evolution most likely took place around thirty-five million years ago when the Earth was enduring a period of global cooling. Colder waters drove more nutrients from deep beneath the ocean up to the surface, which provided whales with a food-rich environment that made living in the ocean more appealing than living on land. The evolution of the whale into an ocean-dwelling mammal was therefore complete. Today, the whale is regarded as a perfect example of Charles Darwin's theory of evolution at work: A creature adapted itself to a new environment and, over time, came to thrive there.

---

**Glossary**

**paleontologist:** a scientist who studies organisms that lived in previous geological time periods

**fluke:** one of the two halves of the triangular tail of a whale

1   According to paragraph 1, which of the following is true of whales?

   Ⓐ They evolved from the hippopotamus and later moved into the water.

   Ⓑ They can be found living in places near both Egypt and Pakistan.

   Ⓒ Their ancestors are believed to have once walked and lived on land.

   Ⓓ It took them more than fifty million years to evolve into their present forms.

**The Evolution of the Whale**

¹➔ The whale is the world's largest animal and is well suited to its underwater environment, yet there is evidence it was not originally a water creature but instead evolved from a land species approximately fifty million years ago. This comes from fossils paleontologists have uncovered in places such as Egypt and Pakistan, which were previously underwater. A close examination of these fossils has proven that an ancient species of whales once had both legs and numerous similarities to the modern-day hippopotamus. As a result, scientists today accept that a hippopotamus-like creature moved into the ocean around fifty million years ago and, over the course of millions of years, evolved into the modern whale.

---

**Glossary** ⊖

**paleontologist:** a scientist who studies organisms that lived in previous geological time periods

**2** In stating that no evidence came to light, the author means that no evidence

Ⓐ disappeared

Ⓑ became important

Ⓒ got analyzed

Ⓓ was discovered

**3** Why does the author mention the Tethys Ocean?

Ⓐ To emphasize that its prior existence helps explain the theory of evolution

Ⓑ To explain the presence of whale fossils in areas which are currently land

Ⓒ To point out how the surface of the Earth has changed over time

Ⓓ To note that whales were the dominant creatures that used to live there

**4** According to paragraph 2, what did paleontologists digging in Egypt do?

Ⓐ They proved that the Tethys Ocean had once existed there.

Ⓑ They found a large number of fossils of whales buried there.

Ⓒ They discovered a fossil of a whale that resembled a hippopotamus.

Ⓓ They observed some whales still living that had fins resembling legs.

² ➔ The notion that whales evolved from land animals was regarded as ludicrous ever since Charles Darwin proposed his theory of evolution in the mid-1800s. Although Darwin himself believed whales had evolved in some manner, he could not prove it. In fact, no evidence came to light until the late twentieth century. In the 1980s, American paleontologists working in Pakistan and Egypt found some fossils of whales with legs. They unearthed these fossils on ancient sea beds. Previously in the past, the area that is Pakistan and Egypt today was covered by a body of water called the Tethys Ocean. The ocean encompassed much of the Middle East as well as the Mediterranean Sea. Paleontologists digging in Egypt unearthed more than 1,000 whale fossils in Wadi Hitan. It was there in 1989 that they discovered an ancient species of whale with rear legs, ankles, feet, and toes.

**5** According to paragraph 3, which of the following is NOT true of whales?

   Ⓐ They have ankle bones that are like those of some land-dwelling animals.

   Ⓑ Their blood has properties that are similar to those of blood in camels and deer.

   Ⓒ The animal to which they are the most closely related is the hippopotamus.

   Ⓓ Some of their ancestors had feet and once walked and lived on land.

**6** Which of the following can be inferred from paragraph 3 about whales?

   Ⓐ They are studied by scientists in a wide range of fields.

   Ⓑ They may evolve to walk on land sometime in the future.

   Ⓒ They share a physical resemblance to pigs and deer.

   Ⓓ They are only slightly larger than most hippopotamuses.

[3] ➙ The discovery of legs on a whale led the investigating paleontologists to assume that whales had once walked on land. The particular species that was discovered, however, had never done that. They concluded that its legs were too small and weak to have enabled it to have walked. Additionally, some other features found on the fossils led the paleontologists to believe that the whale had only lived in the water. After their discovery, the team began searching the fossil record for an ancestor of that whale with feet— an animal that had once lived on land but had eventually moved to the sea. Interestingly, years earlier in the 1950s, some scientists learned that whale blood possesses similar properties to the blood of animals in the mammalian order that includes pigs, deer, camels, and hippopotamuses. Then, in the 1990s, a team of molecular biologists determined that the whale's closest living relative is the hippopotamus. Finally, in 2000, some paleontologists noticed that the ankle bones of the fossilized whale were practically identical to those of animals in the family of mammals which hippopotamuses belong to.

**7**  The word abundant in the passage is closest in meaning to

Ⓐ appropriate

Ⓑ nutritious

Ⓒ ample

Ⓓ nearby

**8**  Which of the sentences below best expresses the essential information in the highlighted sentence in the passage? *Incorrect* answer choices change the meaning in important ways or leave out essential information.

ⒶEnvironmental changes that moved nutrients closer to the surface provided so much food for whales that there was no need for them to live on land.

ⒷWhen whales were moving into the water, cooler temperatures in the oceans often brought many nutrients closer to the surface where they lived.

ⒸOne appeal of living in the water was that the oceans were full of nutrients that helped the whales grow to become extremely large in size.

ⒹMost nutrients in the ocean are found deep beneath the surface, but cold water can force these nutrients to move closer to the water's surface.

---

**Glossary**                                          ⊖

**fluke:** one of the two halves of the triangular tail of a whale

---

Nevertheless, experts remain uncertain as to which species was the whale's original ancestor. Thus far, the oldest whale-like fossils found date back fifty million years, so any ancestors of the modern whale must have lived and evolved after that time. Some scientists theorize that a hippopotamus-like ancestor of the whale dwelled in the shallow coastal waters of the Tethys Ocean. There, it found abundant food sources and protection from land predators. Gradually, it started staying in the water more often than on land. Its body shape likely changed to help it adapt to aquatic life. For instance, its nostrils moved back toward the top of its head and became a blowhole while its legs gradually evolved into webbed fins, and its tail transformed into a fluke. This new species might have occasionally returned to land to drink fresh water or to mate and bear young, but after a few more million years, it came to live in the water permanently.

The final stage of evolution most likely took place around thirty-five million years ago when the Earth was enduring a period of global cooling. Colder waters drove more nutrients from deep beneath the ocean up to the surface, which provided whales with a food-rich environment that made living in the ocean more appealing than living on land. The evolution of the whale into an ocean-dwelling mammal was therefore complete. Today, the whale is regarded as a perfect example of Charles Darwin's theory of evolution at work: A creature adapted itself to a new environment and, over time, came to thrive there.

**9** Look at the four squares [ ■ ] that indicate where the following sentence could be added to the passage.

**These animals all share some physical resemblances with one another.**

Where would the sentence best fit?

Click on a square [ ■ ] to add the sentence to the passage.

The discovery of legs on a whale led the investigating paleontologists to assume that whales had once walked on land. The particular species that was discovered, however, had never done that. They concluded that its legs were too small and weak to have enabled it to have walked. Additionally, some other features found on the fossils led the paleontologists to believe that the whale had only lived in the water. After their discovery, the team began searching the fossil record for an ancestor of that whale with feet—an animal that had once lived on land but had eventually moved to the sea. **1** Interestingly, years earlier in the 1950s, some scientists learned that whale blood possesses similar properties to the blood of animals in the mammalian order that includes pigs, deer, camels, and hippopotamuses. **2** Then, in the 1990s, a team of molecular biologists determined that the whale's closest living relative is the hippopotamus. **3** Finally, in 2000, some paleontologists noticed that the ankle bones of the fossilized whale were practically identical to those of animals in the family of mammals which hippopotamuses belong to. **4**

10  **Directions:** An introductory sentence for a brief summary of the passage is provided below. Complete the summary by selecting the THREE answer choices that express the most important ideas of the passage. Some sentences do not belong because they express ideas that are not presented in the passage or are minor ideas in the passage. **This question is worth 2 points.**

Drag your answer choices to the spaces where they belong.
To remove an answer choice, click on it. To review the passage, click on **View Text**.

**Over millions of years, whales evolved from being land-dwelling creatures to being animals that are highly adapted to living in the ocean.**

- 
- 
- 

## Answer Choices

1  The Tethys Ocean, which existed millions of years ago, was one place where the earliest ancestors of whales frequently swam.

2  The discovery of fossils of whales with legs proved that it took a very long time for whales to change their bodies.

3  Whales did not immediately adapt to living in the water but instead took millions of years to do so.

4  When whales moved into the water, many parts of their bodies changed so that living in the water became easier for them.

5  Whales have similarities to a number of creatures that live on land, including hippopotamuses, camels, and deer.

6  Thirty-five million years ago, whales were forced to live completely in the water because global cooling occurred.

TOEFL® MAP **ACTUAL TEST**

?
HELP

◀◀
BACK

▶▶
NEXT

READING

00:36:00 ⦵ HIDE TIME

ACTUAL TEST 01

# The Decline of English Piracy

In England, the heyday of piracy lasted from the sixteenth to the nineteenth centuries. This period was during the great age of sailing ships, when exploration and trade increased the number of ships on the ocean and the values of the cargoes transported. During much of the sixteenth century, English pirates were the scourges of the oceans as they seized cargoes from countless ships. This frequently brought them into conflict with others, especially the Spanish Empire, and it was even a principal cause of a war between England and Spain. However, during the middle of the seventeenth century, English piracy in European waters began declining for several reasons. While it would continue into the 1800s, English piracy was no longer the potent force it had been in the 1500s.

For centuries, the southwestern English counties of Devon and Cornwall were home to many pirate-controlled harbors. Being far from the center of power in London and often operating with the tacit consent of local authorities, the pirates mostly operated with impunity. Indeed, the kings and queens of England frequently relied upon pirate ships to act as privateering vessels in a form of legal piracy that was both a necessary and legitimate part of warfare during that age. English privateers were regularly given letters from the monarchy that legalized their actions during wartime. They were permitted to attack and take ships in the waters around England, thereby disrupting their enemies' trade routes. Several intrepid privateering captains, including Francis Drake, sailed their ships across the Atlantic Ocean all the way to the Caribbean Sea in search of Spanish treasure to plunder. Actions like these eventually resulted in nearly twenty years of war between England and Spain.

One consequence of the war was that the English navy grew in both strength and reputation. In previous centuries, the English navy had expanded during times of war but subsequently disappeared during times of peace. Yet in the sixteenth century, first under King Henry VIII and then under his daughter Elizabeth, the English navy became better established. Its defeat of the immense Spanish Armada in 1588 enhanced its reputation. Service in the navy came to be regarded as a respectable career, so by the early seventeenth century, the navy was made permanent. English monarchs later started believing that transforming pirates into privateers was no longer necessary like it had been in the past and instead started feeling that the navy alone should be responsible for fighting England's wars on the oceans. Simultaneously, many of the great pirate captains were no longer active as some had died, others had aged and retired to enjoy their wealth, and some had even joined the navy to command royal ships or entire fleets.

In its infancy, the English navy was too weak to protect English ships and coastal towns from a new threat: the Barbary Coast pirates. These ruthless seafarers had their homeport at Algiers in North Africa. During the early sixteenth century, they grew in size and scope, pushed out of the Mediterranean Sea, and sailed into the Atlantic Ocean, where they traveled as far as Western Europe and North America. The Barbary Coast pirates were different from European pirates in one major way: They enslaved the people they captured. They typically sailed in galleys, which used sails and oars and were mostly rowed by slaves. There were also slave markets in the Middle East that the pirates filled by capturing people from ships and on coastal raids. In the early seventeenth century, the pirates began boldly raiding the southwestern English coast, including the once-safe havens of English pirates. Dozens—sometimes hundreds—of men, women, and children were captured during these raids, which greatly disrupted English piracy and helped lead to its decline.

Nevertheless, English pirates did not disappear overnight, and many operated in distant waters. But the use of England as a base of operations for piracy was in steep decline by the middle of the seventeenth century. One century later, the English navy was large, powerful, and permanent, and it controlled the waters around England and in many areas far away. By the time the nineteenth century arrived, the use of sanctioned privateers in warfare had been abolished, and English piracy and privateering disappeared for good.

## Glossary

**scourge:** a bane; a person who is the cause of a great deal of punishment or torture

**privateering vessel:** a privately owned ship that has been commissioned by a government to attack enemy ships

**11** The word heyday in the passage is closest in meaning to

   Ⓐ age

   Ⓑ domination

   Ⓒ practice

   Ⓓ peak

**12** According to paragraph 1, England and Spain fought a war because

   Ⓐ the Spanish felt that English pirates constituted a threat to their global holdings

   Ⓑ English pirates were attacking and capturing large numbers of Spanish ships

   Ⓒ England often sent pirates to attack ships that were docked in Spanish harbors

   Ⓓ Spain wanted to capture the English queen in order to end English piracy

**The Decline of English Piracy**

[1] ➜ In England, the heyday of piracy lasted from the sixteenth to the nineteenth centuries. This period was during the great age of sailing ships, when exploration and trade increased the number of ships on the ocean and the values of the cargoes transported. During much of the sixteenth century, English pirates were the scourges of the oceans as they seized cargoes from countless ships. This frequently brought them into conflict with others, especially the Spanish Empire, and it was even a principal cause of a war between England and Spain. However, during the middle of the seventeenth century, English piracy in European waters began declining for several reasons. While it would continue into the 1800s, English piracy was no longer the potent force it had been in the 1500s.

---

**Glossary** ⊖

**scourge:** a bane; a person who is the cause of a great deal of punishment or torture

**13** The word plunder in the passage is closest in meaning to

Ⓐ rob

Ⓑ sink

Ⓒ assault

Ⓓ capture

For centuries, the southwestern English counties of Devon and Cornwall were home to many pirate-controlled harbors. Being far from the center of power in London and often operating with the tacit consent of local authorities, the pirates mostly operated with impunity. Indeed, the kings and queens of England frequently relied upon pirate ships to act as **privateering vessels** in a form of legal piracy that was both a necessary and legitimate part of warfare during that age. English privateers were regularly given letters from the monarchy that legalized their actions during wartime. They were permitted to attack and take ships in the waters around England, thereby disrupting their enemies' trade routes. Several intrepid privateering captains, including Francis Drake, sailed their ships across the Atlantic Ocean all the way to the Caribbean Sea in search of Spanish treasure to plunder. Actions like these eventually resulted in nearly twenty years of war between England and Spain.

**Glossary**     ⊖

**privateering vessel:** a privately owned ship that has been commissioned by a government to attack enemy ships

**14** Why does the author mention the immense Spanish Armada?

Ⓐ To explain how the English under the leadership of Francis Drake destroyed it

Ⓑ To note that its defeat improved the status of the English navy

Ⓒ To mention the year in which the English managed to gain a victory over it

Ⓓ To declare its loss the turning point in the war between England and Spain

**15** Which of the sentences below best expresses the essential information in the highlighted sentence in the passage? *Incorrect* answer choices change the meaning in important ways or leave out essential information.

Ⓐ After some time, the English navy alone became responsible for all of England's fighting forces around the world.

Ⓑ The kings and queens of England utilized pirates as both privateers and sailors in their professional navy.

Ⓒ Many pirates were drafted into the English navy at the request of England's kings and queens.

Ⓓ The rulers of England lost interest in using privateers and relied more on the navy to fight at sea for them.

One consequence of the war was that the English navy grew in both strength and reputation. In previous centuries, the English navy had expanded during times of war but subsequently disappeared during times of peace. Yet in the sixteenth century, first under King Henry VIII and then under his daughter Elizabeth, the English navy became better established. Its defeat of the immense Spanish Armada in 1588 enhanced its reputation. Service in the navy came to be regarded as a respectable career, so by the early seventeenth century, the navy was made permanent. English monarchs later started believing that transforming pirates into privateers was no longer necessary like it had been in the past and instead started feeling that the navy alone should be responsible for fighting England's wars on the oceans. Simultaneously, many of the great pirate captains were no longer active as some had died, others had aged and retired to enjoy their wealth, and some had even joined the navy to command royal ships or entire fleets.

**16** In paragraph 3, the author implies that the English navy

Ⓐ was forced to depend on pirates in order to defeat the Spanish Armada

Ⓑ was responsible for vastly increasing the wealth of England

Ⓒ was not a permanent organization prior to the sixteenth century

Ⓓ seized many pirate ships and outfitted them as navy ships

³➜ One consequence of the war was that the English navy grew in both strength and reputation. In previous centuries, the English navy had expanded during times of war but subsequently disappeared during times of peace. Yet in the sixteenth century, first under King Henry VIII and then under his daughter Elizabeth, the English navy became better established. Its defeat of the immense Spanish Armada in 1588 enhanced its reputation. Service in the navy came to be regarded as a respectable career, so by the early seventeenth century, the navy was made permanent. English monarchs later started believing that transforming pirates into privateers was no longer necessary like it had been in the past and instead started feeling that the navy alone should be responsible for fighting England's wars on the oceans. Simultaneously, many of the great pirate captains were no longer active as some had died, others had aged and retired to enjoy their wealth, and some had even joined the navy to command royal ships or entire fleets.

**17** According to paragraph 4, which of the following is NOT true of the Barbary Coast pirates?

Ⓐ They preferred to kill the people they attacked rather than capture them.

Ⓑ They operated both in the Mediterranean Sea and the Atlantic Ocean.

Ⓒ They seized slaves on their missions and then used the slaves as labor or sold them.

Ⓓ They attacked towns on the coast of England and caused problems there.

**18** According to paragraph 5, which of the following is true of English piracy during the 1800s?

Ⓐ It eventually vanished from England after undergoing many years of decline.

Ⓑ It was forcefully stopped through the actions of the powerful English navy.

Ⓒ It was occasionally permitted to exist during times when England was at war.

Ⓓ It only existed in the guise of privateers that focused on attacking foreign ships.

[4]→ In its infancy, the English navy was too weak to protect English ships and coastal towns from a new threat: the Barbary Coast pirates. These ruthless seafarers had their homeport at Algiers in North Africa. During the early sixteenth century, they grew in size and scope, pushed out of the Mediterranean Sea, and sailed into the Atlantic Ocean, where they traveled as far as Western Europe and North America. The Barbary Coast pirates were different from European pirates in one major way: They enslaved the people they captured. They typically sailed in galleys, which used sails and oars and were mostly rowed by slaves. There were also slave markets in the Middle East that the pirates filled by capturing people from ships and on coastal raids. In the early seventeenth century, the pirates began boldly raiding the southwestern English coast, including the once-safe havens of English pirates. Dozens—sometimes hundreds—of men, women, and children were captured during these raids, which greatly disrupted English piracy and helped lead to its decline.

[5]→ Nevertheless, English pirates did not disappear overnight, and many operated in distant waters. But the use of England as a base of operations for piracy was in steep decline by the middle of the seventeenth century. One century later, the English navy was large, powerful, and permanent, and it controlled the waters around England and in many areas far away. By the time the nineteenth century arrived, the use of sanctioned privateers in warfare had been abolished, and English piracy and privateering disappeared for good.

**19** Look at the four squares [ ■ ] that indicate where the following sentence could be added to the passage.

**Located both on the Atlantic Ocean and the English Channel, they provided pirate ships with easy access to open water.**

Where would the sentence best fit?

Click on a square [ ■ ] to add the sentence to the passage.

■ For centuries, the southwestern English counties of Devon and Cornwall were home to many pirate-controlled harbors. ■ Being far from the center of power in London and often operating with the tacit consent of local authorities, the pirates mostly operated with impunity. ■ Indeed, the kings and queens of England frequently relied upon pirate ships to act as **privateering vessels** in a form of legal piracy that was both a necessary and legitimate part of warfare during that age. ■ English privateers were regularly given letters from the monarchy that legalized their actions during wartime. They were permitted to attack and take ships in the waters around England, thereby disrupting their enemies' trade routes. Several intrepid privateering captains, including Francis Drake, sailed their ships across the Atlantic Ocean all the way to the Caribbean Sea in search of Spanish treasure to plunder. Actions like these eventually resulted in nearly twenty years of war between England and Spain.

| Glossary | ⊖ |
|---|---|

**privateering vessel:** a privately owned ship that has been commissioned by a government to attack enemy ships

20  **Directions:** An introductory sentence for a brief summary of the passage is provided below. Complete the summary by selecting the THREE answer choices that express the most important ideas of the passage. Some sentences do not belong because they express ideas that are not presented in the passage or are minor ideas in the passage. **This question is worth 2 points.**

> Drag your answer choices to the spaces where they belong.
> To remove an answer choice, click on it. To review the passage, click on **View Text.**

**While piracy was once permitted by the English throne, it went into gradual decline and eventually disappeared.**

- ●

- ●

- ●

### Answer Choices

1  Francis Drake was considered a pirate by many, especially the Spanish, whose ships he frequently captured and looted.

2  So many English pirates attacked Spanish ships that the Spanish eventually went to war against England.

3  English monarchs frequently made pirates into privateers, which gave them the right to attack foreign shipping.

4  The Spanish Armada attacked England in 1588, and its defeat by Francis Drake increased the prestige of the young English navy.

5  The rise of the Barbary pirates resulted in great damage to English coastal cities, which helped bring about the end of piracy.

6  The rulers of England began to focus more on building a professional navy than on employing privateers during times of war.

# Role-Playing in Child Development

Most children like to play, and playing is a key component in the learning process for virtually all of them. There are various ways in which children play, but one of the most important is role-playing. This involves a child engaging in an activity during which the individual pretends to be another person. Role-playing helps foster children's imaginations, aids in the developing of language skills, and provides opportunities for children to learn how to plan and perform actions in sequence. Additionally, when role-playing is done by a group of children, those involved engage in social interaction, which also permits them to learn about leadership, negotiation, compromise, and fairness while helping them become more emotionally developed.

Role-playing utilizes children's imaginations and can therefore assume numerous forms. Many children try imitating their parents in one common form of role-playing. For instance, boys may pretend to shave like their fathers or may perform various chores inside and outside their homes. Girls, meanwhile, often imitate their mothers in their daily tasks, particularly if they involve caring for younger siblings. Many girls enjoy playing with baby dolls and pretending that they are mothers caring for children. Other types of role-playing involve more elaborate situations. Children may imagine that they belong to a group of superheroes on an adventure. In doing so, they might dress up in costumes and assume different roles. Sometimes, children imitate real-life situations, such as when they act as if they are cowboys on the range or police officers apprehending criminals. The reenacting of stories that children read in books is also common as is performing for audiences comprised of parents, teachers, classmates, and friends.

All of these actions help children learn. Experts on child development believe that role-playing increases the connections in children's brains that let them learn. Language skills are some of the most important aspects of learning. Playing with other youths enables children to develop their oral communication skills. They become able to organize others and to give directions. Children also develop problem-solving skills when they role-play. Sometimes they must solve puzzles, work out steps that need to be taken to complete a task, and devise plans to act out an adventure or story. In order to do these activities, children may need to make costumes, gather materials, decide on colors and decorations, and put everything together in a cohesive manner. Children frequently use props when role-playing, so they come up with methods to make and utilize these items. All of these actions stimulate children's curiosity about the world and encourage them to learn as much as they can.

Another vital aspect of role-playing is that children's social skills are enhanced. When engaged in group activities, children assume different roles. Some are leaders while others are followers. At times, children will disagree, so they must learn to negotiate and compromise with one another, and they must learn to apologize when they have strong arguments or disagreements as well. Children further learn about cooperation and sharing and, hopefully, begin to understand things from other people's perspectives. Through these activities, children develop more advanced language skills when they learn what they require to accomplish certain goals. They can enhance their vocabulary, develop their sentence structure, and gradually improve other verbal skills.

One final beneficial aspect of role-playing is that it can help children deal with certain actions that may cause them emotional distress, such as the fear they face when going to school for the first time or making a visit to the doctor. If children role-play scenarios such as these beforehand, the dread that they typically experience when doing these actions in reality frequently lessens. For this reason, child development experts encourage parents to allow their children to role-play and even to take part in these activities to help their children master their fears. Parents may also find that, in doing so, the parent-child bond becomes stronger. By increasing the amount of interaction between children and parents and by making these periods of time more entertaining, both children and their parents can decrease the amount of stress in their lives. The end result is that they can both reap the benefits of role-playing.

## Glossary

**costume:** a set of clothes worn for a specific occasion; an outfit
**prop:** an object that is used in a play

21 Which of the following can be inferred from paragraph 1 about role-playing?

Ⓐ Some babies are able to role-play by using their imaginations.

Ⓑ It is something that children learn how to do by watching their parents.

Ⓒ The most effective form of it happens when children role-play together in groups.

Ⓓ Children may engage in role-playing in a wide variety of manners.

22 The word elaborate in the passage is closest in meaning to

Ⓐ pronounced

Ⓑ complicated

Ⓒ imaginative

Ⓓ extended

---

**Role-Playing in Child Development**

[1] ➜ Most children like to play, and playing is a key component in the learning process for virtually all of them. There are various ways in which children play, but one of the most important is role-playing. This involves a child engaging in an activity during which the individual pretends to be another person. Role-playing helps foster children's imaginations, aids in the developing of language skills, and provides opportunities for children to learn how to plan and perform actions in sequence. Additionally, when role-playing is done by a group of children, those involved engage in social interaction, which also permits them to learn about leadership, negotiation, compromise, and fairness while helping them become more emotionally developed.

Role-playing utilizes children's imaginations and can therefore assume numerous forms. Many children try imitating their parents in one common form of role-playing. For instance, boys may pretend to shave like their fathers or may perform various chores inside and outside their homes. Girls, meanwhile, often imitate their mothers in their daily tasks, particularly if they involve caring for younger siblings. Many girls enjoy playing with baby dolls and pretending that they are mothers caring for children. Other types of role-playing involve more elaborate situations. Children may imagine that they belong to a group of superheroes on an adventure. In doing so, they might dress up in costumes and assume different roles. Sometimes, children imitate real-life situations, such as when they act as if they are cowboys on the range or police officers apprehending criminals. The reenacting of stories that children read in books is also common as is performing for audiences comprised of parents, teachers, classmates, and friends.

---

**Glossary** ●

**costume:** a set of clothes worn for a specific occasion; an outfit

**23** The word devise in the passage is closest in meaning to

Ⓐ consider

Ⓑ create

Ⓒ approach

Ⓓ write

**24** In paragraph 3, the author's description of the puzzle-solving skills children learn by role-playing mentions which of the following?

Ⓐ They may figure out what they need to do to perform a certain activity.

Ⓑ They may organize a group of children into groups with varying responsibilities.

Ⓒ They may consult with adults to determine how to solve a particular problem.

Ⓓ They may get together with other children so that they can play together.

**25** According to paragraph 4, which of the following is NOT true of what children learn when engaged in group role-playing activities?

Ⓐ They learn how to look at things from different points of view.

Ⓑ They understand how they can become both leaders and followers.

Ⓒ They acquire a bigger vocabulary and learn to use it in sentences.

Ⓓ They think about the best ways to utilize the resources they possess.

---

³➡ All of these actions help children learn. Experts on child development believe that role-playing increases the connections in children's brains that let them learn. Language skills are some of the most important aspects of learning. Playing with other youths enables children to develop their oral communication skills. They become able to organize others and to give directions. Children also develop problem-solving skills when they role-play. Sometimes they must solve puzzles, work out steps that need to be taken to complete a task, and devise plans to act out an adventure or story. In order to do these activities, children may need to make costumes, gather materials, decide on colors and decorations, and put everything together in a cohesive manner. Children frequently use props when role-playing, so they come up with methods to make and utilize these items. All of these actions stimulate children's curiosity about the world and encourage them to learn as much as they can.

⁴➡ Another vital aspect of role-playing is that children's social skills are enhanced. When engaged in group activities, children assume different roles. Some are leaders while others are followers. At times, children will disagree, so they must learn to negotiate and compromise with one another, and they must learn to apologize when they have strong arguments or disagreements as well. Children further learn about cooperation and sharing and, hopefully, begin to understand things from other people's perspectives. Through these activities, children develop more advanced language skills when they learn what they require to accomplish certain goals. They can enhance their vocabulary, develop their sentence structure, and gradually improve other verbal skills.

---

**Glossary** ⊖

**prop:** an object that is used in a play

26 According to paragraph 4, how can children's language skills improve by role-playing?

Ⓐ Children are able to improve their debating skills by arguing with others.

Ⓑ Children come to learn the meanings of more words when role-playing.

Ⓒ Children develop a better awareness of grammar and how to use words properly.

Ⓓ Children improve their creativity by using language in a variety of ways.

27 Which of the sentences below best expresses the essential information in the highlighted sentence in the passage? *Incorrect* answer choices change the meaning in important ways or leave out essential information.

Ⓐ When children role-play going to school or to the doctor, they no longer have any fear of doing these two activities.

Ⓑ Role-playing can assist children in overcoming fears that might be a source of emotional pain for them.

Ⓒ By role-playing certain activities, children can understand why they are afraid of doing certain activities.

Ⓓ Children who suffer emotional distress when role-playing may not receive any benefits from doing it at all.

28 The word master in the passage is closest in meaning to

Ⓐ appeal to

Ⓑ eliminate

Ⓒ utilize

Ⓓ overcome

[4] ➡ Another vital aspect of role-playing is that children's social skills are enhanced. When engaged in group activities, children assume different roles. Some are leaders while others are followers. At times, children will disagree, so they must learn to negotiate and compromise with one another, and they must learn to apologize when they have strong arguments or disagreements as well. Children further learn about cooperation and sharing and, hopefully, begin to understand things from other people's perspectives. Through these activities, children develop more advanced language skills when they learn what they require to accomplish certain goals. They can enhance their vocabulary, develop their sentence structure, and gradually improve other verbal skills.

One final beneficial aspect of role-playing is that it can help children deal with certain actions that may cause them emotional distress, such as the fear they face when going to school for the first time or making a visit to the doctor. If children role-play scenarios such as these beforehand, the dread that they typically experience when doing these actions in reality frequently lessens. For this reason, child development experts encourage parents to allow their children to role-play and even to take part in these activities to help their children master their fears. Parents may also find that, in doing so, the parent-child bond becomes stronger. By increasing the amount of interaction between children and parents and by making these periods of time more entertaining, both children and their parents can decrease the amount of stress in their lives. The end result is that they can both reap the benefits of role-playing.

29  Look at the four squares [ ■ ] that indicate where the following sentence could be added to the passage.

**For example, this might involve pretending to do yardwork or repairing something broken in the home.**

Where would the sentence best fit?

Click on a square [ ■ ] to add the sentence to the passage.

Role-playing utilizes children's imaginations and can therefore assume numerous forms. Many children try imitating their parents in one common form of role-playing. For instance, boys may pretend to shave like their fathers or may perform various chores inside and outside their homes. **1** Girls, meanwhile, often imitate their mothers in their daily tasks, particularly if they involve caring for younger siblings. **2** Many girls enjoy playing with baby dolls and pretending that they are mothers caring for children. **3** Other types of role-playing involve more elaborate situations. **4** Children may imagine that they belong to a group of superheroes on an adventure. In doing so, they might dress up in costumes and assume different roles. Sometimes, children imitate real-life situations, such as when they act as if they are cowboys on the range or police officers apprehending criminals. The reenacting of stories that children read in books is also common as is performing for audiences comprised of parents, teachers, classmates, and friends.

| Glossary | ⊖ |
|---|---|

**costume:** a set of clothes worn for a specific occasion; an outfit

**30** **Directions:** Select the appropriate sentences from the answer choices and match them to the cause and effect of role-playing by children to which they relate. TWO of the answer choices will NOT be used. **This question is worth 3 points.**

> Drag your answer choices to the spaces where they belong.
> To remove an answer choice, click on it. To review the passage, click on **View Text.**

### Answer Choices

1. Some children are taught how to role-play by their parents.

2. Children become more interested in the world around them.

3. Children have a desire to act like their own parents.

4. Children become able to negotiate with one another.

5. Many children have incredibly vivid imaginations.

6. Children improve their performances and grades at school.

7. Some children have a variety of emotional problems.

### ROLE-PLAYING BY CHILDREN

**Cause**

- 
- 
- 

**Effect**

- 
-

# TOEFL® MAP

# ACTUAL TEST

Reading **1**

02

# Reading Section Directions

This section measures your ability to understand academic passages in English. You will have **72 minutes** to read and answer questions about **4 passages**. A clock at the top of the screen will show you how much time is remaining.

Most questions are worth 1 point but the last question for each passage is worth more than 1 point. The directions for the last question indicate how many points you may receive.

Some passages include a word or phrase that is underlined in blue. Click on the word or phrase to see a definition or an explanation.

When you want to move to the next question, click on **Next**. You may skip questions and go back to them later. If you want to return to previous questions, click on **Back**. You can click on **Review** at any time, and the review screen will show you which questions you have answered and which you have not answered. From this review screen, you may go directly to any question you have already seen in the Reading section.

Click on **Continue** to go on.

# 3D Printing in Surgery

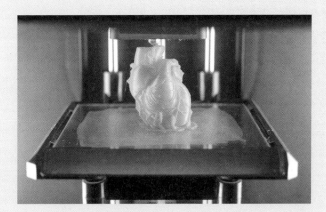

A model of a heart made by 3D printing

One of the more advanced innovations in the medical field is the utilization of 3D printing to assist with surgery. 3D printing refers to the construction of a physical object from a three-dimensional drawing. The drawing is scanned into a 3D printer, which then uses a material—usually plastic—to make very thin layers that are piled on top of one another to create a physical object. A benefit of 3D printing over traditional manufacturing processes is that it allows for greater detailed customization and complexity of physical objects. This advantage makes it an ideal tool for the medical field. Currently, 3D printing is used in the medical industry for two main purposes: to manufacture specific parts for the body and to create models that surgeons can use to assist them in upcoming surgeries.

A practical application for 3D printing in medicine is in the area of orthopedic surgery, mainly in patient-specific implants used in hip and knee replacements. Surgeons make an MRI or CAT scan of the region affected and then construct a three-dimensional drawing of the body part requiring replacement. After that, the surgical team uses a 3D printer to make the part from plastic and finally performs the surgery to insert the implant. By making a personalized part for an individual patient, surgeons can reduce surgery time and complications both during and after an operation. In the past, orthopedic surgeons utilized off-the-shelf replacement parts, and during the operation, they often had to shape the bones with crude methods to make the new part properly fit the patient. In recent years, patient-specific implants manufactured with 3D printers have also been successfully used for patients with jaw and skull fractures caused by accidents.

Another area that 3D printing is utilized in is building training models of internal organs. While every human body has the same general internal structure, there are often unique differences between patients. To reduce surgery time and to improve the chances of a successful operation, surgical teams build and train on 3D models of organs. Perhaps a patient requires liver surgery. The surgical team will conduct scans of the patient's liver and then create an accurate model of it with a 3D printer. The model will be clear and show the internal structure of the liver, including the placement of every blood vessel inside it. If there are any cancerous tumors in the liver, the 3D printer will include them in the model. Prior to the actual operation, the surgical team trains on the model of the liver, thereby ensuring that the patient has the best chance of having a successful surgery. Many medical schools are presently taking advantage of 3D printing to make models for future medical practitioners to train on.

Most 3D-printed models of organs are made of hard plastic. Currently, there is a growing demand for softer models which surgeons and medical students can use to practice actual operations. To make these softer models, a 3D printer must use silicone or hydrogel as the building material. Many surgeons and medical schools also want organ models to bleed to make practicing as realistic as possible. The softer materials have springier properties, which mimic the actual elasticity of patients' organs, and therefore give surgeons a better way to judge how deeply they should slice into an organ. To mimic the properties of human organs, model makers examine the characteristics of real organs removed from patients. As 3D-printed organ model technology advances and models become more realistic, the hope is that one day, 3D printers can be used to construct artificial organs to replace malfunctioning ones.

While 3D printing is a valuable aid in the medical field, there are some problems surrounding its use. One such issue is the cost involved. State-of-the-art 3D printers cost tens of thousands of dollars, so only the wealthiest of hospitals can afford to purchase one of them. Hospitals must also hire or train staff members to use the printer. In addition, the costs of creating 3D-printed implants as well as surgical aid models are not always covered by health insurance providers. This means neither of them is a feasible option for people who have limited access to financial resources.

## Glossary

**orthopedic surgery:** an operation that corrects a problem with the skeletal system, especially the spine, or muscles and ligaments

**hydrogel:** a gel that uses water as its primary liquid

1   In paragraph 1, all of the following questions
are answered EXCEPT:

Ⓐ When did 3D printers start being utilized
by large numbers of people in the field of
medicine?

Ⓑ Why are 3D printers considered to be of
value to people who work in the medical
industry?

Ⓒ What is the primary material that is used
by 3D printers to make various physical
objects?

Ⓓ What is the process for having a drawing
of a physical object added to a 3D
printer?

**3D Printing in Surgery**

[1] ➔ One of the more advanced innovations in
the medical field is the utilization of 3D printing
to assist with surgery. 3D printing refers to the
construction of a physical object from a three-
dimensional drawing. The drawing is scanned
into a 3D printer, which then uses a material—
usually plastic—to make very thin layers that are
piled on top of one another to create a physical
object. A benefit of 3D printing over traditional
manufacturing processes is that it allows for
greater detailed customization and complexity of
physical objects. This advantage makes it an ideal
tool for the medical field. Currently, 3D printing
is used in the medical industry for two main
purposes: to manufacture specific parts for the
body and to create models that surgeons can use
to assist them in upcoming surgeries.

**2** The word crude in the passage is closest in meaning to

Ⓐ untalented

Ⓑ advanced

Ⓒ acceptable

Ⓓ clumsy

**3** According to paragraph 2, 3D printers are used in the medical industry because

Ⓐ they are utilized exclusively for patients suffering from jaw and skull fractures

Ⓑ they can take off-the-shelf replacement parts and shape them into customized pieces

Ⓒ they are capable of creating implants based upon drawings made from medical scans

Ⓓ they eliminate all unexpected complications that arise during the surgical process

² ➜ A practical application for 3D printing in medicine is in the area of orthopedic surgery, mainly in patient-specific implants used in hip and knee replacements. Surgeons make an MRI or CAT scan of the region affected and then construct a three-dimensional drawing of the body part requiring replacement. After that, the surgical team uses a 3D printer to make the part from plastic and finally performs the surgery to insert the implant. By making a personalized part for an individual patient, surgeons can reduce surgery time and complications both during and after an operation. In the past, orthopedic surgeons utilized off-the-shelf replacement parts, and during the operation, they often had to shape the bones with crude methods to make the new part properly fit the patient. In recent years, patient-specific implants manufactured with 3D printers have also been successfully used for patients with jaw and skull fractures caused by accidents.

| Glossary | ● |
| --- | --- |

**orthopedic surgery:** an operation that corrects a problem with the skeletal system, especially the spine, or muscles and ligaments

ACTUAL TEST 02

**4** The word it in the passage refers to

Ⓐ the internal structure

Ⓑ the liver

Ⓒ the placement

Ⓓ every blood vessel

**5** According to paragraph 3, why do surgical teams use models of organs made by 3D printers?

Ⓐ The models can help surgical teams reduce the costs of the operations that they perform.

Ⓑ Surgical teams can use models as references while performing operations on patients.

Ⓒ The models can help surgeons with little experience improve their abilities to do their jobs.

Ⓓ 3D printers can create realistic models of organs which surgical teams can practice on.

³→ Another area that 3D printing is utilized in is building training models of internal organs. While every human body has the same general internal structure, there are often unique differences between patients. To reduce surgery time and to improve the chances of a successful operation, surgical teams build and train on 3D models of organs. Perhaps a patient requires liver surgery. The surgical team will conduct scans of the patient's liver and then create an accurate model of it with a 3D printer. The model will be clear and show the internal structure of the liver, including the placement of every blood vessel inside it. If there are any cancerous tumors in the liver, the 3D printer will include them in the model. Prior to the actual operation, the surgical team trains on the model of the liver, thereby ensuring that the patient has the best chance of having a successful surgery. Many medical schools are presently taking advantage of 3D printing to make models for future medical practitioners to train on.

**6** Which of the sentences below best expresses the essential information in the highlighted sentence in the passage? *Incorrect* answer choices change the meaning in important ways or leave out essential information.

Ⓐ Actual organs are springy in nature, so surgeons have to learn how much they need to cut into those organs by using the models.

Ⓑ The elastic properties of softer materials resemble real organs, and that lets doctors understand better how to conduct an operation.

Ⓒ Soft, elastic models are better than plastic ones since they can help surgeons understand what to do during a medical procedure.

Ⓓ Because surgeons need to know how much they must cut into an organ, a model organ itself must have springy qualities.

**7** In paragraph 4, the author implies that 3D printers

Ⓐ can construct organs that bleed, which lets surgeons conduct realistic practice sessions

Ⓑ have been specially designed to manufacture organs that are made from hydrogel

Ⓒ will soon stop being made solely out of materials such as various types of plastics

Ⓓ are presently unable to construct actual organs that can be utilized in human bodies

[4] ➜ Most 3D-printed models of organs are made of hard plastic. Currently, there is a growing demand for softer models which surgeons and medical students can use to practice actual operations. To make these softer models, a 3D printer must use silicone or hydrogel as the building material. Many surgeons and medical schools also want organ models to bleed to make practicing as realistic as possible. The softer materials have springier properties, which mimic the actual elasticity of patients' organs, and therefore give surgeons a better way to judge how deeply they should slice into an organ. To mimic the properties of human organs, model makers examine the characteristics of real organs removed from patients. As 3D-printed organ model technology advances and models become more realistic, the hope is that one day, 3D printers can be used to construct artificial organs to replace malfunctioning ones.

| **Glossary** | ⊖ |
| --- | --- |

**hydrogel:** a gel that uses water as its primary liquid

**8** The word feasible in the passage is closest in meaning to

   Ⓐ affordable

   Ⓑ common

   Ⓒ practical

   Ⓓ serious

While 3D printing is a valuable aid in the medical field, there are some problems surrounding its use. One such issue is the cost involved. State-of-the-art 3D printers cost tens of thousands of dollars, so only the wealthiest of hospitals can afford to purchase one of them. Hospitals must also hire or train staff members to use the printer. In addition, the costs of creating 3D-printed implants as well as surgical aid models are not always covered by health insurance providers. This means neither of them is a feasible option for people who have limited access to financial resources.

ACTUAL TEST 02

**9** Look at the four squares [ ■ ] that indicate where the following sentence could be added to the passage.

**For instance, heart disease and cancer can cause certain organs in the body to enlarge to sizes much greater than those of healthy individuals.**

Where would the sentence best fit?

Click on a square [ ■ ] to add the sentence to the passage.

Another area that 3D printing is utilized in is building training models of internal organs. **1** While every human body has the same general internal structure, there are often unique differences between patients. **2** To reduce surgery time and to improve the chances of a successful operation, surgical teams build and train on 3D models of organs. **3** Perhaps a patient requires liver surgery. **4** The surgical team will conduct scans of the patient's liver and then create an accurate model of it with a 3D printer. The model will be clear and show the internal structure of the liver, including the placement of every blood vessel inside it. If there are any cancerous tumors in the liver, the 3D printer will include them in the model. Prior to the actual operation, the surgical team trains on the model of the liver, thereby ensuring that the patient has the best chance of having a successful surgery. Many medical schools are presently taking advantage of 3D printing to make models for future medical practitioners to train on.

**10  Directions:** An introductory sentence for a brief summary of the passage is provided below. Complete the summary by selecting the THREE answer choices that express the most important ideas of the passage. Some sentences do not belong because they express ideas that are not presented in the passage or are minor ideas in the passage. **This question is worth 2 points.**

Drag your answer choices to the spaces where they belong.
To remove an answer choice, click on it. To review the passage, click on **View Text**.

**3D printers are presently being effectively used by the medical industry and should increase in value in the future.**

- 
- 
- 

## Answer Choices

1. As 3D printers improve, the model organs they make will become more realistic, and they may be able to make actual physical organs one day.

2. Some surgeons create models of patients' organs in order to practice surgical processes to make sure they go as well as possible.

3. Because 3D printers are so expensive, many hospitals cannot afford the printers or the staff members needed to operate them.

4. Hydrogel, silicone, and other soft materials may be used to create model organs by some 3D printers in the future.

5. Surgeons can use 3D printers to make customized body parts that are then implanted in bodies during operations.

6. People involved in the medical industry were among the first to recognize the potential advantages of 3D printers.

TOEFL® MAP **ACTUAL TEST**

**?**
HELP

◀◀
BACK

▶▶
NEXT

**READING**

00:54:00 ⊖ HIDE TIME

# Primitive Cave Art

A prehistoric cave painting at Lascaux, France

During the past 150 years, people have discovered works of art inside caves in numerous places around Europe, particularly in France and Spain. These works of art comprise three main types: etchings in soft stone, etchings in hard stone, and paintings. Some clay statues have also been found, but they are relatively few in number compared to the other works discovered. Most of the artwork was created on the floors and the walls of caves and consists of representations of animals, some of which are now extinct. Initially, who made the artwork and why were mysteries that baffled experts. Over time, however, thanks to archaeological methods and scientific analysis, many answers have progressively been revealed.

When the first cave art was discovered in the 1860s, nobody knew what to make of it. Some were convinced it was an elaborate hoax whereas others deemed it the work of real artists from a time in the recent past. The answer was much more complex. Radiocarbon dating of the materials used in the artwork and organic material found in the caves established the time of its creation to have been between 40,000 and 10,000 B.C. The majority of the art was determined to have been made from 18,000 to 10,000 B.C. During this period, the people known as the Magdalenians lived in Western Europe. Their name derives from a site in France where some remains of their primitive society were discovered. Cave art attributed to the Magdalenians includes the works found in the famous Lascaux Cave in France.

It is believed that the Magdalenians first made drawings in soft mud by using their fingers, perhaps in imitation of animal claw marks. Sometimes the mud hardened and preserved these handmade images. From this experience, early men learned to carve into soft stone with various stone tools. The later development of harder flint-based tools enabled them to shape harder rocks. In some etchings, the finished works are almost like bas-reliefs in that they protrude many centimeters from the surfaces of the rocks. Although the cave paintings are better known, these etchings are much more numerous, consisting of almost triple the number of paintings at some sites. Art historians theorize that one reason there are so many is that engraving was not nearly as labor intensive as making paintings or drawings.

It may seem odd that engraving was easier than painting, but during prehistoric times, all paint was handmade and required additional materials to make it bind to rock. Primitive men used only a few colors in their works—primarily black, red, white, yellow, and brown. The sources of some of these paints are known. For instance, red was derived from iron oxide, black from magnesium dioxide or burned pine or juniper, and white from mica. The fact that mortars and pestles have been found at some sites provides evidence that prehistoric painters used them to grind minerals and other materials into fine powders. After doing that, they added water to containers made from shells or bones to mix the paint. The artists then utilized vegetable and animal oils to make the paint bind to their rocky canvases. To apply the paint, the artists are believed to have used brushes made from plant or animal matter, but none have survived, so archaeologists can merely speculate about this matter. What has survived, however, are hollow bone tubes through which paint was blown onto rock in a fine spray to make it spread evenly.

Many paintings are located deep inside caves, which must have required some type of effort to provide light during their creation. Like modern painters, prehistoric artists likely employed some type of scaffolding to help them reach high places on cave walls. The socket holes found in the walls of some caves were probably made for this purpose, and the heights of the nearby paintings lend credence to that theory. All of this work was labor intensive, and it is certain that cave artists did not do everything by themselves. Perhaps some communities had teams of people who worked to gather the materials for the paints and the brushes, to make torches to light the caves, and to build structures that enabled the artists to reach high places.

## Glossary

**pestle:** a tool utilized with a mortar to grind substances into a fine powder

**scaffolding:** a temporary structure used to elevate a person while that individual is doing work above the ground

11  In paragraph 1, the author implies that experts in cave art

Ⓐ have discovered all of the existing examples of cave art

Ⓑ have more that they need to learn about the artwork

Ⓒ can recreate some of the cave art images they have found

Ⓓ now completely understand why people made cave art

12  The word hoax in the passage is closest in meaning to

Ⓐ deception

Ⓑ undertaking

Ⓒ exhibition

Ⓓ endeavor

13  According to paragraph 2, experts know when a lot of cave art was made because

Ⓐ they have precise records that were kept by the Magdalenians

Ⓑ they have compared it with prehistoric artwork found elsewhere

Ⓒ they have unearthed artifacts in caves and know how old the items are

Ⓓ they have conducted scientific tests in order to date the artwork

## Primitive Cave Art

¹→ During the past 150 years, people have discovered works of art inside caves in numerous places around Europe, particularly in France and Spain. These works of art comprise three main types: etchings in soft stone, etchings in hard stone, and paintings. Some clay statues have also been found, but they are relatively few in number compared to the other works discovered. Most of the artwork was created on the floors and the walls of caves and consists of representations of animals, some of which are now extinct. Initially, who made the artwork and why were mysteries that baffled experts. Over time, however, thanks to archaeological methods and scientific analysis, many answers have progressively been revealed.

²→ When the first cave art was discovered in the 1860s, nobody knew what to make of it. Some were convinced it was an elaborate hoax whereas others deemed it the work of real artists from a time in the recent past. The answer was much more complex. Radiocarbon dating of the materials used in the artwork and organic material found in the caves established the time of its creation to have been between 40,000 and 10,000 B.C. The majority of the art was determined to have been made from 18,000 to 10,000 B.C. During this period, the people known as the Magdalenians lived in Western Europe. Their name derives from a site in France where some remains of their primitive society were discovered. Cave art attributed to the Magdalenians includes the works found in the famous Lascaux Cave in France.

ACTUAL TEST **02**

**14** The word them in the passage refers to

Ⓐ these handmade images

Ⓑ early men

Ⓒ various stone tools

Ⓓ harder flint-based tools

**15** According to paragraph 3, which of the following is NOT true of how some cave art was made?

Ⓐ People used their fingers in order to make certain kinds of designs in mud.

Ⓑ Artists employed hard rocks to cut into other rocks that were softer.

Ⓒ Tools were utilized to cut into certain types of soft stones inside caves.

Ⓓ Hard rocks were etched into by people who were using tools made of flint.

[3]→ It is believed that the Magdalenians first made drawings in soft mud by using their fingers, perhaps in imitation of animal claw marks. Sometimes the mud hardened and preserved these handmade images. From this experience, early men learned to carve into soft stone with various stone tools. The later development of harder flint-based tools enabled them to shape harder rocks. In some etchings, the finished works are almost like bas-reliefs in that they protrude many centimeters from the surfaces of the rocks. Although the cave paintings are better known, these etchings are much more numerous, consisting of almost triple the number of paintings at some sites. Art historians theorize that one reason there are so many is that engraving was not nearly as labor intensive as making paintings or drawings.

**16** The author uses hollow bone tubes as an example of

(A) objects that were required to mix the paint used for prehistoric artwork

(B) tools used by men when they were making works of art in caves

(C) types of brushes that artists utilized to paint the walls of some caves

(D) forms of artwork that have been dug up in caves with art on their walls

**17** According to paragraph 4, the paint that prehistoric artists used was able to adhere to cave walls because

(A) the brushes that the artists painted with were made of special materials

(B) the particles added to the paint were ground to a fine powder

(C) it was partially composed of either vegetable or animal oil

(D) only natural materials such as pine, juniper, and mica were used

⁴→ It may seem odd that engraving was easier than painting, but during prehistoric times, all paint was handmade and required additional materials to make it bind to rock. Primitive men used only a few colors in their works—primarily black, red, white, yellow, and brown. The sources of some of these paints are known. For instance, red was derived from iron oxide, black from magnesium dioxide or burned pine or juniper, and white from mica. The fact that mortars and **pestles** have been found at some sites provides evidence that prehistoric painters used them to grind minerals and other materials into fine powders. After doing that, they added water to containers made from shells or bones to mix the paint. The artists then utilized vegetable and animal oils to make the paint bind to their rocky canvases. To apply the paint, the artists are believed to have used brushes made from plant or animal matter, but none have survived, so archaeologists can merely speculate about this matter. What has survived, however, are hollow bone tubes through which paint was blown onto rock in a fine spray to make it spread evenly.

---

**Glossary**    ●

**pestle:** a tool utilized with a mortar to grind substances into a fine powder

**18** In stating that the heights of the nearby paintings lend credence to that theory, the author means that the theory

Ⓐ needs to be revised

Ⓑ is relatively new

Ⓒ is believable

Ⓓ has few supporters

Many paintings are located deep inside caves, which must have required some type of effort to provide light during their creation. Like modern painters, prehistoric artists likely employed some type of scaffolding to help them reach high places on cave walls. The socket holes found in the walls of some caves were probably made for this purpose, and the heights of the nearby paintings lend credence to that theory. All of this work was labor intensive, and it is certain that cave artists did not do everything by themselves. Perhaps some communities had teams of people who worked to gather the materials for the paints and the brushes, to make torches to light the caves, and to build structures that enabled the artists to reach high places.

**Glossary** ⊖

**scaffolding :** a temporary structure used to elevate a person while that individual is doing work above the ground

**19** Look at the four squares [■] that indicate where the following sentence could be added to the passage.

**In some cases, blood was also employed to make paint.**

Where would the sentence best fit?

Click on a square [■] to add the sentence to the passage.

It may seem odd that engraving was easier than painting, but during prehistoric times, all paint was handmade and required additional materials to make it bind to rock. **1** Primitive men used only a few colors in their works—primarily black, red, white, yellow, and brown. **2** The sources of some of these paints are known. **3** For instance, red was derived from iron oxide, black from magnesium dioxide or burned pine or juniper, and white from mica. **4** The fact that mortars and **pestles** have been found at some sites provides evidence that prehistoric painters used them to grind minerals and other materials into fine powders. After doing that, they added water to containers made from shells or bones to mix the paint. The artists then utilized vegetable and animal oils to make the paint bind to their rocky canvases. To apply the paint, the artists are believed to have used brushes made from plant or animal matter, but none have survived, so archaeologists can merely speculate about this matter. What has survived, however, are hollow bone tubes through which paint was blown onto rock in a fine spray to make it spread evenly.

---

**Glossary**                                            ⊖

**pestle:** a tool utilized with a mortar to grind substances into a fine powder

20 **Directions:** An introductory sentence for a brief summary of the passage is provided below. Complete the summary by selecting the THREE answer choices that express the most important ideas of the passage. Some sentences do not belong because they express ideas that are not presented in the passage or are minor ideas in the passage. **This question is worth 2 points.**

Drag your answer choices to the spaces where they belong.
To remove an answer choice, click on it. To review the passage, click on **View Text**.

**A number of different types of ancient artwork that were made either by using primitive tools or paints have been found in many caves in Europe.**

- 
- 
- 

## Answer Choices

1. Lascaux Cave in France contains some of the most fascinating examples of cave art to be seen in all of Europe.

2. Artists utilized natural materials, such as plant or animal matter, to create the paints that they made their art with.

3. The Magdalenians were a group of people who lived in Europe and made cave art thousands of years ago.

4. It is highly likely that the artists were assisted by teams of individuals who had duties such as providing light for the artists.

5. By using both soft and hard stone tools, primitive men were able to make etchings in the walls of caves.

6. The majority of the cave art that has been discovered in Europe was created more than 10,000 years ago.

# Human Internal Body Temperatures

Humans are warm-blooded animals that produce heat through internal mechanisms. Like most mammals, humans do this by converting the food they eat into energy. While humans may be influenced by external temperatures, particularly in extreme heat and cold, the human body has ways to adapt to these conditions that enable it to survive. Additionally, humans can maintain their body temperatures through other means, including clothing, using fire in cold weather, and imbibing fluids in hot weather. Without these internal and external coping mechanisms, humans could not survive in certain harsh environments.

Thermoregulation is the term used to describe the human body's ability to control its internal temperature. Although a human's average body temperature is around thirty-seven degrees Celsius, various parts of the body maintain different temperatures. At the body's core—the head, the chest, and the abdomen—the temperature is slightly higher than in the extremities—the arms and the legs. The reason is that people's most vital organs are in their head, chest, and abdomen. The three most important organs for human survival are the brain, the heart, and the liver, so the body attempts to ensure that these organs function as well as possible.

As blood flows throughout the body, it carries heat through the arteries to the outer limbs and increases the temperature of the veins as the blood returns to the inner body. But in very cold weather, the body contracts the outer blood vessels near the skin, which makes them receive less blood and thereby keeps the warm blood closer to the important inner organs. This can result in a person developing pale skin and frostbite once the moisture in the skin and the outer flesh freezes. Before this occurs, however, the body can utilize two defensive mechanisms. First, the muscles near the hairs on the body contract, causing the hairs to rise and the person's skin to develop goose bumps. The rising hairs help trap heat in the body. Second, the brain sends signals to other muscles to begin contracting rapidly, causing the person to shiver, which produces more body heat.

Yet sometimes a person may be exposed to frigid temperatures for a long period of time and is additionally unable to gain access to an external heat source such as hot food or fire. When no heat is available, the body begins to shut down. It pools as much warm blood as possible into the brain, the heart, and the liver, which gives the person the opportunity to survive longer. Eventually, though, the person will experience hypothermia and then become incoherent and unable to function. Unless drastic measures are taken to increase the amount of heat in the body, that individual will die.

The body also has ways of dealing with extremely hot weather conditions. When a person exercises, that individual's inner body temperature rises. Body hairs lie flat to prevent heat from being trapped. The flowing of blood toward the surface of the skin increases, which thereby transfers more heat out of the body. The body also produces sweat to keep its temperature from rising too much. Fluids travel out of the sweat glands to the surface of the skin and then spread out. This causes a cooling effect as the inner heat evaporates more rapidly. However, there is a negative tradeoff in that the more the body sweats, the more fluids it loses. Unless these fluids are replaced, dehydration will result if the body's internal level of fluids becomes too low. In very hot places such as deserts, the body is exposed to massive doses of heat due to the effects of the sun's radiant heat energy on the skin. Unless a person actively attempts to reduce the amount of heat that individual is exposed to, the internal organs may become so hot that they cease functioning properly.

The human body has limits in how cold or hot it can become. If a person's core body temperature falls beneath thirty-two degrees Celsius, unconsciousness will ensue. At around twenty-six degrees Celsius, death is almost always inevitable. As for heat, any temperature above forty degrees Celsius will lead to severe illness while few people have ever survived internal body temperatures that have risen above forty-four degrees Celsius.

---

## Glossary

**artery :** one of the major blood vessels that carries blood throughout the body

**dehydration :** the loss of water from the body

21  The word coping in the passage is closest in meaning to

Ⓐ survival

Ⓑ breathing

Ⓒ contraction

Ⓓ circulation

### Human Internal Body Temperatures

Humans are warm-blooded animals that produce heat through internal mechanisms. Like most mammals, humans do this by converting the food they eat into energy. While humans may be influenced by external temperatures, particularly in extreme heat and cold, the human body has ways to adapt to these conditions that enable it to survive. Additionally, humans can maintain their body temperatures through other means, including clothing, using fire in cold weather, and imbibing fluids in hot weather. Without these internal and external coping mechanisms, humans could not survive in certain harsh environments.

22 The author mentions Thermoregulation in order to

Ⓐ explain its connection with the body's abdomen

Ⓑ compare its effects on the body's internal organs

Ⓒ provide the definition of a physiological term

Ⓓ account for temperature loss in humans

23 According to paragraph 2, the body maintains different internal temperatures because

Ⓐ its extremities require more heat than other parts of the body

Ⓑ a person's head is the most important part of the body

Ⓒ the blood closest to the heart is harder to keep cool

Ⓓ it keeps some organs at higher temperatures than others

24 In paragraph 2, the author implies that a person's arms and legs

Ⓐ require more blood than the chest and head do

Ⓑ lack organs that are critical to an individual's survival

Ⓒ receive blood that contains fewer nutrients than other places

Ⓓ need a relatively small amount of blood to work properly

² ➡ Thermoregulation is the term used to describe the human body's ability to control its internal temperature. Although a human's average body temperature is around thirty-seven degrees Celsius, various parts of the body maintain different temperatures. At the body's core—the head, the chest, and the abdomen—the temperature is slightly higher than in the extremities—the arms and the legs. The reason is that people's most vital organs are in their head, chest, and abdomen. The three most important organs for human survival are the brain, the heart, and the liver, so the body attempts to ensure that these organs function as well as possible.

25  Which of the sentences below best expresses the essential information in the highlighted sentence in the passage? *Incorrect* answer choices change the meaning in important ways or leave out essential information.

Ⓐ When parts of the body contract, this prevents blood from circulating as it instead remains closer to crucial organs.

Ⓑ Blood vessels closer to the skin get less blood when the weather is cold, so more warm blood surrounds various organs.

Ⓒ In times of cold weather, the body's inner organs require a larger supply of blood than they do in warm weather.

Ⓓ The body's blood vessels begin to contract, so they continue pumping blood near the skin as well as the organs.

26  The word pools in the passage is closest in meaning to

Ⓐ collects

Ⓑ manufactures

Ⓒ protects

Ⓓ heats

As blood flows throughout the body, it carries heat through the arteries to the outer limbs and increases the temperature of the veins as the blood returns to the inner body. But in very cold weather, the body contracts the outer blood vessels near the skin, which makes them receive less blood and thereby keeps the warm blood closer to the important inner organs. This can result in a person developing pale skin and frostbite once the moisture in the skin and the outer flesh freezes. Before this occurs, however, the body can utilize two defensive mechanisms. First, the muscles near the hairs on the body contract, causing the hairs to rise and the person's skin to develop goose bumps. The rising hairs help trap heat in the body. Second, the brain sends signals to other muscles to begin contracting rapidly, causing the person to shiver, which produces more body heat.

Yet sometimes a person may be exposed to frigid temperatures for a long period of time and is additionally unable to gain access to an external heat source such as hot food or fire. When no heat is available, the body begins to shut down. It pools as much warm blood as possible into the brain, the heart, and the liver, which gives the person the opportunity to survive longer. Eventually, though, the person will experience hypothermia and then become incoherent and unable to function. Unless drastic measures are taken to increase the amount of heat in the body, that individual will die.

---

**Glossary**                                                   ⊖

**artery:** one of the major blood vessels that carries blood throughout the body

27  According to paragraph 5, heat can get transferred out of the body when

   Ⓐ more blood in the body than usual flows closer to a person's skin

   Ⓑ an individual is exposed to the sun's heat for an extended period of time

   Ⓒ a person consumes enough fluids to replace those that are lost by sweating

   Ⓓ the body's organs begin to use less of the blood that is flowing near them

28  In paragraph 6, the author's description of how the body responds to extreme weather conditions mentions all of the following EXCEPT:

   Ⓐ the temperature at which a person might pass out

   Ⓑ the temperature at which a person might die

   Ⓒ the temperature at which a person might become ill

   Ⓓ the temperature at which a person might vomit

29  Look at the four squares [ ■ ] that indicate where the following sentence could be added to the passage.

**This is the primary reason why individuals engaged in athletic events are urged to drink large amounts of liquids.**

Where would the sentence best fit?

Click on a square [ ■ ] to add the sentence to the passage.

⁵➙ The body also has ways of dealing with extremely hot weather conditions. When a person exercises, that individual's inner body temperature rises. Body hairs lie flat to prevent heat from being trapped. The flowing of blood toward the surface of the skin increases, which thereby transfers more heat out of the body. The body also produces sweat to keep its temperature from rising too much. Fluids travel out of the sweat glands to the surface of the skin and then spread out. This causes a cooling effect as the inner heat evaporates more rapidly. **1** However, there is a negative tradeoff in that the more the body sweats, the more fluids it loses. **2** Unless these fluids are replaced, dehydration will result if the body's internal level of fluids becomes too low. **3** In very hot places such as deserts, the body is exposed to massive doses of heat due to the effects of the sun's radiant heat energy on the skin. **4** Unless a person actively attempts to reduce the amount of heat that individual is exposed to, the internal organs may become so hot that they cease functioning properly.

⁶➙ The human body has limits in how cold or hot it can become. If a person's core body temperature falls beneath thirty-two degrees Celsius, unconsciousness will ensue. At around twenty-six degrees Celsius, death is almost always inevitable. As for heat, any temperature above forty degrees Celsius will lead to severe illness while few people have ever survived internal body temperatures that have risen above forty-four degrees Celsius.

| **Glossary** | ⊖ |
|---|---|
| **dehydration:** the loss of water from the body | |

30 **Directions:** Select the appropriate sentences from the answer choices and match them to the extreme weather condition to which they relate. TWO of the answer choices will NOT be used. **This question is worth 3 points.**

> Drag your answer choices to the spaces where they belong.
> To remove an answer choice, click on it. To review the passage, click on **View Text**.

**Answer Choices**                    **EXTREME WEATHER CONDITION**

1 A person's skin may become somewhat pale.                    **Cold**

2 An individual may lose consciousness.                    •

3 The body begins to sweat.                    •

4 The brain may cause a person to shiver.                    •

5 The body relies on thermoregulation.

6 The hair on a person's body may be flat.                    **Heat**

7 The heart pumps blood to the body much faster.                    •

                    •

# Giorgio Vasari

A fresco painted by Giorgio Vasari in 1579

The origins of the academic field of art history can be traced back to the work of Italian painter and architect Giorgio Vasari. His 1550 book entitled *The Lives of the Most Eminent Painters, Sculptors, and Architects* is considered one of the first attempts to chronicle the lives of the artists of his day. Vasari is famed for coining the term *renaissance* to describe the new style of art which existed during his lifetime and of which he was also a practitioner.

Vasari was born in the town of Arezzo in the Tuscany region of Italy in 1511. He was the oldest of six children and belonged to a family with a long history of involvement in the arts. He received a well-rounded education with an emphasis on Latin and learned drawing from a famed French designer of stained-glass windows. In 1524, he moved to Florence to continue his education in the arts. Vasari's family had connections with the famed Medici banking family. In his new home, he studied alongside the children of the Medici family and was also apprenticed to Michelangelo for a short time. Tragedy struck when Vasari was sixteen as his father died of the plague, and being the oldest son, Vasari took over the family's affairs. Due to that event, he developed a lifelong desire for financial security for himself and his family, which he successfully attained through his friendship with and the patronage of the Medici family. He spent most of his adult life in Florence, where the Medici family often employed him on various projects. He would later die in Florence in 1574.

As an artist, Vasari is considered a member of the Mannerism Period of the Late Renaissance. During his lifetime, he was well known as an artist and had a large following, including many students who themselves later achieved fame. However, modern-day critics believe that Vasari's style was largely copied from the masters who preceded him, especially his friend Michelangelo.

Vasari was also noted for his architectural work, including the remodeling of many churches and the design and the construction of homes for the Medici family. In the final decade of his life, Vasari was directly employed by the Vatican to work on decorating several churches. Today, however, his legacy centers mainly on his historical work *The Lives of the Most Eminent Painters, Sculptors, and Architects*.

Vasari was well versed in Latin and ancient literature, and thus, when he wrote his biography of artists, he may have been influenced by the works of ancient Roman writers such as Plutarch and Vitruvius. While Vasari claimed that he wanted the book to serve as the foundation of the education of future artists, some believe he began the book in an attempt to salvage his reputation, which was in decline in the late 1540s due to his difficult personality. He was also worried about his patrons, the Medici, because he had not yet been accepted into the inner circle of the family despite his long ties to them. Finally, in 1554, the head of the family asked Vasari to join them, thereby cementing the Medici's patronage of him.

*The Lives of the Most Eminent Painters, Sculptors, and Architects* covered the lives of artists over a 300-year period from the thirteenth to sixteenth centuries. Vasari wrote about the lives of hundreds of artists, including famous individuals such as Leonardo da Vinci and Michelangelo. The majority, however, were from the Florence region, and Vasari gave little space to artists in other areas until the second edition in 1568, when he included some Venetian artists such as Titian. The book became household reading among the rich and powerful of Florence, yet even in his own time, Vasari was criticized for some inaccuracies in the book and for his embellishing of certain events. Sometimes he even put himself in the middle of history. For example, he claimed to have saved Michelangelo's statue *David* from an angry mob. He additionally engaged in self-promotion in the book as he included a lengthy biography of himself and his family at the end. Despite these shortcomings, the work has been praised in the centuries following Vasari's death as the best source of information on artists of the Renaissance.

## Glossary

**stained-glass window:** glass that has been colored through various methods and is used for windows in churches, cathedrals, and other similar places

**biography:** a book which tells about the life of a person, often someone of importance

**31** According to paragraph 1, which of the following is true of Giorgio Vasari?

(A) Much of the new style of art popular during his life was taught to others by him.

(B) He created the type of art made during a period whose name he came up with.

(C) Most people know him for his work as a painter rather than for his work as a writer.

(D) He was considered a leading Italian architect during the Renaissance.

**32** According to paragraph 2, Giorgio Vasari wanted to be financially secure because

(A) he realized that working as an artist would not always earn him very much money

(B) he envied the wealthy lifestyles of his friends who were in the Medici family

(C) he had many children and wanted to be sure he could take care of all of them

(D) he was greatly affected by the death of his father during his teenage years

## Giorgio Vasari

**1 →** The origins of the academic field of art history can be traced back to the work of Italian painter and architect Giorgio Vasari. His 1550 book entitled *The Lives of the Most Eminent Painters, Sculptors, and Architects* is considered one of the first attempts to chronicle the lives of the artists of his day. Vasari is famed for coining the term *renaissance* to describe the new style of art which existed during his lifetime and of which he was also a practitioner.

**2 →** Vasari was born in the town of Arezzo in the Tuscany region of Italy in 1511. He was the oldest of six children and belonged to a family with a long history of involvement in the arts. He received a well-rounded education with an emphasis on Latin and learned drawing from a famed French designer of stained-glass windows. In 1524, he moved to Florence to continue his education in the arts. Vasari's family had connections with the famed Medici banking family. In his new home, he studied alongside the children of the Medici family and was also apprenticed to Michelangelo for a short time. Tragedy struck when Vasari was sixteen as his father died of the plague, and being the oldest son, Vasari took over the family's affairs. Due to that event, he developed a lifelong desire for financial security for himself and his family, which he successfully attained through his friendship with and the patronage of the Medici family. He spent most of his adult life in Florence, where the Medici family often employed him on various projects. He would later die in Florence in 1574.

### Glossary ⊖

**stained-glass window:** glass that has been colored through various methods and is used for windows in churches, cathedrals, and other similar places

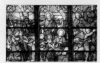

**33** In paragraph 3, the author's description of Giorgio Vasari mentions all of the following EXCEPT:

(A) the number and types of paintings that he created during his entire art career

(B) the school of artwork that he was said to have belonged to during his life

(C) the main reason that most people still remember him in the present time

(D) the types of buildings that he designed and renovated as an architect

**34** In paragraph 3, the author implies that Giorgio Vasari

(A) is not considered to have been an original artist by modern-day experts

(B) should have authored more books since he was a talented writer

(C) had the potential to be a greater artist than Michelangelo ever was

(D) built a following of supporters bigger than those of other contemporary artists

**35** In paragraph 4, why does the author mention Plutarch and Vitruvius?

(A) To claim that Giorgio Vasari consulted their works when writing his own book

(B) To point out the names of two Roman writers whose works were read by Giorgio Vasari

(C) To name two individuals whose writing affected Giorgio Vasari in a positive manner

(D) To compare their works with the most famous book written by Giorgio Vasari

³→ As an artist, Vasari is considered a member of the Mannerism Period of the Late Renaissance. During his lifetime, he was well known as an artist and had a large following, including many students who themselves later achieved fame. However, modern-day critics believe that Vasari's style was largely copied from the masters who preceded him, especially his friend Michelangelo. Vasari was also noted for his architectural work, including the remodeling of many churches and the design and the construction of homes for the Medici family. In the final decade of his life, Vasari was directly employed by the Vatican to work on decorating several churches. Today, however, his legacy centers mainly on his historical work *The Lives of the Most Eminent Painters, Sculptors, and Architects.*

⁴→ Vasari was well versed in Latin and ancient literature, and thus, when he wrote his biography of artists, he may have been influenced by the works of ancient Roman writers such as Plutarch and Vitruvius. While Vasari claimed that he wanted the book to serve as the foundation of the education of future artists, some believe he began the book in an attempt to salvage his reputation, which was in decline in the late 1540s due to his difficult personality. He was also worried about his patrons, the Medici, because he had not yet been accepted into the inner circle of the family despite his long ties to them. Finally, in 1554, the head of the family asked Vasari to join them, thereby cementing the Medici's patronage of him.

| **Glossary** ⊖ |
| --- |
| **biography:** a book which tells about the life of a person, often someone of importance |

**36** The word salvage in the passage is closest in meaning to

  (A) monitor

  (B) enhance

  (C) alter

  (D) rescue

**37** In paragraph 5, the author uses Titian as an example of

  (A) an artist from outside Florence who was featured in the second edition of Giorgio Vasari's book

  (B) one of the greatest and most famous artists who lived during the entire Italian Renaissance

  (C) an artist whose life and work Giorgio Vasari had a great deal of influence upon

  (D) one artist about whom Giorgio Vasari made several mistakes when he was writing his book

**38** The word embellishing in the passage is closest in meaning to

  (A) interpreting

  (B) describing

  (C) exaggerating

  (D) approving

Vasari was well versed in Latin and ancient literature, and thus, when he wrote his biography of artists, he may have been influenced by the works of ancient Roman writers such as Plutarch and Vitruvius. While Vasari claimed that he wanted the book to serve as the foundation of the education of future artists, some believe he began the book in an attempt to salvage his reputation, which was in decline in the late 1540s due to his difficult personality. He was also worried about his patrons, the Medici, because he had not yet been accepted into the inner circle of the family despite his long ties to them. Finally, in 1554, the head of the family asked Vasari to join them, thereby cementing the Medici's patronage of him.

5 ➡ *The Lives of the Most Eminent Painters, Sculptors, and Architects* covered the lives of artists over a 300-year period from the thirteenth to sixteenth centuries. Vasari wrote about the lives of hundreds of artists, including famous individuals such as Leonardo da Vinci and Michelangelo. The majority, however, were from the Florence region, and Vasari gave little space to artists in other areas until the second edition in 1568, when he included some Venetian artists such as Titian. The book became household reading among the rich and powerful of Florence, yet even in his own time, Vasari was criticized for some inaccuracies in the book and for his embellishing of certain events. Sometimes he even put himself in the middle of history. For example, he claimed to have saved Michelangelo's statue *David* from an angry mob. He additionally engaged in self-promotion in the book as he included a lengthy biography of himself and his family at the end. Despite these shortcomings, the work has been praised in the centuries following Vasari's death as the best source of information on artists of the Renaissance.

---

**Glossary** ⊖

**biography:** a book which tells about the life of a person, often someone of importance

39 Look at the four squares [ ■ ] that indicate where the following sentence could be added to the passage.

**Some of its members were among the most powerful and influential individuals not just in the city but also in Italy as a whole for centuries.**

Where would the sentence best fit?

Click on a square [ ■ ] to add the sentence to the passage.

---

Vasari was born in the town of Arezzo in the Tuscany region of Italy in 1511. He was the oldest of six children and belonged to a family with a long history of involvement in the arts. **1** He received a well-rounded education with an emphasis on Latin and learned drawing from a famed French designer of <u>stained-glass windows</u>. **2** In 1524, he moved to Florence to continue his education in the arts. **3** Vasari's family had connections with the famed Medici banking family. **4** In his new home, he studied alongside the children of the Medici family and was also apprenticed to Michelangelo for a short time. Tragedy struck when Vasari was sixteen as his father died of the plague, and being the oldest son, Vasari took over the family's affairs. Due to that event, he developed a lifelong desire for financial security for himself and his family, which he successfully attained through his friendship with and the patronage of the Medici family. He spent most of his adult life in Florence, where the Medici family often employed him on various projects. He would later die in Florence in 1574.

---

**Glossary** ⊖

**stained-glass window:** glass that has been colored through various methods and is used for windows in churches, cathedrals, and other similar places

**40** **Directions:** An introductory sentence for a brief summary of the passage is provided below. Complete the summary by selecting the THREE answer choices that express the most important ideas of the passage. Some sentences do not belong because they express ideas that are not presented in the passage or are minor ideas in the passage. **This question is worth 2 points.**

> Drag your answer choices to the spaces where they belong.
> To remove an answer choice, click on it. To review the passage, click on **View Text**.

**Giorgio Vasari was an important artist in the sixteenth century who also wrote an influential book about artists.**

- •
- •
- •

## Answer Choices

1. The Medici family served as Giorgio Vasari's patron and provided him with the financial security he needed to be an artist.

2. Giorgio Vasari believed that the preservation of art was important and was responsible for saving the statue *David* from destruction.

3. Michelangelo and Leonardo da Vinci were two Renaissance artists whose works heavily influenced Giorgio Vasari.

4. Giorgio Vasari not only painted but also worked as an architect, designing and remodeling many buildings for the Medici family.

5. *The Lives of the Most Eminent Painters, Sculptors, and Architects* is considered an important work in the field of art history.

6. Giorgio Vasari was born in Tuscany but spent most of his life both living and working in the city of Florence.

ACTUAL TEST 02

03

# Reading Section Directions

This section measures your ability to understand academic passages in English. You will have **54 minutes** to read and answer questions about **3 passages**. A clock at the top of the screen will show you how much time is remaining.

Most questions are worth 1 point but the last question for each passage is worth more than 1 point. The directions for the last question indicate how many points you may receive.

Some passages include a word or phrase that is underlined in blue. Click on the word or phrase to see a definition or an explanation.

When you want to move to the next question, click on **Next**. You may skip questions and go back to them later. If you want to return to previous questions, click on **Back**. You can click on **Review** at any time, and the review screen will show you which questions you have answered and which you have not answered. From this review screen, you may go directly to any question you have already seen in the Reading section.

Click on **Continue** to go on.

# Cloud Components

Clouds are regular sights in places around the world. They are responsible for rain, snow, and various other types of precipitation that fall to the ground at times. While clouds themselves are primarily comprised of water vapor, they attach themselves to tiny particles in the atmosphere. These particles themselves may be a variety of substances.

The Earth's atmosphere is filled with water vapor that manifests itself in extremely small droplets that people are mostly unable to see with the naked eye. However, when clouds form, the water vapor becomes visible. The reason is that the water vapor attaches itself to particles floating in the atmosphere. They are typically motes of dust. The water vapor droplets then converge and form clouds of varying shapes and sizes throughout the different layers of the atmosphere. Over time, as more and more water vapor droplets come together, they increase the size of their cloud until it reaches a point that it is so heavy that it releases its water, which falls to the ground as precipitation.

The particles in the atmosphere that are primarily responsible for helping create clouds are common dust. There is a massive amount of dust in the atmosphere. It is often invisible, but, at times, it may be observed as smoke, smog, and haze. When the sun rises and sets, its reddish color is the result of its light passing through this dust and having some of its colored wavelengths blocked so that, as a result, people mostly see the red wavelength. This dust has both human and natural sources. The human sources can be anything that puts dust into the atmosphere, including farming, forestry, mining, and manufacturing. The natural sources consist of forest fires, volcanic activity, and erosion that blows dust into the air, among others. Additionally, the atmosphere contains organic matter. For example, when forest fires occur, some organic matter from plants is sent into the atmosphere. Likewise, pollen and seeds that blow off plants are sometimes found in the air and may become parts of clouds when water vapor attaches itself to them and rises into the atmosphere.

Clouds may also be partially formed of salt particles and ice nuclei. Salt particles are mostly found in the air near the oceans and are responsible for many of the clouds that form over oceans far from land and high levels of atmospheric dust. The salt enters the atmosphere through evaporation or in the guise of ocean spray when salt water collides with the shore. At sea, the convergence of hot and cold air can result in dense banks of fog that form from water vapor and salt particles. As for ice nuclei, they are supercooled water droplets which have formed around a particle of dust, organic matter, or even bacteria. Forming high in the atmosphere, these ice nuclei create ice crystals that can fall as snow or ice or sometimes as rain if the lower atmospheric levels are warmer. In addition, they are responsible for much of the electrical transference between clouds that causes lightning.

Scientists have also learned that bacteria may be a part of cloud formations. More than twenty-five years ago, it was proposed that bacteria could form ice nuclei and then spread to other parts of the world by falling to the ground along with rain and snow. While this theory was at first disregarded, there is a growing body of evidence that this, in fact, happens. Various forms of bacteria common to plants have been collected from ice samples in many different places, even in the Earth's Polar Regions in places where there are no plants. It seems that the bacteria are blown into the atmosphere, form ice nuclei, which then become ice crystals, and later fall as rain or snow and land in new areas. Despite sounding somewhat farfetched, many scientists agree that this is happening. Indeed, considering how organisms frequently find ways to reproduce and spread to new territories, it seems logical for bacteria to use clouds to move into other regions. In doing so, they act as just another component—one of many—in the clouds floating high in the sky.

Glossary

**mote:** a small particle, often of dust; a speck
**nucleus:** a core; a center

ACTUAL TEST 03

**1** According to paragraph 1, which of the following is true of clouds?

   Ⓐ The greatest part of them consists of water vapor.

   Ⓑ There is nowhere in the world that clouds have not been.

   Ⓒ Clouds that drop rain and clouds that drop snow look different.

   Ⓓ All clouds vary in the amount of water that they contain.

**2** The word converge in the passage is closest in meaning to

   Ⓐ evaporate

   Ⓑ rise

   Ⓒ unite

   Ⓓ expand

**3** In paragraph 2, the author of the passage implies that clouds

   Ⓐ filled with water are likely to cause rain to fall

   Ⓑ typically form for only a short amount of time

   Ⓒ created in the upper atmosphere are more likely to be thin

   Ⓓ containing large amounts of dust drop very much rain

**Cloud Components**

¹➜ Clouds are regular sights in places around the world. They are responsible for rain, snow, and various other types of precipitation that fall to the ground at times. While clouds themselves are primarily comprised of water vapor, they attach themselves to tiny particles in the atmosphere. These particles themselves may be a variety of substances.

²➜ The Earth's atmosphere is filled with water vapor that manifests itself in extremely small droplets that people are mostly unable to see with the naked eye. However, when clouds form, the water vapor becomes visible. The reason is that the water vapor attaches itself to particles floating in the atmosphere. They are typically motes of dust. The water vapor droplets then converge and form clouds of varying shapes and sizes throughout the different layers of the atmosphere. Over time, as more and more water vapor droplets come together, they increase the size of their cloud until it reaches a point that it is so heavy that it releases its water, which falls to the ground as precipitation.

**Glossary** ⊖

**mote:** a small particle, often of dust; a speck

**4** The word It in the passage refers to

Ⓐ The atmosphere

Ⓑ Common dust

Ⓒ A massive amount

Ⓓ The sun

**5** Why does the author mention smoke, smog, and haze?

Ⓐ To stress that all three of them can be found at fairly low altitudes

Ⓑ To blame them for increasing the amount of air pollution around the world

Ⓒ To name some of the various manifestations of dust in the atmosphere

Ⓓ To explain how they can sometimes be responsible for forming clouds

The particles in the atmosphere that are primarily responsible for helping create clouds are common dust. There is a massive amount of dust in the atmosphere. It is often invisible, but, at times, it may be observed as smoke, smog, and haze. When the sun rises and sets, its reddish color is the result of its light passing through this dust and having some of its colored wavelengths blocked so that, as a result, people mostly see the red wavelength. This dust has both human and natural sources. The human sources can be anything that puts dust into the atmosphere, including farming, forestry, mining, and manufacturing. The natural sources consist of forest fires, volcanic activity, and erosion that blows dust into the air, among others. Additionally, the atmosphere contains organic matter. For example, when forest fires occur, some organic matter from plants is sent into the atmosphere. Likewise, pollen and seeds that blow off plants are sometimes found in the air and may become parts of clouds when water vapor attaches itself to them and rises into the atmosphere.

**6** According to paragraph 4, which of the following is NOT true of ice nuclei?

Ⓐ They may be responsible for snow falling to the ground.

Ⓑ They are a combination of water vapor and another substance.

Ⓒ A part of them may sometimes be comprised of a living organism.

Ⓓ They have little to do with the creation of lightning in clouds.

⁴➔ Clouds may also be partially formed of salt particles and ice nuclei. Salt particles are mostly found in the air near the oceans and are responsible for many of the clouds that form over oceans far from land and high levels of atmospheric dust. The salt enters the atmosphere through evaporation or in the guise of ocean spray when salt water collides with the shore. At sea, the convergence of hot and cold air can result in dense banks of fog that form from water vapor and salt particles. As for ice nuclei, they are supercooled water droplets which have formed around a particle of dust, organic matter, or even bacteria. Forming high in the atmosphere, these ice nuclei create ice crystals that can fall as snow or ice or sometimes as rain if the lower atmospheric levels are warmer. In addition, they are responsible for much of the electrical transference between clouds that causes lightning.

ACTUAL TEST **03**

---

**Glossary** ⊖

**nucleus:** a core; a center

**7** The word farfetched in the passage is closest in meaning to

Ⓐ measured

Ⓑ alien

Ⓒ inappropriate

Ⓓ unbelievable

**8** According to paragraph 5, which of the following is true of bacteria?

Ⓐ They sometimes get carried to new places by becoming parts of clouds.

Ⓑ Their role in the creation of some clouds is no longer in dispute.

Ⓒ They can move quickly around the world when they unite with water vapor.

Ⓓ They have been known to reproduce while they are floating in clouds.

⁵ ➤ Scientists have also learned that bacteria may be a part of cloud formations. More than twenty-five years ago, it was proposed that bacteria could form ice nuclei and then spread to other parts of the world by falling to the ground along with rain and snow. While this theory was at first disregarded, there is a growing body of evidence that this, in fact, happens. Various forms of bacteria common to plants have been collected from ice samples in many different places, even in the Earth's Polar Regions in places where there are no plants. It seems that the bacteria are blown into the atmosphere, form ice nuclei, which then become ice crystals, and later fall as rain or snow and land in new areas. Despite sounding somewhat farfetched, many scientists agree that this is happening. Indeed, considering how organisms frequently find ways to reproduce and spread to new territories, it seems logical for bacteria to use clouds to move into other regions. In doing so, they act as just another component—one of many—in the clouds floating high in the sky.

**9**  Look at the four squares [ ■ ] that indicate where the following sentence could be added to the passage.

**Smoke that comes from factories is a major source of this dust.**

Where would the sentence best fit?

Click on a square [ ■ ] to add the sentence to the passage.

The particles in the atmosphere that are primarily responsible for helping create clouds are common dust. There is a massive amount of dust in the atmosphere. It is often invisible, but, at times, it may be observed as smoke, smog, and haze. When the sun rises and sets, its reddish color is the result of its light passing through this dust and having some of its colored wavelengths blocked so that, as a result, people mostly see the red wavelength. This dust has both human and natural sources. The human sources can be anything that puts dust into the atmosphere, including farming, forestry, mining, and manufacturing. **1** The natural sources consist of forest fires, volcanic activity, and erosion that blows dust into the air, among others. **2** Additionally, the atmosphere contains organic matter. **3** For example, when forest fires occur, some organic matter from plants is sent into the atmosphere. **4** Likewise, pollen and seeds that blow off plants are sometimes found in the air and may become parts of clouds when water vapor attaches itself to them and rises into the atmosphere.

ACTUAL TEST **03**

10 **Directions:** An introductory sentence for a brief summary of the passage is provided below. Complete the summary by selecting the THREE answer choices that express the most important ideas of the passage. Some sentences do not belong because they express ideas that are not presented in the passage or are minor ideas in the passage. **This question is worth 2 points.**

Drag your answer choices to the spaces where they belong.
To remove an answer choice, click on it. To review the passage, click on **View Text**.

**Clouds are a combination of water vapor and other substances.**

- 
- 
- 

## Answer Choices

1. Scientists are conducting research on how bacteria can appear in places where they are not normally found.

2. In places near the oceans, salt can be a major component of the clouds that are created.

3. The sun appears to change in the evening because of the presence of dust in the air.

4. Some scientists argue that bacteria can form ice nuclei and thereby become parts of clouds.

5. Clouds assume only a few different shapes and sizes throughout the Earth's atmosphere.

6. The most common substance that water vapor bonds with to form clouds is dust.

# Rome: From Republic to Empire

A battle scene from the Arch of Constantine marble panel in Rome

Rome emerged as a center of power on the Italian peninsula by the banks of the Tiber River sometime around 500 B.C. After an early period of monarchy, the Roman people overthrew their leaders, established a culture that employed a system of democratic beliefs, and created an entity that would become known as the Roman Republic. Their political principles were based on an unwritten constitution that established a number of political offices with central powers and a system of checks and balances that limited those powers. At the apex of this system was the powerful Roman Senate, yet it too had limits on its authority. Over time, the Senate evolved into a representative body of the most powerful families in Rome. Despite controlling most aspects of Roman life, the Senate could never manage the political intrigue and infighting among its members and other powerful Roman families, which would prove to be its undoing. A power struggle in the first century B.C. led to a period of instability that eventually resulted in the death of the Roman Republic and the founding of the Roman Empire.

Julius Caesar was at the center of this period of conflict. One of Rome's greatest military commanders, Caesar was involved in several political intrigues, which made him numerous enemies in the Senate. When the Senate banned Caesar from entering Rome in 49 B.C., he led his veteran army from Gaul—modern-day France—to the Italian peninsula and advanced on Rome. With only a weak army of recruits who had no hope of defeating Caesar's seasoned veterans, the Senate and its military leaders fled the city. After a short civil war, Caesar defeated his enemies and became the ruler of Rome. He invested the power of many political offices in his own person and ruled as a virtual dictator for five years. Caesar's acts deprived the Senate of much of its authority and set in motion the process for all of Rome's power to be held by a single individual. In response, the Senate reacted violently to the loss of its power and prestige, and many of its members played a central role in Caesar's assassination in 44 B.C.

Following Caesar's death, a new period of instability and civil war started. Octavian, Caesar's nephew and adopted heir, established an alliance with Caesar's trusted friend and lieutenant Mark Anthony. Having expected to be named Caesar's heir instead of the young Octavian, Anthony managed to hold his jealousy in check while the two men worked together to defeat those who had been responsible for Caesar's assassination. Once this was accomplished, Anthony came out against Octavian by joining forces with the Egyptian queen Cleopatra, who had been romantically involved with Caesar prior to his death. At the great naval battle of Actium in 31 B.C., Octavian's forces defeated Anthony and Cleopatra. By 29 B.C., the civil war was over, and the way was clear for Octavian to complete Caesar's work. He returned to Rome in triumph, adopted the name Augustus, and became Rome's first emperor.

Over the next few decades until his death in 14 A.D., Augustus transformed Rome from a republic to an empire and successfully concentrated power into the emperor's hands. Augustus set three precedents which were to become characteristic of future Roman emperors. First, Octavian appointed people who were loyal to him alone to positions of power throughout the empire. Second, he maintained the respect of the citizens of Rome, which provided him with a strong power base. Third, he ensured the loyalty of the Roman legions, so he used them to prevent the Senate from recapturing its former powers. Additionally, Augustus followed Caesar's example and adopted an heir, whom he trained to become the future emperor. In doing so, he guaranteed a smooth transition of power following his death.

So long as competent rulers sat on the throne, the Roman Empire was successful. The emperors who immediately followed Augustus imitated his custom of adopting heirs and training them well. Eventually, the position became hereditary though, and too many later emperors were weak and poorly trained. They relied excessively on the Roman people and the legions to maintain power. Still, the Roman Empire lasted for nearly five hundred years until barbarian hordes overran its borders and brought it to an end.

## Glossary

**intrigue:** a conspiracy; a plot
**legion:** a military unit in the Roman army

**11** Which of the sentences below best expresses the essential information in the highlighted sentence in the passage? *Incorrect* answer choices change the meaning in important ways or leave out essential information.

- Ⓐ Because so many Roman families were powerful, their members often engaged in various squabbles, which helped weaken the Roman Republic.

- Ⓑ The Senate could not stop various powerful people from engaging in intrigue, which later caused its downfall in spite of all the power it had.

- Ⓒ The Senate was responsible for taking care of Rome, but too many powerful families were only interested in how they themselves could benefit.

- Ⓓ The Senate was finally removed from power when its members began to care less about running Rome than they did their various political intrigues.

**Rome: From Republic to Empire**

Rome emerged as a center of power on the Italian peninsula by the banks of the Tiber River sometime around 500 B.C. After an early period of monarchy, the Roman people overthrew their leaders, established a culture that employed a system of democratic beliefs, and created an entity that would become known as the Roman Republic. Their political principles were based on an unwritten constitution that established a number of political offices with central powers and a system of checks and balances that limited those powers. At the apex of this system was the powerful Roman Senate, yet it too had limits on its authority. Over time, the Senate evolved into a representative body of the most powerful families in Rome. Despite controlling most aspects of Roman life, the Senate could never manage the political intrigue and infighting among its members and other powerful Roman families, which would prove to be its undoing. A power struggle in the first century B.C. led to a period of instability that eventually resulted in the death of the Roman Republic and the founding of the Roman Empire.

ACTUAL TEST **03**

**12** The author discusses Julius Caesar in paragraph 2 in order to

(A) explain why his assassination in 44 B.C. was justified

(B) blame him for abandoning his duty when he overthrew the republic

(C) show which of his actions led to the end of the Roman Republic

(D) describe the ill will that existed between him and the Senate

**13** The word virtual in the passage is closest in meaning to

(A) practical

(B) legitimate

(C) benevolent

(D) cruel

**14** According to paragraph 2, which of the following is true of Julius Caesar?

(A) He consolidated the power of Rome into one person's hands.

(B) He was assassinated in a plot by all of the members of the Senate.

(C) He conquered Gaul and other lands and then added them to the republic.

(D) He dissolved the Senate and ordered that it no longer meet.

²➜ Julius Caesar was at the center of this period of conflict. One of Rome's greatest military commanders, Caesar was involved in several political intrigues, which made him numerous enemies in the Senate. When the Senate banned Caesar from entering Rome in 49 B.C., he led his veteran army from Gaul—modern-day France—to the Italian peninsula and advanced on Rome. With only a weak army of recruits who had no hope of defeating Caesar's seasoned veterans, the Senate and its military leaders fled the city. After a short civil war, Caesar defeated his enemies and became the ruler of Rome. He invested the power of many political offices in his own person and ruled as a virtual dictator for five years. Caesar's acts deprived the Senate of much of its authority and set in motion the process for all of Rome's power to be held by a single individual. In response, the Senate reacted violently to the loss of its power and prestige, and many of its members played a central role in Caesar's assassination in 44 B.C.

---

**Glossary** ⊖

**intrigue:** a conspiracy; a plot

**15** Why does the author mention Actium?

   Ⓐ To give the name of the first battle of the Roman civil war

   Ⓑ To explain where Mark Anthony was defeated

   Ⓒ To credit Octavian with achieving a great military victory

   Ⓓ To provide the date when the battle was fought

**16** According to paragraph 3, Octavian and Mark Anthony fought one another because

   Ⓐ Octavian refused to share any of his power with Mark Anthony

   Ⓑ Mark Anthony had been involved in the assassination of Julius Caesar

   Ⓒ Octavian disliked the fact that Mark Anthony was allied with Cleopatra

   Ⓓ Mark Anthony had wanted to be selected as Julius Caesar's heir

³➡ Following Caesar's death, a new period of instability and civil war started. Octavian, Caesar's nephew and adopted heir, established an alliance with Caesar's trusted friend and lieutenant Mark Anthony. Having expected to be named Caesar's heir instead of the young Octavian, Anthony managed to hold his jealousy in check while the two men worked together to defeat those who had been responsible for Caesar's assassination. Once this was accomplished, Anthony came out against Octavian by joining forces with the Egyptian queen Cleopatra, who had been romantically involved with Caesar prior to his death. At the great naval battle of Actium in 31 B.C., Octavian's forces defeated Anthony and Cleopatra. By 29 B.C., the civil war was over, and the way was clear for Octavian to complete Caesar's work. He returned to Rome in triumph, adopted the name Augustus, and became Rome's first emperor.

ACTUAL TEST **03**

**17** The phrase characteristic of in the passage is closest in meaning to

(A) possible to

(B) distinctive of

(C) required for

(D) imagined by

**18** In paragraph 4, the author's description of Octavian's actions while emperor mentions all of the following EXCEPT:

(A) The manner in which he stopped the Senate from regaining power

(B) Who he appointed to various positions of power in the empire

(C) How he trained his son to assume the duties of emperor after he died

(D) How he managed to obtain the support of the people of Rome

⁴→ Over the next few decades until his death in 14 A.D., Augustus transformed Rome from a republic to an empire and successfully concentrated power into the emperor's hands. Augustus set three precedents which were to become characteristic of future Roman emperors. First, Octavian appointed people who were loyal to him alone to positions of power throughout the empire. Second, he maintained the respect of the citizens of Rome, which provided him with a strong power base. Third, he ensured the loyalty of the Roman legions, so he used them to prevent the Senate from recapturing its former powers. Additionally, Augustus followed Caesar's example and adopted an heir, whom he trained to become the future emperor. In doing so, he guaranteed a smooth transition of power following his death.

---

**Glossary**                                                          ⊖

**legion :** a military unit in the Roman army

**19** Look at the four squares [ ■ ] that indicate where the following sentence could be added to the passage.

**They not only lost the battle but also lost their lives in the process.**

Where would the sentence best fit?

Click on a square [ ■ ] to add the sentence to the passage.

Following Caesar's death, a new period of instability and civil war started. Octavian, Caesar's nephew and adopted heir, established an alliance with Caesar's trusted friend and lieutenant Mark Anthony. Having expected to be named Caesar's heir instead of the young Octavian, Anthony managed to hold his jealousy in check while the two men worked together to defeat those who had been responsible for Caesar's assassination. Once this was accomplished, Anthony came out against Octavian by joining forces with the Egyptian queen Cleopatra, who had been romantically involved with Caesar prior to his death. **1** At the great naval battle of Actium in 31 B.C., Octavian's forces defeated Anthony and Cleopatra. **2** By 29 B.C., the civil war was over, and the way was clear for Octavian to complete Caesar's work. **3** He returned to Rome in triumph, adopted the name Augustus, and became Rome's first emperor. **4**

20 **Directions:** Select the appropriate sentences from the answer choices and match them to the period of Roman history to which they relate. TWO of the answer choices will NOT be used. **This question is worth 3 points.**

Drag your answer choices to the spaces where they belong.
To remove an answer choice, click on it. To review the passage, click on **View Text**.

| **Answer Choices** | **PERIOD OF ROMAN HISTORY** |
|---|---|
| ① Octavian and Mark Anthony joined forces in battle. | **Roman Republic** |
| ② Eventually, Roman rulers came to be determined by their parentage. | • |
| ③ Rome became a great power on the Italian peninsula. | • |
| ④ The people of Rome became loyal to Augustus. | **Roman Empire** |
| ⑤ Julius Caesar was assassinated by a conspiracy of senators. | • |
| ⑥ Rome was governed primarily by democratic principles. | • |
| ⑦ An heir was chosen and trained to become the next ruler of Rome. | • |

TOEFL® MAP **ACTUAL TEST**

?
HELP

◄◄
BACK

►►
NEXT

READING

00:18:00 ⊝ HIDE TIME

# Carnivorous Plants

Carnivorous Venus flytraps and sundews

Plants require nourishment like all other living organisms, and most get it from the soil by absorbing nutrients such as nitrogen. They additionally convert the chlorophyll found in their leaves into glucose with the assistance of sunlight in the process known as photosynthesis. Nevertheless, some plants are carnivorous, so they devour small creatures such as insects to get the nourishment they need to sustain them. These carnivorous plants mostly accomplish this by attracting animals, trapping them, digesting them, and then absorbing their nutrients.

At present, botanists have identified and named more than 600 carnivorous plants. To be classified as one, the plant must have a means of trapping and holding prey, a method of digesting that prey, and a way of absorbing the nutrients that can be obtained from the digesting of its prey. A few plants possess some, but not all, of these characteristics, so they are therefore not considered carnivorous. Botanists also disagree on the mechanism of digestion. Some think that a plant must utilize enzymes which it produces to digest insects to be considered carnivorous. Yet one class of plants traps insects and uses bacteria that the plants themselves do not produce when they digest their prey, so some botanists insist that they are not actually carnivorous plants. There are more than 300 of these types of borderline carnivorous plants, which have been termed protocarnivorous plants.

In general, carnivorous plants grow in regions with poor soil conditions, such as bogs and areas with rocky terrain. Thus they have adapted and survived through the acquiring of nutrients from other sources—namely, insects. The methods utilized to attract insects vary from plant to plant. Some use sweet nectar to lure insects into their traps while others depend on enticing smells or their physical appearances to gain the attention of passing insects. Once attracted to the plants, the insects are typically ensnared by their traps.

There are five traps most commonly employed by carnivorous plants: pitfall traps, snapping traps, sticky traps, suction traps, and lobster pot traps. The pitfall trap is typically employed by carnivorous plants such as the pitcher plant. The pitcher plant is tubelike and has an opening that attracts insects in some manner. Once the insect is on the plant, its waxy surface causes it to fall down and to slip into the opening. Most of the time, the insect cannot crawl out of the trap. Snapping traps, such as those used by the Venus flytrap, have parts—like leaves—that can close rapidly and trap insects before they are able to escape. While the Venus flytrap is a relatively well-known carnivorous plant, it is in fact one of only two plants that utilize the snapping-trap mechanism.

Instead, sticky traps are much more common. Plants that utilize sticky traps have a glue-like substance on their surface that ensnares insects and prevents them from escaping. Suction traps are frequently utilized by plants growing near water. These create a vacuum when a bladder inside the plant is squeezed. Passing insects are literally sucked into the plant along with the water. Finally, lobster pot traps operate on the same principles as a lobster pot, hence the name. Insects can crawl into the plant but cannot crawl back out. Tiny hairs on the plants' surfaces point only in one direction, which allows insects to enter, but when they try to leave, the hairs prevent them from escaping. With the exception of the snapping trap, every type of trap that carnivorous plants employ has a number of varieties.

Once an insect is trapped in a carnivorous plant, it is slowly digested by enzymes in the plant's interior. The nutrients enter the plant by one of three methods. First, most carnivorous plants have a protective layer called a cuticle, which is waxy. But some carnivorous plants lack this waxy lining, so the nutrients are absorbed directly into them. Other carnivorous plants have specialized cell structures that open temporarily to permit the nutrients to pass through the cuticle. Finally, a third type of carnivorous plants has permanent breaks in the cuticle to allow for the passing of nutrients. Whatever the case, the nutrients are eventually absorbed, which permits the plants to obtain the nutrition they need to continue living.

---

Glossary

**mechanism:** a process; a way of doing something
**bog:** a swampy area; an area of land that is wet and has spongy ground

**21** According to paragraph 1, why are some plants carnivorous?

Ⓐ They are unable to extract sufficient amounts of nitrogen from the soil.

Ⓑ They need to create glucose and other nutrients from the bodies of insects.

Ⓒ They require the nourishment that the animals they trap can provide them.

Ⓓ They live in regions that lack enough sunlight for them to use photosynthesis.

**22** Why does the author mention protocarnivorous plants?

Ⓐ To provide the name of some plants which are not truly carnivorous

Ⓑ To explain that they rely more upon photosynthesis than upon captured insects

Ⓒ To claim that they contain enzymes that help them digest their prey

Ⓓ To compare their numbers with those of other types of carnivorous plants

**23** According to paragraph 2, some botanists consider a plant to be carnivorous when

Ⓐ it absorbs bacteria from the bodies of dead animals

Ⓑ it both digests and absorbs the prey that it captures

Ⓒ it makes use of the enzymes that are found in certain animals

Ⓓ it eats either live or dead animals that it finds and captures

**Carnivorous Plants**

[1] → Plants require nourishment like all other living organisms, and most get it from the soil by absorbing nutrients such as nitrogen. They additionally convert the chlorophyll found in their leaves into glucose with the assistance of sunlight in the process known as photosynthesis. Nevertheless, some plants are carnivorous, so they devour small creatures such as insects to get the nourishment they need to sustain them. These carnivorous plants mostly accomplish this by attracting animals, trapping them, digesting them, and then absorbing their nutrients.

[2] → At present, botanists have identified and named more than 600 carnivorous plants. To be classified as one, the plant must have a means of trapping and holding prey, a method of digesting that prey, and a way of absorbing the nutrients that can be obtained from the digesting of its prey. A few plants possess some, but not all, of these characteristics, so they are therefore not considered carnivorous. Botanists also disagree on the mechanism of digestion. Some think that a plant must utilize enzymes which it produces to digest insects to be considered carnivorous. Yet one class of plants traps insects and uses bacteria that the plants themselves do not produce when they digest their prey, so some botanists insist that they are not actually carnivorous plants. There are more than 300 of these types of borderline carnivorous plants, which have been termed protocarnivorous plants.

**Glossary**

**mechanism:** a process; a way of doing something

**24** The word enticing in the passage is closest in meaning to

(A) pleasant

(B) powerful

(C) appealing

(D) exotic

**25** The author's description of the pitfall trap in paragraph 4 mentions all of the following EXCEPT:

(A) the method that the trap itself uses to catch insects

(B) the shape of the trap that the plants utilize

(C) the connection that it has with the Venus flytrap

(D) the type of plants that it is commonly employed by

**26** In paragraph 4, the author implies that snapping traps

(A) are the least common method of ensnarement used by carnivorous plants

(B) are highly effective, which is why the Venus flytrap is so well known

(C) work much better against crawling insects than they do against flying ones

(D) may become ineffective if the insect that gets trapped is very small

In general, carnivorous plants grow in regions with poor soil conditions, such as bogs and areas with rocky terrain. Thus they have adapted and survived through the acquiring of nutrients from other sources—namely, insects. The methods utilized to attract insects vary from plant to plant. Some use sweet nectar to lure insects into their traps while others depend on enticing smells or their physical appearances to gain the attention of passing insects. Once attracted to the plants, the insects are typically ensnared by their traps.

⁴→ There are five traps most commonly employed by carnivorous plants: pitfall traps, snapping traps, sticky traps, suction traps, and lobster pot traps. The pitfall trap is typically employed by carnivorous plants such as the pitcher plant. The pitcher plant is tubelike and has an opening that attracts insects in some manner. Once the insect is on the plant, its waxy surface causes it to fall down and to slip into the opening. Most of the time, the insect cannot crawl out of the trap. Snapping traps, such as those used by the Venus flytrap, have parts—like leaves—that can close rapidly and trap insects before they are able to escape. While the Venus flytrap is a relatively well-known carnivorous plant, it is in fact one of only two plants that utilize the snapping-trap mechanism.

---

**Glossary** ⊖

**bog:** a swampy area; an area of land that is wet and has spongy ground

27 According to paragraph 5, which of the following is true of suction traps?

Ⓐ Some of them have been known to capture animals as big as lobsters.

Ⓑ They rely upon a substance that is like glue to ensnare their prey.

Ⓒ The plants that utilize them can grow to be enormous in size.

Ⓓ Carnivorous plants that live in watery regions are likely to have them.

28 According to paragraph 6, some carnivorous plants have cuts in their cuticles because

Ⓐ a plant with a cuticle that totally surrounds it cannot acquire any nutrients

Ⓑ they do not get enough nutrition for their cuticles to be complete

Ⓒ the openings enable nutrients to be absorbed into the interiors of the plants

Ⓓ the cuts provide places for the plants' enzymes to digest the captured prey

29 Look at the four squares [ ■ ] that indicate where the following sentence could be added to the passage.

**The corkscrew plant uses this method as the hairs basically force insects backward into a chamber, where they are then digested.**

Where would the sentence best fit?

Click on a square [ ■ ] to add the sentence to the passage.

⁵➡ Instead, sticky traps are much more common. Plants that utilize sticky traps have a glue-like substance on their surface that ensnares insects and prevents them from escaping. Suction traps are frequently utilized by plants growing near water. These create a vacuum when a bladder inside the plant is squeezed. Passing insects are literally sucked into the plant along with the water. Finally, lobster pot traps operate on the same principles as a lobster pot, hence the name. **1** Insects can crawl into the plant but cannot crawl back out. **2** Tiny hairs on the plants' surfaces point only in one direction, which allows insects to enter, but when they try to leave, the hairs prevent them from escaping. **3** With the exception of the snapping trap, every type of trap that carnivorous plants employ has a number of varieties. **4**

⁶➡ Once an insect is trapped in a carnivorous plant, it is slowly digested by enzymes in the plant's interior. The nutrients enter the plant by one of three methods. First, most carnivorous plants have a protective layer called a cuticle, which is waxy. But some carnivorous plants lack this waxy lining, so the nutrients are absorbed directly into them. Other carnivorous plants have specialized cell structures that open temporarily to permit the nutrients to pass through the cuticle. Finally, a third type of carnivorous plants has permanent breaks in the cuticle to allow for the passing of nutrients. Whatever the case, the nutrients are eventually absorbed, which permits the plants to obtain the nutrition they need to continue living.

ACTUAL TEST **03**

**30 Directions:** An introductory sentence for a brief summary of the passage is provided below. Complete the summary by selecting the THREE answer choices that express the most important ideas of the passage. Some sentences do not belong because they express ideas that are not presented in the passage or are minor ideas in the passage. **This question is worth 2 points.**

> Drag your answer choices to the spaces where they belong.
> To remove an answer choice, click on it. To review the passage, click on **View Text**.

**Carnivorous plants rely upon a variety of methods to trap insects and then to digest them in order to absorb their nutrients.**

- •
- •
- •

## Answer Choices

1. Carnivorous plants typically employ one of the five primary types of traps to capture insects.

2. There are at least 600 species of carnivorous plants and another 300 species of protocarnivorous plants.

3. Botanists frequently disagree over what qualifies a plant to be considered truly carnivorous in nature.

4. Carnivorous plants must often ensnare organisms because they live in places with unsuitable growing conditions.

5. The Venus flytrap is the most famous of all carnivorous plants, and it also uses a trap that is quite common.

6. When a plant digests an animal, the nutrients in that animal's body are then absorbed into the plant and used to support it.

# TOEFL® MAP

## ACTUAL TEST  Reading 1

04

## Reading Section Directions

This section measures your ability to understand academic passages in English. You will have **72 minutes** to read and answer questions about **4 passages**. A clock at the top of the screen will show you how much time is remaining.

Most questions are worth 1 point but the last question for each passage is worth more than 1 point. The directions for the last question indicate how many points you may receive.

Some passages include a word or phrase that is <u>underlined</u> in blue. Click on the word or phrase to see a definition or an explanation.

When you want to move to the next question, click on **Next**. You may skip questions and go back to them later. If you want to return to previous questions, click on **Back**. You can click on **Review** at any time, and the review screen will show you which questions you have answered and which you have not answered. From this review screen, you may go directly to any question you have already seen in the Reading section.

Click on **Continue** to go on.

ACTUAL TEST 04

# The Earth's Climate in the Cambrian Period

Anomalocaris, a creature from the Cambrian Period

The Earth's climate has changed during the planet's long existence. Sometimes it was much colder than today while at other times, the temperature was much hotter. One time when there were significant climate differences from modern times was the Cambrian Period. It lasted from 541 to 285 million years ago and was a part of a longer geological time period called the Paleozoic Era. The Cambrian Period was a time with much hotter temperatures, resulting in a climate which was much more amenable to newer life forms than previous periods. This led to a significant change in the types of organisms on the Earth. Single-celled organisms mostly gave way to multi-celled complex lifeforms, including the first shellfish and vertebrates. As a result of this expansion in the number of lifeforms, scientists call this event the Cambrian Explosion.

Scientists theorize that the average global temperature during the Cambrian Period was approximately twenty-two degrees Celsius. This compares to the present-day average of fourteen degrees Celsius. The temperature was thought to have been so high due to the greenhouse effect caused by the sun's heat being trapped near the Earth's surface for an extended period of time. This theory was unproven for decades until a recent study in Great Britain managed to find a way to measure temperatures during the Cambrian Period. The most common way for scientists to determine the temperature and the climate in the past is to examine tree rings and ice cores. However, trees did not exist then, and scientists have yet to discover any ice cores more than a few million years old.

In order to discover temperatures during the Cambrian Period, the British team of scientists studied oxygen levels in fossils. They examined two oxygen isotopes, oxygen-16, which is very common on the Earth, and the rarer isotope oxygen-18. Organisms in the Cambrian Period mostly lived in the oceans, where they absorbed oxygen from sea water into their shells and bones. The evaporation and condensation rates of water are slightly different depending upon which oxygen isotope is present. By examining the ratio of the two different isotopes in these fossils, scientists could judge the temperatures as well as the resulting climate during the Cambrian Period.

The use of fossils was necessary in this study due to the properties of calcium carbonate and calcium phosphate, which can absorb oxygen, in shells and bones. However, the researchers initially found only one set of fossils for which this technique managed to produce the desired results. This was an early form of vertebrate called a conodont. Unfortunately, this organism only existed in the late Cambrian Period, so the fossil was not useful for studying the temperatures and the climate at the start of the Cambrian Period. Recently, a team in Britain was able to use fossils from the shellfish group called brachiopods, which were fossilized in limestone in Britain between 510 and 520 million years ago. This method yielded data showing that temperatures in the early Cambrian Period at the Earth's high northern latitudes were consistently between twenty and twenty-five degrees Celsius. This data was then used to extrapolate worldwide average temperatures, which in turn gave weight to the theory of a greenhouse-like effect on the Earth during this time. Furthermore, the theory of a greenhouse climate was bolstered when the temperature data was compared and found to be similar to better known periods of greenhouse-like effects during the Mesozoic and Cenozoic eras.

One result of this rise in temperatures during the Cambrian Period was the mass introduction of new lifeforms. Prior to this period, most lifeforms lived in oceans and were single-celled organisms. A few million years before the Cambrian Period began, these forms gradually began evolving into multi-cellular organisms, yet this was a slow process. However, with the rise in global temperatures, conditions became more favorable, so a greater number of multi-cellular organisms, including shellfish and vertebrates, developed during the Cambrian Period. As a result of the mineral compositions of shells and bones in these creatures, the world's first significant fossilizations of organisms started. Beginning in the Cambrian Period, the fossil record becomes rich with lifeforms that were the precursors to many modern lifeforms. These fossils in turn allow scientists to better understand the Earth's past climate.

## Glossary

**ice core:** a sample of ice removed from a glacier or ice sheet
**isotope:** one of two or more atoms of an element with the same atomic number but a different number of neutrons in its nucleus

1   In paragraph 1, why does the author mention the Paleozoic Era?

   Ⓐ To point out some of the differences between geological eras and periods

   Ⓑ To state that the Cambrian Period took place during one part of that era

   Ⓒ To argue that there were fewer multi-celled organisms than previously thought then

   Ⓓ To remark that geologists do not know enough about that geological era

2   The phrase amenable to in the passage is closest in meaning to

   Ⓐ consistent with

   Ⓑ approachable to

   Ⓒ sufficient for

   Ⓓ agreeable to

**The Climate in the Cambrian Period**

[1]→ The Earth's climate has changed during the planet's long existence. Sometimes it was much colder than today while at other times, the temperature was much hotter. One time when there were significant climate differences from modern times was the Cambrian Period. It lasted from 541 to 285 million years ago and was a part of a longer geological time period called the Paleozoic Era. The Cambrian Period was a time with much hotter temperatures, resulting in a climate which was much more amenable to newer life forms than previous periods. This led to a significant change in the types of organisms on the Earth. Single-celled organisms mostly gave way to multi-celled complex lifeforms, including the first shellfish and vertebrates. As a result of this expansion in the number of lifeforms, scientists call this event the Cambrian Explosion.

ACTUAL TEST 04

**3**  According to paragraph 2, the average temperature during the Cambrian Period was so high because

Ⓐ some of the heat from the sun remained near the Earth's surface for a long time

Ⓑ more of the sun's heat was able to reach the Earth due to a relative lack of clouds

Ⓒ the Earth's orbit made it travel much closer to the sun than it does in modern times

Ⓓ the greenhouse effect caused ice sheets and glaciers to melt and made the Earth warmer

**4**  According to paragraph 3, scientists were able to determine temperatures during the Cambrian Period by

Ⓐ studying both tree rings and ice cores and analyzing the oxygen isotopes found within them

Ⓑ figuring out how much oxygen existed in the atmosphere during that time

Ⓒ analyzing the amounts of different types of oxygen isotopes in fossils of water creatures

Ⓓ studying how much water evaporated and condensed in places all around the world

² → Scientists theorize that the average global temperature during the Cambrian Period was approximately twenty-two degrees Celsius. This compares to the present-day average of fourteen degrees Celsius. The temperature was thought to have been so high due to the greenhouse effect caused by the sun's heat being trapped near the Earth's surface for an extended period of time. This theory was unproven for decades until a recent study in Great Britain managed to find a way to measure temperatures during the Cambrian Period. The most common way for scientists to determine the temperature and the climate in the past is to examine tree rings and ice cores. However, trees did not exist then, and scientists have yet to discover any ice cores more than a few million years old.

³ → In order to discover temperatures during the Cambrian Period, the British team of scientists studied oxygen levels in fossils. They examined two oxygen isotopes, oxygen-16, which is very common on the Earth, and the rarer isotope oxygen-18. Organisms in the Cambrian Period mostly lived in the oceans, where they absorbed oxygen from sea water into their shells and bones. The evaporation and condensation rates of water are slightly different depending upon which oxygen isotope is present. By examining the ratio of the two different isotopes in these fossils, scientists could judge the temperatures as well as the resulting climate during the Cambrian Period.

---

**Glossary**

**ice core:** a sample of ice removed from a glacier or ice sheet

**isotope:** one of two or more atoms of an element with the same atomic number but a different number of neutrons in its nucleus

**5** In paragraph 4, the author uses a conodont as an example of

Ⓐ a fossil from the past that was found to have absorbed oxygen in its shell and bones

Ⓑ the most typical animal from the Cambrian Period that has been found in fossilized form

Ⓒ an organism that lived during the entire Cambrian Period but thrived at the end of that period

Ⓓ an animal whose fossils have been found in great number in various parts of Britain

**6** The word yielded in the passage is closest in meaning to

Ⓐ surrendered

Ⓑ analyzed

Ⓒ repeated

Ⓓ provided

**7** In paragraph 4, which of the following can be inferred about the Cambrian Period?

Ⓐ It was the hottest period of time during the Earth's entire history.

Ⓑ The most common animals that existed during it were vertebrates living in the oceans.

Ⓒ Scientists do not know as much about it as they do the Mesozoic and Cenozoic eras.

Ⓓ Only a relatively small number of fossils of animals that lived during it have been found.

⁴➡ The use of fossils was necessary in this study due to the properties of calcium carbonate and calcium phosphate, which can absorb oxygen, in shells and bones. However, the researchers initially found only one set of fossils for which this technique managed to produce the desired results. This was an early form of vertebrate called a conodont. Unfortunately, this organism only existed in the late Cambrian Period, so the fossil was not useful for studying the temperatures and the climate at the start of the Cambrian Period. Recently, a team in Britain was able to use fossils from the shellfish group called brachiopods, which were fossilized in limestone in Britain between 510 and 520 million years ago. This method yielded data showing that temperatures in the early Cambrian Period at the Earth's high northern latitudes were consistently between twenty and twenty-five degrees Celsius. This data was then used to extrapolate worldwide average temperatures, which in turn gave weight to the theory of a greenhouse-like effect on the Earth during this time. Furthermore, the theory of a greenhouse climate was bolstered when the temperature data was compared and found to be similar to better known periods of greenhouse-like effects during the Mesozoic and Cenozoic eras.

ACTUAL TEST **04**

**8**   In paragraph 5, all of the following questions are answered EXCEPT:

   Ⓐ What were some types of animals that began to exist during the Cambrian Period?

   Ⓑ What parts of the world have scientists found fossils from the Cambrian Period in?

   Ⓒ What was one important effect of the high temperatures that existed during the Cambrian Period?

   Ⓓ What allowed a large number of animals to begin to be fossilized during the Cambrian Period?

**9**   Look at the four squares [ ■ ] that indicate where the following sentence could be added to the passage.

   **Called the Cambrian Explosion, this period is considered one of the most vital times in the Earth's history since the ancestors of so many modern-day organisms appeared during it.**

   Where would the sentence best fit?

   Click on a square [ ■ ] to add the sentence to the passage.

---

⁵➜ One result of this rise in temperatures during the Cambrian Period was the mass introduction of new lifeforms. Prior to this period, most lifeforms lived in oceans and were single-celled organisms. A few million years before the Cambrian Period began, these forms gradually began evolving into multi-cellular organisms, yet this was a slow process. However, with the rise in global temperatures, conditions became more favorable, so a greater number of multi-cellular organisms, including shellfish and vertebrates, developed during the Cambrian Period. **1** As a result of the mineral compositions of shells and bones in these creatures, the world's first significant fossilizations of organisms started. **2** Beginning in the Cambrian Period, the fossil record becomes rich with lifeforms that were the precursors to many modern lifeforms. **3** These fossils in turn allow scientists to better understand the Earth's past climate. **4**

10 **Directions:** An introductory sentence for a brief summary of the passage is provided below. Complete the summary by selecting the THREE answer choices that express the most important ideas of the passage. Some sentences do not belong because they express ideas that are not presented in the passage or are minor ideas in the passage. **This question is worth 2 points.**

> Drag your answer choices to the spaces where they belong.
> To remove an answer choice, click on it. To review the passage, click on **View Text**.

**The Cambrian Period was a time when global temperatures were warm, so new organisms developed during this age.**

- 
- 
- 

## Answer Choices

1. It is difficult for scientists to study the Cambrian Period because it took place hundreds of millions of years ago.

2. Some fossils from the Cambrian Period have been found to contain traces of oxygen-16 and oxygen-18.

3. Greater numbers of vertebrates lived during the Mesozoic and Cenozoic eras than lived during the Cambrian Period.

4. The warmer temperatures of the Cambrian Period allowed new organisms such as shellfish and vertebrates to develop.

5. Many new lifeforms from the Cambrian Period were fossilized, thereby allowing scientists to learn more about this time.

6. Scientists believe the Earth's temperature was warm during the Cambrian Period because of a greenhouse-like effect that happened then.

# Premature Aging

Many people eventually grow old and die. But there are some children who age at such a rapid rate that their bodies exhibit signs of aging while they are still in their youth. This is the result of a disease known as progeria. People who suffer from progeria do not develop in the same manner as the vast majority of children. Instead, children with this disease exhibit various features of the elderly and are particularly susceptible to maladies that afflict the old, such as cardiovascular ones. Very few individuals who suffer from progeria succeed at living past the age of twenty-one as the average age of death from this disease is thirteen. Unfortunately, since it is exceedingly rare, few funds are being spent on finding a cure for it, which makes it likely that one will not be found for quite some time.

Fewer than fifty cases of progeria have been diagnosed anywhere in the world. The disease is caused by a defect in a person's genetic code in the protein Lamin A. This protein holds the nuclei of cells together, but the defect makes the nuclei unstable, which results in a person rapidly aging. Because so few people suffer from this disease, medical experts are uncertain exactly how or why the Lamin A protein becomes defective. It is not believed that progeria is hereditary despite the fact that there are two cases in which a family had more than one child with it. Instead, most cases seemingly strike at random. Likewise, there is no ethnicity or nation that has many more cases than others; this is unlike other rare diseases, which frequently affect a particular ethnic or racial group more than others. As a result, it is impossible to create a test for early detection to determine who is likely to bear a child with progeria.

A family with a normal healthy child has no way of knowing if progeria will afflict the boy or girl. The reason is that progeria's symptoms do not manifest until a child is between ten and twenty-four months old. At that time, certain features of rapid aging become noticeable. These include limited growth, a loss of body fat and hair, stiffness in the joints, and the appearance of aging skin. Children with progeria also appear to have pinched faces and develop small facial features with more rounded bald heads, which give them the appearance of elderly people. Common health issues for children with progeria are hip dislocations, heart disease, and strokes, all of which are problems that the elderly typically suffer from. Doctors estimate that progeria sufferers age at a rate eight to ten times faster than healthy children. Most sufferers die between the ages of eight and twenty-one while only a few live any longer than that.

Once a child starts exhibiting signs of progeria, a genetic test can determine if this is indeed the disease the child has. While doctors can determine its existence, they cannot cure it, so its sufferers all eventually succumb to death. Currently, researchers looking for a cure are concentrating on reversing the abnormality which affects the nuclei of cells. One method under consideration is the use of drugs that help eliminate some types of cancer. These tests are only in their initial stages though, so it will likely take at least several more years before a viable cure exists. In the meantime, those children presently dealing with progeria are attempting to extend their lives through controlled diets and the taking of medication to treat heart disease.

Part of the reason why medical researchers have been unable to find a cure for progeria is that it happens so infrequently. Because there are but a handful of progeria cases, neither expert medical researchers nor funds are attracted to the cause. The lion's share of expertise and research money instead goes to diseases such as cancer, which affects an exponentially greater number of people. Nevertheless, progeria has recently attracted the interest of some members of the medical community because research on it may offer clues into why people age. Some speculate that if researchers find a way to cure progeria, they might also learn how to slow advanced aging in adults.

---

## Glossary

**cardiovascular:** relating to the heart and blood vessels
**hereditary:** genetic; transmissible

**11** The word susceptible in the passage is closest in meaning to

(A) resistant

(B) opposed

(C) reactive

(D) vulnerable

**12** The author discusses Lamin A in paragraph 2 in order to

(A) focus on the genetic makeup of that particular protein

(B) describe what doctors believe causes a person to get progeria

(C) mention that it is only found in the bodies of some individuals

(D) explain why there are so few cases of progeria around the world

**13** In paragraph 2, the author implies that progeria

(A) behaves differently from other rare diseases that affect people

(B) will likely become a more common disease in the future

(C) requires an accurate test before scientists can understand it better

(D) probably affects more people than doctors are aware of

| **Glossary**                                              ⊖ |
| --- |
| **cardiovascular:** relating to the heart and blood vessels |
| **hereditary:** genetic; transmissible |

**Premature Aging**

Many people eventually grow old and die. But there are some children who age at such a rapid rate that their bodies exhibit signs of aging while they are still in their youth. This is the result of a disease known as progeria. People who suffer from progeria do not develop in the same manner as the vast majority of children. Instead, children with this disease exhibit various features of the elderly and are particularly susceptible to maladies that afflict the old, such as cardiovascular ones. Very few individuals who suffer from progeria succeed at living past the age of twenty-one as the average age of death from this disease is thirteen. Unfortunately, since it is exceedingly rare, few funds are being spent on finding a cure for it, which makes it likely that one will not be found for quite some time.

2 ➡ Fewer than fifty cases of progeria have been diagnosed anywhere in the world. The disease is caused by a defect in a person's genetic code in the protein Lamin A. This protein holds the nuclei of cells together, but the defect makes the nuclei unstable, which results in a person rapidly aging. Because so few people suffer from this disease, medical experts are uncertain exactly how or why the Lamin A protein becomes defective. It is not believed that progeria is hereditary despite the fact that there are two cases in which a family had more than one child with it. Instead, most cases seemingly strike at random. Likewise, there is no ethnicity or nation that has many more cases than others; this is unlike other rare diseases, which frequently affect a particular ethnic or racial group more than others. As a result, it is impossible to create a test for early detection to determine who is likely to bear a child with progeria.

**14** In paragraph 3, why does the author mention hip dislocations, heart disease, and strokes?

Ⓐ To name some of the problems that people with progeria often have

Ⓑ To blame these health issues for the deaths of many people with progeria

Ⓒ To claim that the elderly must deal with these problems more than progeria sufferers

Ⓓ To explain why most progeria sufferers die when they are still quite young

**15** In paragraph 3, the author's description of the features of progeria mentions all of the following EXCEPT:

Ⓐ the ages when most of the sufferers of the disease pass away

Ⓑ the facial appearances of the people who suffer from it

Ⓒ the pain that people with the disease are forced to endure

Ⓓ the age period people are in when it begins to affect them

³→ A family with a normal healthy child has no way of knowing if progeria will afflict the boy or girl. The reason is that progeria's symptoms do not manifest until a child is between ten and twenty-four months old. At that time, certain features of rapid aging become noticeable. These include limited growth, a loss of body fat and hair, stiffness in the joints, and the appearance of aging skin. Children with progeria also appear to have pinched faces and develop small facial features with more rounded bald heads, which give them the appearance of elderly people. Common health issues for children with progeria are hip dislocations, heart disease, and strokes, all of which are problems that the elderly typically suffer from. Doctors estimate that progeria sufferers age at a rate eight to ten times faster than healthy children. Most sufferers die between the ages of eight and twenty-one while only a few live any longer than that.

ACTUAL TEST **04**

109

**16** The word viable in the passage is closest in meaning to

  Ⓐ feasible

  Ⓑ transparent

  Ⓒ respectable

  Ⓓ immediate

**17** According to paragraph 4, doctors lack a cure for progeria because

  Ⓐ finding a cure for it is more difficult than finding a cure for cancer

  Ⓑ the genetic makeup of the disease is too complex for them to understand

  Ⓒ taking heart disease medicine is sufficient for those with progeria

  Ⓓ they have just begun to conduct tests in order to find one

**18** Which of the following can be inferred from paragraph 5 about progeria?

  Ⓐ Larger amounts of money will likely be spent researching it in the future.

  Ⓑ Some doctors are abandoning cancer research in order to begin studying it.

  Ⓒ There is a hospital being built that will be used only for progeria patients.

  Ⓓ A few of the medical profession's top researchers are working to try to cure it.

---

[4] → Once a child starts exhibiting signs of progeria, a genetic test can determine if this is indeed the disease the child has. While doctors can determine its existence, they cannot cure it, so its sufferers all eventually succumb to death. Currently, researchers looking for a cure are concentrating on reversing the abnormality which affects the nuclei of cells. One method under consideration is the use of drugs that help eliminate some types of cancer. These tests are only in their initial stages though, so it will likely take at least several more years before a viable cure exists. In the meantime, those children presently dealing with progeria are attempting to extend their lives through controlled diets and the taking of medication to treat heart disease.

[5] → Part of the reason why medical researchers have been unable to find a cure for progeria is that it happens so infrequently. Because there are but a handful of progeria cases, neither expert medical researchers nor funds are attracted to the cause. The lion's share of expertise and research money instead goes to diseases such as cancer, which affects an exponentially greater number of people. Nevertheless, progeria has recently attracted the interest of some members of the medical community because research on it may offer clues into why people age. Some speculate that if researchers find a way to cure progeria, they might also learn how to slow advanced aging in adults.

19  Look at the four squares [ ■ ] that indicate where the following sentence could be added to the passage.

**A ten-year-old child with progeria would therefore be similar in some regards to a person several decades older.**

Where would the sentence best fit?

Click on a square [ ■ ] to add the sentence to the passage.

A family with a normal healthy child has no way of knowing if progeria will afflict the boy or girl. The reason is that progeria's symptoms do not manifest until a child is between ten and twenty-four months old. At that time, certain features of rapid aging become noticeable. These include limited growth, a loss of body fat and hair, stiffness in the joints, and the appearance of aging skin. Children with progeria also appear to have pinched faces and develop small facial features with more rounded bald heads, which give them the appearance of elderly people. **1** Common health issues for children with progeria are hip dislocations, heart disease, and strokes, all of which are problems that the elderly typically suffer from. **2** Doctors estimate that progeria sufferers age at a rate eight to ten times faster than healthy children. **3** Most sufferers die between the ages of eight and twenty-one while only a few live any longer than that. **4**

ACTUAL TEST 04

20 **Directions:** An introductory sentence for a brief summary of the passage is provided below. Complete the summary by selecting the THREE answer choices that express the most important ideas of the passage. Some sentences do not belong because they express ideas that are not presented in the passage or are minor ideas in the passage. **This question is worth 2 points.**

> Drag your answer choices to the spaces where they belong.
> To remove an answer choice, click on it. To review the passage, click on **View Text**.

**Progeria is a rare disease that causes rapid aging in children and is thus far incurable.**

- •
- •
- •

**Answer Choices**

1. Because there is no cure for progeria, everyone who gets it eventually dies.

2. A problem with a protein in the body is believed to be the cause of progeria.

3. Scientists are aware of fewer than twenty cases of progeria in the world.

4. Doctors argue that more money needs to be spent on finding a cure for progeria.

5. Progeria does not appear to affect people of one ethnicity more than any other.

6. People who suffer from progeria begin to take on the appearances of elderly individuals.

TOEFL® MAP **ACTUAL TEST**

?
HELP

◀◀
BACK

▶▶
NEXT

READING

00:36:00 ⊖ HIDE TIME

# Early Types of Clocks

A sundial located in the ancient city of Tarragona, Spain

Clocks are ubiquitous in the present day and range from simple wristwatches to atomic clocks which people use to keep accurate time. However, clocks were not always that common, so early men frequently relied upon the movements of **heavenly bodies** and the passing of the seasons to measure time. But stargazing and keeping track of the seasons were employed to measure large units of time—months and years. As life became more complex and civilizations arose though, it gradually became necessary to keep track of time on a daily basis. Accordingly, throughout human history, a number of different types of clocks have been used.

Among the earliest clocks made by humans were sundials. They were limited in that they could not be used after the sun had set and the shadows that sundials cast depend upon the latitude at which a person is. Resultantly, sundials could only be utilized to keep track of the local time during daylight hours, which made them unreliable and relatively ineffective. These limitations inspired humans to attempt to develop clocks of a mechanical nature. The first dependable mechanical clock was the water clock. It was a relatively simple device that measured the passage of time with flowing water. A water clock was either an inflow or outflow type. An inflow water clock introduced water into a container that was marked in order to indicate how much time had passed as determined by the rising level of the water. An outflow clock made use of the same concept except for the fact that the water level in the container fell. Water clocks were created by the ancient Egyptians thousands of years ago, and many other early societies either independently invented them or learned about them from other civilizations. During ancient times, water clocks were most commonly used to time astronomical events for religious ceremonies, particularly those that occurred at night.

For centuries, water clocks were the most advanced types of timekeeping mechanisms that humans managed to construct. It was not until the 1400s that a new type of clock, one which used spring power, was developed. Power from a mechanical spring that was wound tightly and then unleashed was able to move gears that turned the hands on a clock face. Spring-powered clocks had several advantages over water clocks. First, by employing spring power, smaller clocks—even those that people could carry—were able to be made. Additionally, spring-powered clocks did not need to be filled and unfilled with water. Yet they had two drawbacks. First, spring-powered clocks had to be rewound once the spring unwound. Second, as the spring was unwinding, its power progressively diminished, so the force of the spring was less than it was at the beginning of the process. This led to spring-powered clocks becoming inaccurate. Various attempts were made at providing mechanical solutions, but spring-powered clocks were not perfected until the mid-1700s.

During the 1600s, some clockmakers began using swinging weights in the form of a pendulum to move gears. Pendulum clocks depended on accurate mathematical formulas that judged the desired length of the swinging arm and the amount of weight at the end. By this motion, the gears were moved, and the clock recorded the time. Pendulum clocks proved to be so accurate that minute hands—and eventually second hands—were added to clock faces. This was not the case for early spring-powered clocks; however, pendulum clocks could only be utilized for large timekeeping devices, so clockmakers did not abandon using spring power for smaller clocks and watches.

Spring-powered watches became popular during the 1600s and 1700s. At first, they looked like small clocks, but these proved to be too cumbersome, so over time, watches that were flat and could fit into a man's pocket were made. These pocket watches, as they were called, were fashionable for men but not for women. Eventually, by the late 1800s, small watches with a strap on them were being worn by women on their wrists whereas most men refused to wear them. Then, during World War I, which lasted from 1914 to 1918, many soldiers found wristwatches to be practical while they were fighting, so the wristwatch took off in popularity after the war.

---

**Glossary**

**heavenly body:** a natural object visible in the sky, including the sun, the stars, the planets, and their moons
**pendulum:** a swinging lever on a clock that helps regulate it

**21** According to paragraph 1, people in the past watched the stars because

  Ⓐ it enabled them to keep track of the passing of time in small units

  Ⓑ they utilized them in order to measure the passage of time

  Ⓒ they needed to determine the accuracy of the clocks that they had

  Ⓓ few of them had watches which they could use to check the time

**22** In paragraph 1, the author implies that the stars

  Ⓐ move almost as much as the planets do during the course of a year

  Ⓑ remain in the same positions all throughout the sky each night

  Ⓒ inspired people to create time-keeping inventions such as clocks

  Ⓓ cannot be used at all for telling what time it is during the day

**Early Types of Clocks**

[1] → Clocks are ubiquitous in the present day and range from simple wristwatches to atomic clocks which people use to keep accurate time. However, clocks were not always that common, so early men frequently relied upon the movements of heavenly bodies and the passing of the seasons to measure time. But stargazing and keeping track of the seasons were employed to measure large units of time—months and years. As life became more complex and civilizations arose though, it gradually became necessary to keep track of time on a daily basis. Accordingly, throughout human history, a number of different types of clocks have been used.

ACTUAL TEST **04**

---

**Glossary**   ⊖

**heavenly body :** a natural object visible in the sky, including the sun, the stars, the planets, and their moons

**23** In paragraph 2, the author uses sundials as an example of

(A) an ideal method of measuring time during daylight hours

(B) a type of clock that replaced primitive water clocks

(C) the best that human ingenuity could do in ancient times

(D) an early type of clock that had many disadvantages

**24** Which of the sentences below best expresses the essential information in the highlighted sentence in the passage? *Incorrect* answer choices change the meaning in important ways or leave out essential information.

(A) People in many old civilizations, including ancient Egypt, either invented water clocks or were taught about them by others.

(B) The ancient Egyptians first invented water clocks, and then they taught people in other cultures how to build them.

(C) By building water clocks during ancient times, people such as the Egyptians were able accurately to measure time.

(D) A lot of past civilizations learned about water clocks, which increased their knowledge of machinery and made them more advanced.

²→ Among the earliest clocks made by humans were sundials. They were limited in that they could not be used after the sun had set and the shadows that sundials cast depend upon the latitude at which a person is. Resultantly, sundials could only be utilized to keep track of the local time during daylight hours, which made them unreliable and relatively ineffective. These limitations inspired humans to attempt to develop clocks of a mechanical nature. The first dependable mechanical clock was the water clock. It was a relatively simple device that measured the passage of time with flowing water. A water clock was either an inflow or outflow type. An inflow water clock introduced water into a container that was marked in order to indicate how much time had passed as determined by the rising level of the water. An outflow clock made use of the same concept except for the fact that the water level in the container fell. Water clocks were created by the ancient Egyptians thousands of years ago, and many other early societies either independently invented them or learned about them from other civilizations. During ancient times, water clocks were most commonly used to time astronomical events for religious ceremonies, particularly those that occurred at night.

25 According to paragraph 2, which of the following is NOT true of water clocks?

Ⓐ They were first made by people who lived thousands of years in the past.

Ⓑ Some of them measured time according to rising water levels.

Ⓒ Most had several intricate parts that made them complex machines.

Ⓓ People used them to keep track of when to hold various ceremonies.

² ➔ Among the earliest clocks made by humans were sundials. They were limited in that they could not be used after the sun had set and the shadows that sundials cast depend upon the latitude at which a person is. Resultantly, sundials could only be utilized to keep track of the local time during daylight hours, which made them unreliable and relatively ineffective. These limitations inspired humans to attempt to develop clocks of a mechanical nature. The first dependable mechanical clock was the water clock. It was a relatively simple device that measured the passage of time with flowing water. A water clock was either an inflow or outflow type. An inflow water clock introduced water into a container that was marked in order to indicate how much time had passed as determined by the rising level of the water. An outflow clock made use of the same concept except for the fact that the water level in the container fell. Water clocks were created by the ancient Egyptians thousands of years ago, and many other early societies either independently invented them or learned about them from other civilizations. During ancient times, water clocks were most commonly used to time astronomical events for religious ceremonies, particularly those that occurred at night.

**26** According to paragraph 3, spring-powered clocks were better than water clocks because

- Ⓐ they were not subject to rusting like all water clocks were
- Ⓑ their springs permitted them always to tell time accurately
- Ⓒ it was possible to build them small enough to become portable
- Ⓓ they contained many fewer moving parts than water clocks

[3]→ For centuries, water clocks were the most advanced types of timekeeping mechanisms that humans managed to construct. It was not until the 1400s that a new type of clock, one which used spring power, was developed. Power from a mechanical spring that was wound tightly and then unleashed was able to move gears that turned the hands on a clock face. Spring-powered clocks had several advantages over water clocks. First, by employing spring power, smaller clocks—even those that people could carry—were able to be made. Additionally, spring-powered clocks did not need to be filled and unfilled with water. Yet they had two drawbacks. First, spring-powered clocks had to be rewound once the spring unwound. Second, as the spring was unwinding, its power progressively diminished, so the force of the spring was less than it was at the beginning of the process. This led to spring-powered clocks becoming inaccurate. Various attempts were made at providing mechanical solutions, but spring-powered clocks were not perfected until the mid-1700s.

27 According to paragraph 4, pendulum clocks often had second hands because

Ⓐ the mathematical formulas that pendulum clocks used kept track of seconds

Ⓑ clockmakers felt that measuring seconds increased the values of the clocks

Ⓒ people were interested in knowing precisely what time it was at all times

Ⓓ it was possible for them to keep track of time down to the second

28 The word cumbersome in the passage is closest in meaning to

Ⓐ intricate

Ⓑ costly

Ⓒ bulky

Ⓓ advanced

⁴➡ During the 1600s, some clockmakers began using swinging weights in the form of a pendulum to move gears. Pendulum clocks depended on accurate mathematical formulas that judged the desired length of the swinging arm and the amount of weight at the end. By this motion, the gears were moved, and the clock recorded the time. Pendulum clocks proved to be so accurate that minute hands—and eventually second hands—were added to clock faces. This was not the case for early spring-powered clocks; however, pendulum clocks could only be utilized for large timekeeping devices, so clockmakers did not abandon using spring power for smaller clocks and watches.

Spring-powered watches became popular during the 1600s and 1700s. At first, they looked like small clocks, but these proved to be too cumbersome, so over time, watches that were flat and could fit into a man's pocket were made. These pocket watches, as they were called, were fashionable for men but not for women. Eventually, by the late 1800s, small watches with a strap on them were being worn by women on their wrists whereas most men refused to wear them. Then, during World War I, which lasted from 1914 to 1918, many soldiers found wristwatches to be practical while they were fighting, so the wristwatch took off in popularity after the war.

ACTUAL TEST **04**

---

**Glossary**                                    ⊖

**pendulum:** a swinging lever on a clock that helps regulate it

29 Look at the four squares [ ■ ] that indicate where the following sentence could be added to the passage.

**This was during the height of the Renaissance, when Europeans were making great advances in many fields.**

Where would the sentence best fit?

Click on a square [ ■ ] to add the sentence to the passage.

For centuries, water clocks were the most advanced types of timekeeping mechanisms that humans managed to construct. It was not until the 1400s that a new type of clock, one which used spring power, was developed. **1** Power from a mechanical spring that was wound tightly and then unleashed was able to move gears that turned the hands on a clock face. **2** Spring-powered clocks had several advantages over water clocks. **3** First, by employing spring power, smaller clocks— even those that people could carry—were able to be made. **4** Additionally, spring-powered clocks did not need to be filled and unfilled with water. Yet they had two drawbacks. First, spring-powered clocks had to be rewound once the spring unwound. Second, as the spring was unwinding, its power progressively diminished, so the force of the spring was less than it was at the beginning of the process. This led to spring-powered clocks becoming inaccurate. Various attempts were made at providing mechanical solutions, but spring-powered clocks were not perfected until the mid-1700s.

**30** **Directions:** Select the appropriate statements from the answer choices and match them to the type of clock to which they relate. TWO of the answer choices will NOT be used. **This question is worth 3 points.**

> Drag your answer choices to the spaces where they belong.
> To remove an answer choice, click on it. To review the passage, click on **View Text**.

### Answer Choices

1. Could be either an inflow or an outflow device

2. Was used as a time-measuring device in ancient Egypt

3. Had minute and second hands in its earliest form

4. Had to be rewound at certain times to ensure accuracy

5. Was worn by women on their wrists in the 1800s

6. Was the first mechanical clock that was reliable

7. Contained a pendulum that swung back and forth

### TYPE OF CLOCK

**Water Clock**

- •
- •
- •

**Spring-Powered Clock**

- •
- •

ACTUAL TEST 04

# The Aztec Temple in Mexico City

The ruins of Templo Mayor in Mexico City, Mexico

In pre-Columbian America, there were three great empires: the Aztec, the Maya, and the Inca. The Aztec Empire, which was centered on the land occupied by present-day Mexico City, was by far the most violent of the three. The Aztecs expanded their territory and influence on other tribes through conquest. During battles, Aztec soldiers frequently sought to capture, not kill, their enemies. These prisoners were later slaughtered by the thousands in ritual human sacrifices in Aztec temples. The greatest of these was Templo Mayor, located in the heart of the Aztec capital Tenochtitlan.

Templo Mayor was approximately fifty meters high and served as the centerpiece of a large plaza in Tenochtitlan. At its apex stood two temples, one to the Aztec god of rain and the other to the Aztec god of the sun and war. In front of both temples, captured enemies were ritualistically sacrificed to appease both gods. When the Spanish conquistadors under Hernan Cortez conquered the Aztecs in 1521, they tore down the temple. Over time, its foundation and many artifacts were covered up, and Mexico City eventually rose around it. Lost for more than 500 years, the ruins of the temple were finally unearthed in 1978. Despite encountering numerous difficulties working in the middle of a sprawling metropolis, since its discovery, archaeologists have been digging on the temple site and have uncovered many impressive Aztec remains and relics.

One major discovery was that Templo Mayor was not the only temple to have been built there. In fact, the remains of seven temples, all of which are pyramid shaped with steep steps, have been excavated. The first was constructed around 1325, and later Aztec rulers sought to show off their power and prestige by rebuilding and expanding Templo Mayor. The final design—the one the Spanish razed—consisted of the main temple with two shrines on top and many smaller pyramids and outer buildings in the plaza.

Thus far, the greatest find at the Templo Mayor site is a chamber located at the foot of the main temple. It was covered by a large stone slab which featured a carved image of the Aztec earth goddess. Underneath the stone was a multilayered chamber where each layer had several items placed on it as offerings to the gods. Included in these items were animal carcasses, gold and jade jewelry, and seashells. The sacrificed animals were birds and mammals, particularly eagles and dogs. In one of the lowest levels, archaeologists found a dog bedecked in luxurious jewels, which prompted them to dub the beast Aristo-Dog. At first, the archaeologists thought that they had discovered a royal tomb and that the dog had been placed there to serve as a companion and guide for its dead master on his journey in the afterlife; however, no human remains were found there, so the purpose of Aristo-Dog remains a mystery.

For the archaeologists, working on a dig site in the middle of Mexico City with its millions of people has brought its own set of problems. In 1978, when the decision was made to unearth the temple, thirteen modern buildings stood on the site. The Mexican government paid off the owners and knocked the buildings down, which cleared the site. However, diggers have had to contend with sewers, gas lines, electrical cables, and the ruins of other buildings from the past. During the past three decades, progress has been slow but steady, and enough artifacts have been found to fill a small museum nearby.

The Mexican government has made an enormous effort to excavate Templo Mayor. One reason for this is the mystical attachment many Mexicans feel toward their Aztec ancestors. To them, the Aztecs represent a connection to the past prior to the arrival of the Spanish. Yet some question whether the Aztecs should be revered or even if the temple should be excavated. Templo Mayor served an evil purpose, some say, and the sacrifice of humans was morally reprehensible. Indeed, chemical analyses of the temple's stones prove that a tremendous amount of blood was shed there. Nevertheless, many Mexicans argue that Aztec society should not be judged based on the sentiments of modern-day people, so they claim the digging needs to continue.

## Glossary

**apex:** the highest point; the top of a place

**carcass:** the corpse of a dead animal

**31** The author mentions Mexico City in paragraph 1 in order to

Ⓐ claim that it was the capital city of the entire Aztec Empire

Ⓑ stress its historical importance to the Aztec Empire

Ⓒ state where the heart of the Aztec Empire once existed

Ⓓ discuss the city's history during pre-Columbian times

**32** In paragraph 2, the author of the passage implies that Tenochtitlan

Ⓐ served as the capital city of the Aztecs for more than half a millennium

Ⓑ was the only place where the Aztecs built temples dedicated to their gods

Ⓒ was located in the same place that Mexico City was founded

Ⓓ was the last Aztec city to be captured by the Spanish conquistadors

## The Aztec Temple in Mexico City

[1] ➜ In pre-Columbian America, there were three great empires: the Aztec, the Maya, and the Inca. The Aztec Empire, which was centered on the land occupied by present-day Mexico City, was by far the most violent of the three. The Aztecs expanded their territory and influence on other tribes through conquest. During battles, Aztec soldiers frequently sought to capture, not kill, their enemies. These prisoners were later slaughtered by the thousands in ritual human sacrifices in Aztec temples. The greatest of these was Templo Mayor, located in the heart of the Aztec capital Tenochtitlan.

[2] ➜ Templo Mayor was approximately fifty meters high and served as the centerpiece of a large plaza in Tenochtitlan. At its apex stood two temples, one to the Aztec god of rain and the other to the Aztec god of the sun and war. In front of both temples, captured enemies were ritualistically sacrificed to appease both gods. When the Spanish conquistadors under Hernan Cortez conquered the Aztecs in 1521, they tore down the temple. Over time, its foundation and many artifacts were covered up, and Mexico City eventually rose around it. Lost for more than 500 years, the ruins of the temple were finally unearthed in 1978. Despite encountering numerous difficulties working in the middle of a sprawling metropolis, since its discovery, archaeologists have been digging on the temple site and have uncovered many impressive Aztec remains and relics.

**Glossary** ⊖

**apex:** the highest point; the top of a place

**33** The word razed in the passage is closest in meaning to

Ⓐ captured

Ⓑ reconstructed

Ⓒ demolished

Ⓓ appropriated

**34** According to paragraph 3, Templo Mayor became larger over time because

Ⓐ the gold the Aztecs won in their battles was used to pay for the renovations

Ⓑ it was destroyed by the Spanish and then subsequently rebuilt by them

Ⓒ the temple had to be made larger to permit human sacrifices to take place

Ⓓ Aztec rulers sought to enlarge it to prove to others how strong they were

³➡ One major discovery was that Templo Mayor was not the only temple to have been built there. In fact, the remains of seven temples, all of which are pyramid shaped with steep steps, have been excavated. The first was constructed around 1325, and later Aztec rulers sought to show off their power and prestige by rebuilding and expanding Templo Mayor. The final design—the one the Spanish razed—consisted of the main temple with two shrines on top and many smaller pyramids and outer buildings in the plaza.

ACTUAL TEST 04

**35** The phrase bedecked in in the passage is closest in meaning to

Ⓐ comprised of

Ⓑ concealing

Ⓒ decorated with

Ⓓ made by

**36** According to paragraph 4, which of the following is true of the chamber found in Templo Mayor?

Ⓐ The remains of several dogs wearing jewels were found in one of its lower levels.

Ⓑ Every layer in the chamber contained large numbers of dead birds or mammals.

Ⓒ A variety of sacrificial items were found placed in some of its different levels.

Ⓓ The remains of some Aztec rulers were discovered buried alongside Aristo-Dog.

**37** According to paragraph 5, the Mexican government purchased some buildings in 1978 in order to

Ⓐ construct a museum where the buildings had once been located

Ⓑ clear an area to enable the excavation of Templo Mayor to start

Ⓒ allow archaeologists to avoid electrical lines while they were digging

Ⓓ let experts examine the area as they searched for Templo Mayor

4 ➜ Thus far, the greatest find at the Templo Mayor site is a chamber located at the foot of the main temple. It was covered by a large stone slab which featured a carved image of the Aztec earth goddess. Underneath the stone was a multilayered chamber where each layer had several items placed on it as offerings to the gods. Included in these items were animal carcasses, gold and jade jewelry, and seashells. The sacrificed animals were birds and mammals, particularly eagles and dogs. In one of the lowest levels, archaeologists found a dog bedecked in luxurious jewels, which prompted them to dub the beast Aristo-Dog. At first, the archaeologists thought that they had discovered a royal tomb and that the dog had been placed there to serve as a companion and guide for its dead master on his journey in the afterlife; however, no human remains were found there, so the purpose of Aristo-Dog remains a mystery.

5 ➜ For the archaeologists, working on a dig site in the middle of Mexico City with its millions of people has brought its own set of problems. In 1978, when the decision was made to unearth the temple, thirteen modern buildings stood on the site. The Mexican government paid off the owners and knocked the buildings down, which cleared the site. However, diggers have had to contend with sewers, gas lines, electrical cables, and the ruins of other buildings from the past. During the past three decades, progress has been slow but steady, and enough artifacts have been found to fill a small museum nearby.

| **Glossary** ⊖ |
| --- |
| **carcass:** the corpse of a dead animal |

126

**38** According to paragraph 6, the Mexican government is focused on excavating the Templo Mayor site because

Ⓐ the Mexican people voted to conduct research on what was found there

Ⓑ they are interested in attaining valuable relics from the dig site

Ⓒ many Mexicans believe that they have a connection with the Aztecs

Ⓓ it is the most important of all ancient Aztec sites located thus far

⁶➜ The Mexican government has made an enormous effort to excavate Templo Mayor. One reason for this is the mystical attachment many Mexicans feel toward their Aztec ancestors. To them, the Aztecs represent a connection to the past prior to the arrival of the Spanish. Yet some question whether the Aztecs should be revered or even if the temple should be excavated. Templo Mayor served an evil purpose, some say, and the sacrifice of humans was morally reprehensible. Indeed, chemical analyses of the temple's stones prove that a tremendous amount of blood was shed there. Nevertheless, many Mexicans argue that Aztec society should not be judged based on the sentiments of modern-day people, so they claim the digging needs to continue.

ACTUAL TEST **04**

TOEFL® MAP **ACTUAL TEST**

REVIEW

HELP

BACK

NEXT

**READING** | Question 39 of 40

00:18:00 ⊖ HIDE TIME

**39** Look at the four squares [ ■ ] that indicate where the following sentence could be added to the passage.

**Archaeologists have some theories about it but have not proven anything yet.**

Where would the sentence best fit?

Click on a square [ ■ ] to add the sentence to the passage.

Thus far, the greatest find at the Templo Mayor site is a chamber located at the foot of the main temple. It was covered by a large stone slab which featured a carved image of the Aztec earth goddess. Underneath the stone was a multilayered chamber where each layer had several items placed on it as offerings to the gods. Included in these items were animal <u>carcasses</u>, gold and jade jewelry, and seashells. **1** The sacrificed animals were birds and mammals, particularly eagles and dogs. **2** In one of the lowest levels, archaeologists found a dog bedecked in luxurious jewels, which prompted them to dub the beast Aristo-Dog. **3** At first, the archaeologists thought that they had discovered a royal tomb and that the dog had been placed there to serve as a companion and guide for its dead master on his journey in the afterlife; however, no human remains were found there, so the purpose of Aristo-Dog remains a mystery. **4**

---

**Glossary**                                          ⊖

**carcass:** the corpse of a dead animal

**40** **Directions:** An introductory sentence for a brief summary of the passage is provided below. Complete the summary by selecting the THREE answer choices that express the most important ideas of the passage. Some sentences do not belong because they express ideas that are not presented in the passage or are minor ideas in the passage. **This question is worth 2 points.**

Drag your answer choices to the spaces where they belong.
To remove an answer choice, click on it. To review the passage, click on **View Text**.

**Templo Mayor, an important place of worship in the Aztec Empire, has been undergoing excavations since its discovery in 1978.**

- 
- 
- 

### Answer Choices

1. Archaeologists working at the temple have found many relics, including ones made of jewels and seashells.

2. Mexico City was built on the site of Tenochtitlan, which has made finding buried Aztec buildings somewhat easy.

3. Some Mexicans oppose the unearthing of Templo Mayor because of the bloodthirsty habits of the Aztec people.

4. A museum full of relics found at the site of the temple has been established for people to learn about Aztec culture.

5. Prisoners captured by the Aztecs in battle were taken to Templo Mayor and sacrificed to various Aztec gods.

6. The Mexican government facilitated the examination of the temple site by purchasing the buildings that were on top of it.

ACTUAL TEST 04

# TOEFL® MAP

## ACTUAL TEST Reading 1

05

# Reading Section Directions

This section measures your ability to understand academic passages in English. You will have **54 minutes** to read and answer questions about **3 passages**. A clock at the top of the screen will show you how much time is remaining.

Most questions are worth 1 point but the last question for each passage is worth more than 1 point. The directions for the last question indicate how many points you may receive.

Some passages include a word or phrase that is <u>underlined</u> in blue. Click on the word or phrase to see a definition or an explanation.

When you want to move to the next question, click on **Next**. You may skip questions and go back to them later. If you want to return to previous questions, click on **Back**. You can click on **Review** at any time, and the review screen will show you which questions you have answered and which you have not answered. From this review screen, you may go directly to any question you have already seen in the Reading section.

Click on **Continue** to go on.

# The Blue Holes of the Bahamas

A blue hole in the Bahamas

In the Bahamas, a group of islands east of Florida and north of Cuba, lies an extensive series of unique caves known as blue holes. From the surface, they are deceptively beautiful as most of them are dark blue in color. These caves extend down from the land's surface and are filled mostly with salt water but have a layer of fresh rainwater on top. This is a result of their location near the ocean yet not precisely in it. As a result, blue hole caves have developed distinctive ecosystems. They present experts with many insights into various fields of science but also provide challenges to divers, for while blue holes may be beautiful, they are also perilous. Nevertheless, dive teams willingly accept these risks as they hurry to investigate the depths of blue holes since the holes may not be around for much longer.

The Bahamian blue holes formed as a result of cave-ins on land. They are types of sinkholes with openings to the sky and underground passages connected to the ocean. Many have a depth of around thirty meters, but one descends 180 meters beneath the surface, making it one of the world's deepest underwater caves. So far, more than 2,000 blue holes have been identified, yet a mere 200 have been explored extensively. The exposure to rain from the sky and sea water from below gives blue holes a special composition because they have a layer each of fresh and salt water. In a typical blue hole, the top layer, which is approximately ten meters, is fresh water. Meanwhile, the middle layer, which is between ten and thirty meters, is composed of a mixture of fresh and salt water while the bottom layer, which can be a few meters or tens of meters deep, is pure salt water.

The fresh water on the top prevents the bottom layer of salt water from getting oxygen from the atmosphere. In the lower levels, bacteria that do not depend on oxygen for survival thrive. They form

133

a layer just beneath the freshwater level. These bacteria need light from the sun but cannot tolerate oxygen. As a byproduct of the form of photosynthesis which they utilize, the bacteria produce hydrogen sulfide, a toxic gas. This gas represents the greatest danger to divers exploring blue holes since it is lethal to humans, who can only handle it in small doses. Divers must quickly pass through the layer of hydrogen sulfide, for if they linger too long, the gas will penetrate their suits, enter their skin, and eventually make it to both their lungs and bloodstream, where it can cause serious health problems and even death.

Yet divers persist in exploring blue holes since their unique ecosystems can provide scientists with knowledge of how life formed on the Earth billions of years ago. Their oxygen-deprived environments are similar to what the Earth was like when it formed. The world in its infancy had no free-standing oxygen, and, for its first billion years, all lifeforms existed in the oceans and did not breathe oxygen. Therefore, by studying the bacteria found in Bahamian blue holes, scientists hope to attain a better understanding of how life evolved from organisms that did not breathe oxygen to those that required it to survive. Additionally, by examining blue hole ecosystems, scientists may be able to learn how life could evolve on planets lacking oxygen. Another advantage of blue holes is that their oxygen-deprived environments preserve fossils exceptionally well. So far, scientists have discovered 3,000-year-old fossils of the extinct Cuban crocodile, fossils of extinct birds, and even the remains of humans belonging to tribes that disappeared once the Europeans came to the New World.

Scientists are rushing to complete their studies, however, because they fear that life in blue holes may not last much longer. When the level of the ocean rises, blue holes become subjected to an influx of sea water from the top. Many are located near the sea, so they will soon be underwater. When this occurs, the delicate balance of fresh and salt water, which creates the conditions required for the blue hole ecosystem, will be destroyed. Over time, if the ocean level continues to rise, then blue holes will eventually become pure saltwater caves.

---

**Glossary**

**sinkhole:** a hole that forms in solid rock due to the action of water
**free-standing:** independent

1   The word perilous in the passage is closest in meaning to

   Ⓐ ubiquitous

   Ⓑ extensive

   Ⓒ dangerous

   Ⓓ transparent

2   In paragraph 1, the author implies that blue holes

   Ⓐ should be off limits to divers because they are not safe

   Ⓑ are situated in regions in both the Bahamas and Cuba

   Ⓒ have more life in them than the average coral reef

   Ⓓ do not exist on a permanent basis but are only temporary

3   According to paragraph 2, which of the following is NOT true of the layers that make up Bahamian blue holes?

   Ⓐ The bottom layer of a blue hole contains salt water.

   Ⓑ The uppermost layer is filled only with fresh water.

   Ⓒ The lowest of the three layers is always the largest.

   Ⓓ The middle layer is usually at least as big as the top layer.

**The Blue Holes of the Bahamas**

[1] ➜ In the Bahamas, a group of islands east of Florida and north of Cuba, lies an extensive series of unique caves known as blue holes. From the surface, they are deceptively beautiful as most of them are dark blue in color. These caves extend down from the land's surface and are filled mostly with salt water but have a layer of fresh rainwater on top. This is a result of their location near the ocean yet not precisely in it. As a result, blue hole caves have developed distinctive ecosystems. They present experts with many insights into various fields of science but also provide challenges to divers, for while blue holes may be beautiful, they are also perilous. Nevertheless, dive teams willingly accept these risks as they hurry to investigate the depths of blue holes since the holes may not be around for much longer.

[2] ➜ The Bahamian blue holes formed as a result of cave-ins on land. They are types of sinkholes with openings to the sky and underground passages connected to the ocean. Many have a depth of around thirty meters, but one descends 180 meters beneath the surface, making it one of the world's deepest underwater caves. So far, more than 2,000 blue holes have been identified, yet a mere 200 have been explored extensively. The exposure to rain from the sky and sea water from below gives blue holes a special composition because they have a layer each of fresh and salt water. In a typical blue hole, the top layer, which is approximately ten meters, is fresh water. Meanwhile, the middle layer, which is between ten and thirty meters, is composed of a mixture of fresh and salt water while the bottom layer, which can be a few meters or tens of meters deep, is pure salt water.

**Glossary**                                                    ⊖

sinkhole: a hole that forms in solid rock due to the action of water

ACTUAL TEST **05**

**4** Which of the sentences below best expresses the essential information in the highlighted sentence in the passage? *Incorrect* answer choices change the meaning in important ways or leave out essential information.

Ⓐ Because divers want to avoid any kind of exposure to the harmful gas, they do not swim anywhere near it.

Ⓑ The divers who insist upon swimming in water with hydrogen sulfide almost always wind up dying due to their actions.

Ⓒ One characteristic of hydrogen sulfide is that it can cause a number of health problems in anyone exposed to it.

Ⓓ The gas may result in all sorts of problems to passing divers, so they swiftly move through the layer in which it is found.

**5** In paragraph 3, the author implies that the bacteria found in blue holes

Ⓐ will suffer harm if they become exposed to oxygen

Ⓑ have thus far not been discovered anywhere else in the world

Ⓒ are responsible for the deaths of divers every year

Ⓓ function properly even when not exposed to light

³➜ The fresh water on the top prevents the bottom layer of salt water from getting oxygen from the atmosphere. In the lower levels, bacteria that do not depend on oxygen for survival thrive. They form a layer just beneath the freshwater level. These bacteria need light from the sun but cannot tolerate oxygen. As a byproduct of the form of photosynthesis which they utilize, the bacteria produce hydrogen sulfide, a toxic gas. This gas represents the greatest danger to divers exploring blue holes since it is lethal to humans, who can only handle it in small doses. Divers must quickly pass through the layer of hydrogen sulfide, for if they linger too long, the gas will penetrate their suits, enter their skin, and eventually make it to both their lungs and bloodstream, where it can cause serious health problems and even death.

**6** According to paragraph 4, scientists can learn about the past when studying blue holes because

  Ⓐ some animals once thought to be extinct have been seen living in them

  Ⓑ their lack of oxygen makes their circumstances similar to those on other planets

  Ⓒ the conditions in them are similar to those on the Earth billions of years ago

  Ⓓ bacteria that existed in the Earth's infancy sometimes make their homes in them

**7** The word delicate in the passage is closest in meaning to

  Ⓐ temporary

  Ⓑ exquisite

  Ⓒ fragile

  Ⓓ sustained

**8** According to paragraph 5, blue holes may be destroyed in the future because

  Ⓐ fragile cave systems are causing some of the blue holes to collapse

  Ⓑ they are being eroded by the water that fills them

  Ⓒ not enough rain is falling to keep parts of them filled with fresh water

  Ⓓ the water in the ocean has started reaching higher levels

⁴→ Yet divers persist in exploring blue holes since their unique ecosystems can provide scientists with knowledge of how life formed on the Earth billions of years ago. Their oxygen-deprived environments are similar to what the Earth was like when it formed. The world in its infancy had no free-standing oxygen, and, for its first billion years, all lifeforms existed in the oceans and did not breathe oxygen. Therefore, by studying the bacteria found in Bahamian blue holes, scientists hope to attain a better understanding of how life evolved from organisms that did not breathe oxygen to those that required it to survive. Additionally, by examining blue hole ecosystems, scientists may be able to learn how life could evolve on planets lacking oxygen. Another advantage of blue holes is that their oxygen-deprived environments preserve fossils exceptionally well. So far, scientists have discovered 3,000-year-old fossils of the extinct Cuban crocodile, fossils of extinct birds, and even the remains of humans belonging to tribes that disappeared once the Europeans came to the New World.

⁵→ Scientists are rushing to complete their studies, however, because they fear that life in blue holes may not last much longer. When the level of the ocean rises, blue holes become subjected to an influx of sea water from the top. Many are located near the sea, so they will soon be underwater. When this occurs, the delicate balance of fresh and salt water, which creates the conditions required for the blue hole ecosystem, will be destroyed. Over time, if the ocean level continues to rise, then blue holes will eventually become pure saltwater caves.

**Glossary** ⊖

**free-standing:** independent

ACTUAL TEST **05**

9 Look at the four squares [ ■ ] that indicate where the following sentence could be added to the passage.

**This makes blue holes of interest to individuals in the field of astronomy.**

Where would the sentence best fit?

Click on a square [ ■ ] to add the sentence to the passage.

Yet divers persist in exploring blue holes since their unique ecosystems can provide scientists with knowledge of how life formed on the Earth billions of years ago. Their oxygen-deprived environments are similar to what the Earth was like when it formed. The world in its infancy had no free-standing oxygen, and, for its first billion years, all lifeforms existed in the oceans and did not breathe oxygen. Therefore, by studying the bacteria found in Bahamian blue holes, scientists hope to attain a better understanding of how life evolved from organisms that did not breathe oxygen to those that required it to survive. **1** Additionally, by examining blue hole ecosystems, scientists may be able to learn how life could evolve on planets lacking oxygen. **2** Another advantage of blue holes is that their oxygen-deprived environments preserve fossils exceptionally well. **3** So far, scientists have discovered 3,000-year-old fossils of the extinct Cuban crocodile, fossils of extinct birds, and even the remains of humans belonging to tribes that disappeared once the Europeans came to the New World. **4**

**Glossary** ⊖

**free-standing:** independent

**10** **Directions:** An introductory sentence for a brief summary of the passage is provided below. Complete the summary by selecting the THREE answer choices that express the most important ideas of the passage. Some sentences do not belong because they express ideas that are not presented in the passage or are minor ideas in the passage. **This question is worth 2 points.**

Drag your answer choices to the spaces where they belong.
To remove an answer choice, click on it. To review the passage, click on **View Text**.

**Bahamian blue holes are unique ecosystems that are important scientifically but are in danger of no longer existing soon.**

- •
- •
- •

## Answer Choices

1. Most blue holes are fairly shallow, but there are some that are more than 100 meters deep.

2. Scientists fear that future environmental conditions may cause some blue holes to disappear.

3. By studying blue holes, experts hope to learn about what the Earth was like soon after it was created.

4. The combination of fresh and salt water in blue holes creates an ecosystem unlike anything else on the planet.

5. Divers must be wary when they are investigating blue holes because they are filled with dangers.

6. Some unique fossils have been found in blue holes, and these have increased people's knowledge of the past.

ACTUAL TEST 05

# Egyptology

Hieroglyphs written on the Rosetta Stone

Egyptology refers to the study of the remains of ancient Egyptian civilization. Due to Egypt's geographical location in the midst of a desert, the hot, dry climate has left it with one of the best-preserved of all ancient civilizations. Its myriad monuments, temples, pyramids, and tombs have attracted explorers, treasure hunters, and tourists since ancient times. Even prior to the end of the ancient period, it was the subject of study. Greek historian Herodotus, who lived from 484 to 430 B.C., wrote about the ancient Egyptians, and countless others have emulated him over the years. However, it was not until the nineteenth century that Egyptology began in earnest as professional archaeologists began unlocking many of ancient Egypt's long-kept secrets.

Egypt was fought over and passed from one conqueror to the next for more than 2,000 years following the decline of the ancient kingdom of the pharaohs. Its early conquerors—the Persians, Macedonians, Romans, and Arabs—all explored and exploited ancient Egypt's remains. In addition, grave robbers have been a constant problem for centuries even into the modern era as they are more interested in finding treasure for the sake of becoming wealthy than for preserving relics and learning more about ancient Egyptian culture and history. Finally, as time passed, the language of ancient Egypt was forgotten, many of its sites were buried beneath the sand, and new buildings were constructed over old ones.

As a result, much of Egypt's past seemed lost forever. Yet this changed in 1798 with the arrival of a French invasion force led by Napoleon Bonaparte. A scientific team whose sole purpose was to explore Egypt accompanied Napoleon's army. The team's greatest find was the Rosetta Stone, a stone slab that was inscribed with three languages: ancient Greek, demotic, and hieroglyphics.

The writing on the Rosetta Stone contained the same message composed in all three languages. This became the key to interpreting the hieroglyphics of ancient Egypt. Two men, Thomas Young of England and Jean-Francois Champollion of France, were instrumental in unlocking the secrets of hieroglyphics. By comparing the hieroglyphic symbols to the Greek and demotic texts, they gradually learned to read the ancient language. Their work enabled those who came after them to interpret the hieroglyphics carved on many of Egypt's monuments and temples. This has led to a greater understanding of the history of ancient Egypt as well as the ancient world in general.

During the 1800s, the study of Egyptology increased as many explorers—mostly from Europe and the United States—visited places throughout Egypt. Unfortunately, many were amateurs with limited funds, so they were forced to use low-paid unskilled local laborers at dig sites. This resulted in many sites being damaged and relics being lost through negligence and haste. One man, William Flinders Petrie of England, set a high standard for Egyptologists though. While an amateur, he was meticulous in his explorations and employed a scientific approach to archaeology. He refused to rush, and he taught the workers at his sites to dig carefully and to uncover remains without causing damage. Flinders Petrie's greatest work was the exploration and excavation of the great Pyramid of Giza in the early 1880s. He spent most of his later years in Egypt and was the mentor of Howard Carter, who discovered the most renowned of Egyptian sites, the tomb of King Tutankhamen, in 1922. Flinders Petrie is often considered the father of modern Egyptology and the scientific archaeological method. The standards he set have been rigorously followed and improved upon ever since he began employing them.

Most modern Egyptologists have been French, British, and Americans, not Egyptians, so many of the artifacts they uncovered are displayed in museums in their home countries. Now that Egypt is free of foreign occupiers, the Egyptians have begun to reassert their rights over their ancient ancestors. While foreign archaeologists are still permitted to dig, the Egyptians are applying pressure to foreign museums and collectors to return many of their artifacts. Some have been returned, but many remain in other countries. The Egyptians have responded by refusing permits for some foreign archaeologists who want to dig in the country. This has led to something of a slowdown in archaeological excavations in recent years.

Glossary

**treasure hunter:** a person who attempts to find objects of value in order to sell them
**hieroglyphics:** a pictographic script that was utilized by the ancient Egyptians

**11** The author discusses Herodotus in paragraph 1 in order to

Ⓐ stress that the Greeks felt Egyptian history was important

Ⓑ mention that he is widely considered the father of history

Ⓒ provide the years when he was born and died

Ⓓ state that he had written about Egypt during his lifetime

**12** According to paragraph 1, people have long visited Egypt because

Ⓐ individuals such as Herodotus have encouraged them to go

Ⓑ it is easy to become wealthy by finding buried treasure there

Ⓒ they are interested in learning about its history and culture

Ⓓ the museums in the country exhibit a great number of relics

**13** The word exploited in the passage is closest in meaning to

Ⓐ utilized

Ⓑ desired

Ⓒ uncovered

Ⓓ stole

### Egyptology

¹➡ Egyptology refers to the study of the remains of ancient Egyptian civilization. Due to Egypt's geographical location in the midst of a desert, the hot, dry climate has left it with one of the best-preserved of all ancient civilizations. Its myriad monuments, temples, pyramids, and tombs have attracted explorers, treasure hunters, and tourists since ancient times. Even prior to the end of the ancient period, it was the subject of study. Greek historian Herodotus, who lived from 484 to 430 B.C., wrote about the ancient Egyptians, and countless others have emulated him over the years. However, it was not until the nineteenth century that Egyptology began in earnest as professional archaeologists began unlocking many of ancient Egypt's long-kept secrets.

Egypt was fought over and passed from one conqueror to the next for more than 2,000 years following the decline of the ancient kingdom of the pharaohs. Its early conquerors—the Persians, Macedonians, Romans, and Arabs—all explored and exploited ancient Egypt's remains. In addition, grave robbers have been a constant problem for centuries even into the modern era as they are more interested in finding treasure for the sake of becoming wealthy than for preserving relics and learning more about ancient Egyptian culture and history. Finally, as time passed, the language of ancient Egypt was forgotten, many of its sites were buried beneath the sand, and new buildings were constructed over old ones.

---

**Glossary** ⊖

**treasure hunter:** a person who attempts to find objects of value in order to sell them

14  Which of the sentences below best expresses the essential information in the highlighted sentence in the passage? *Incorrect* answer choices change the meaning in important ways or leave out essential information.

Ⓐ Knowledge of Egyptian culture has increased slowly due to the work of grave robbers, who have stolen numerous invaluable artifacts.

Ⓑ A large number of grave robbers search for tombs throughout Egypt in order to find their contents so that they can steal anything of value.

Ⓒ Archaeologists recognize the importance to Egyptian culture of preventing grave robbers from stealing treasures from ancient tombs.

Ⓓ For hundreds of years, grave robbers have engaged in looting to make money rather than to improve people's knowledge of Egypt.

15  According to paragraph 3, which of the following is true of the Rosetta Stone?

Ⓐ A message was written on it in three languages, including hieroglyphics.

Ⓑ The stone was taken to France when Napoleon's army returned home.

Ⓒ It was discovered by French archaeologist Jean-Francois Champollion.

Ⓓ The hieroglyphics carved on it differed from those carved on many temples.

**Glossary** ⊖

**hieroglyphics:** a pictographic script that was utilized by the ancient Egyptians

Egypt was fought over and passed from one conqueror to the next for more than 2,000 years following the decline of the ancient kingdom of the pharaohs. Its early conquerors—the Persians, Macedonians, Romans, and Arabs—all explored and exploited ancient Egypt's remains. In addition, grave robbers have been a constant problem for centuries even into the modern era as they are more interested in finding treasure for the sake of becoming wealthy than for preserving relics and learning more about ancient Egyptian culture and history. Finally, as time passed, the language of ancient Egypt was forgotten, many of its sites were buried beneath the sand, and new buildings were constructed over old ones.

[3]➜ As a result, much of Egypt's past seemed lost forever. Yet this changed in 1798 with the arrival of a French invasion force led by Napoleon Bonaparte. A scientific team whose sole purpose was to explore Egypt accompanied Napoleon's army. The team's greatest find was the Rosetta Stone, a stone slab that was inscribed with three languages: ancient Greek, demotic, and hieroglyphics. The writing on the Rosetta Stone contained the same message composed in all three languages. This became the key to interpreting the hieroglyphics of ancient Egypt. Two men, Thomas Young of England and Jean-Francois Champollion of France, were instrumental in unlocking the secrets of hieroglyphics. By comparing the hieroglyphic symbols to the Greek and demotic texts, they gradually learned to read the ancient language. Their work enabled those who came after them to interpret the hieroglyphics carved on many of Egypt's monuments and temples. This has led to a greater understanding of the history of ancient Egypt as well as the ancient world in general.

ACTUAL TEST **05**

**16** The word meticulous in the passage is closest in meaning to

(A) slow

(B) skilled

(C) precise

(D) regulated

**17** Which of the following can be inferred from paragraph 4 about Howard Carter?

(A) He became famous following his discovery of King Tutankhamen's tomb.

(B) He made more important discoveries in Egypt than William Flinders Petrie.

(C) His methods of archaeology sometimes damaged the sites that he was examining.

(D) There were some people who considered him to be a grave robber.

[4] ➜ During the 1800s, the study of Egyptology increased as many explorers—mostly from Europe and the United States—visited places throughout Egypt. Unfortunately, many were amateurs with limited funds, so they were forced to use low-paid unskilled local laborers at dig sites. This resulted in many sites being damaged and relics being lost through negligence and haste. One man, William Flinders Petrie of England, set a high standard for Egyptologists though. While an amateur, he was meticulous in his explorations and employed a scientific approach to archaeology. He refused to rush, and he taught the workers at his sites to dig carefully and to uncover remains without causing damage. Flinders Petrie's greatest work was the exploration and excavation of the great Pyramid of Giza in the early 1880s. He spent most of his later years in Egypt and was the mentor of Howard Carter, who discovered the most renowned of Egyptian sites, the tomb of King Tutankhamen, in 1922. Flinders Petrie is often considered the father of modern Egyptology and the scientific archaeological method. The standards he set have been rigorously followed and improved upon ever since he began employing them.

**18** According to paragraph 5, some foreign archaeologists are being refused permits to dig in Egypt because

Ⓐ a few of them have been accused of stealing artifacts and then selling them

Ⓑ they were caught using improper digging methods on their previous visits

Ⓒ museums from the archaeologists' countries refuse to return relics to Egypt

Ⓓ the Egyptian government prefers that Egyptian archaeologists do more digging

⁵➜ Most modern Egyptologists have been French, British, and Americans, not Egyptians, so many of the artifacts they uncovered are displayed in museums in their home countries. Now that Egypt is free of foreign occupiers, the Egyptians have begun to reassert their rights over their ancient ancestors. While foreign archaeologists are still permitted to dig, the Egyptians are applying pressure to foreign museums and collectors to return many of their artifacts. Some have been returned, but many remain in other countries. The Egyptians have responded by refusing permits for some foreign archaeologists who want to dig in the country. This has led to something of a slowdown in archaeological excavations in recent years.

ACTUAL TEST **05**

**19** Look at the four squares [ ■ ] that indicate where the following sentence could be added to the passage.

**This enabled him to preserve the places he excavated, which helped considerably advance the field of Egyptology.**

Where would the sentence best fit?

Click on a square [ ■ ] to add the sentence to the passage.

During the 1800s, the study of Egyptology increased as many explorers—mostly from Europe and the United States—visited places throughout Egypt. Unfortunately, many were amateurs with limited funds, so they were forced to use low-paid unskilled local laborers at dig sites. This resulted in many sites being damaged and relics being lost through negligence and haste. One man, William Flinders Petrie of England, set a high standard for Egyptologists though. While an amateur, he was meticulous in his explorations and employed a scientific approach to archaeology. He refused to rush, and he taught the workers at his sites to dig carefully and to uncover remains without causing damage. **1** Flinders Petrie's greatest work was the exploration and excavation of the great Pyramid of Giza in the early 1880s. **2** He spent most of his later years in Egypt and was the mentor of Howard Carter, who discovered the most renowned of Egyptian sites, the tomb of King Tutankhamen, in 1922. **3** Flinders Petrie is often considered the father of modern Egyptology and the scientific archaeological method. **4** The standards he set have been rigorously followed and improved upon ever since he began employing them.

**20** **Directions:** An introductory sentence for a brief summary of the passage is provided below. Complete the summary by selecting the THREE answer choices that express the most important ideas of the passage. Some sentences do not belong because they express ideas that are not presented in the passage or are minor ideas in the passage. **This question is worth 2 points.**

Drag your answer choices to the spaces where they belong.
To remove an answer choice, click on it. To review the passage, click on **View Text**.

**Egyptology concerns the study of ancient Egyptian history and is often carried out through archaeological digs.**

- 
- 
- 

## Answer Choices

1. Herodotus was one of the first people to be concerned about ancient Egypt and to write about it.

2. Howard Carter and William Flinders Petrie were two of the first men to excavate ancient Egyptian ruins.

3. Thanks to the Rosetta Stone, experts can now read hieroglyphics and thus learn more about Egypt's past.

4. William Flinders Petrie introduced methods to archaeology that helped preserve sites which were being excavated.

5. Because the Egyptian government will not let some archaeologists dig in the country, there are few excavations going on at the present.

6. By examining ancient tombs, temples, and other sites, people have learned a great deal about ancient Egypt.

ACTUAL TEST 05

147

# The Outer Solar System

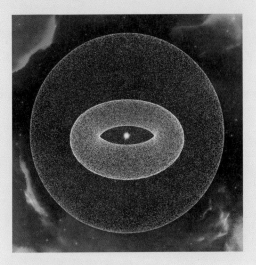

The Kuiper Belt and the Oort Cloud

The inner solar system consists of the sun, eight planets and their moons, and the countless other celestial bodies that orbit the sun between the planets. There are also innumerable objects in the realm beyond the last planet in the region that has been termed the outer solar system. These objects include several dwarf planets and their moons, comets, and various small icy and rocky objects that are too small to be classified as either.

The boundary of the solar system is the limit of the sun's gravitational pull since any objects that get caught by its gravity will begin to orbit the sun. So far, the most distant object discovered that orbits the sun is approximately sixty-eight astronomical units (AU) from the sun, yet some astronomers believe that the sun's pull may extend even further than that. One AU is equivalent to the distance of Earth from the sun—roughly 150 million kilometers. Astronomers refer to the region of space where the majority of these faraway objects orbit the sun as the Kuiper Belt.

The most distant visible object that is still a part of the solar system is Eris, the largest dwarf planet, which is located sixty-three AU from the sun. It is so far from the sun that it completes a single orbit in 560 Earth years. Astronomers have thus far identified five dwarf planets, which have been given that moniker since they are large celestial objects that do not fit the criteria to be considered an actual planet. Pluto, which was once called the ninth planet, had its status downgraded to that of a dwarf planet in 2006 and belongs to the outer solar system. Yet Pluto is not always so distant from the sun, and its elliptical orbit at times places it closer to the sun than

Neptune, the farthest from the sun of the eight planets. Besides Pluto and Eris, the other dwarf planets are Ceres, Haumea, and Makemake. Ceres actually resides in the asteroid belt between Mars and Jupiter. Haumea, meanwhile, is approximately forty-three AU from the sun and completes a single orbit in 285 years while Makemake is around forty-six AU from the sun and takes 310 years to orbit it. Every distant dwarf planet is small, rocky, and cold and is covered in frozen substances, most likely methane.

Pluto, Haumea, and Makemake are all located within the Kuiper Belt. The Kuiper Belt, astronomers theorize, is a donut-shaped region between thirty and fifty AU from the sun. It contains around 70,000 objects, many of which are merely small icy bodies. Astronomers believe that they are the remains of the materials that were used during the creation of the solar system billions of years ago. Comets continually move into and out of the Kuiper Belt as they orbit the sun. Some of their orbits are very long and irregular, but others, such as Halley's Comet, engage in relatively short orbits that can be predicted with some regularity.

As for Eris, it exists slightly outside the Kuiper Belt although some astronomers claim it is located inside that area. Others, however, believe that Eris is located in the Oort Cloud. This is a region that theoretically extends up to 50,000 AU from the sun. Its existence was first proposed by Dutch astronomer Jan Oort in the 1950s. Oort believed that all comets had to have originated from somewhere, so he theorized a region where they formed. Later, they were diverted from their courses by gravitational forces and then moved into the inner solar system. The majority of objects that may be in the Oort Cloud are too small and distant to be seen with modern telescopes.

In fact, the actual existence of the Oort Cloud is mostly based upon a theoretical belief since the long-term comets that orbit the sun must come from somewhere. Beyond the Oort Cloud lies the vast emptiness of space that leads to other stars located light years away from the solar system. How far past the Oort Cloud the sun's gravitational pull extends is uncertain though. It is a question that cannot be answered until modern science makes more technological advances.

Glossary

**celestial:** heavenly; relating to the sky or outer space
**gravitational pull:** the attraction that one object exerts on another

**The Outer Solar System**

The inner solar system consists of the sun, eight planets and their moons, and the countless other celestial bodies that orbit the sun between the planets. There are also innumerable objects in the realm beyond the last planet in the region that has been termed the outer solar system. These objects include several dwarf planets and their moons, comets, and various small icy and rocky objects that are too small to be classified as either.

² ➝ The boundary of the solar system is the limit of the sun's gravitational pull since any objects that get caught by its gravity will begin to orbit the sun. So far, the most distant object discovered that orbits the sun is approximately sixty-eight astronomical units (AU) from the sun, yet some astronomers believe that the sun's pull may extend even further than that. One AU is equivalent to the distance of Earth from the sun—roughly 150 million kilometers. Astronomers refer to the region of space where the majority of these faraway objects orbit the sun as the Kuiper Belt.

21  The word innumerable in the passage is closest in meaning to

Ⓐ varied

Ⓑ indisputable

Ⓒ individual

Ⓓ countless

22  According to paragraph 2, which of the following is true of the Kuiper Belt?

Ⓐ Some of the planets travel through it as they orbit the sun.

Ⓑ There are many objects within it that revolve around the sun.

Ⓒ It extends all the way out to sixty-eight AU from the sun.

Ⓓ It covers an area spanning approximately 150 million kilometers.

| Glossary | ⊖ |
| --- | --- |

**celestial:** heavenly; relating to the sky or outer space
**gravitational pull:** the attraction that one object exerts on another

**23** In paragraph 3, why does the author mention Eris?

(A) To emphasize that it is one of the five dwarf planets in the solar system

(B) To claim that nothing else visible in the solar system is farther from the sun

(C) To compare its characteristics with those of the other known dwarf planets

(D) To emphasize the number of years it takes to complete one orbit of the sun

**24** According to paragraph 3, Pluto is sometimes closer to the sun than Neptune because

(A) the sun's gravity causes a permanent change in Pluto's orbit

(B) the elliptical orbit of Neptune brings it into the outer solar system

(C) it has an oval orbit that can take it into the inner solar system

(D) it has an orbit that forces it to pass several of the planets in the solar system

**25** In paragraph 3, the author implies that Ceres

(A) is the dwarf planet that is the most similar to Makemake

(B) is large enough to be considered a planet by many astronomers

(C) is different from the other four dwarf planets in some ways

(D) has a gravitational force that is much stronger than Pluto's

³→ The most distant visible object that is still a part of the solar system is Eris, the largest dwarf planet, which is located sixty-three AU from the sun. It is so far from the sun that it completes a single orbit in 560 Earth years. Astronomers have thus far identified five dwarf planets, which have been given that moniker since they are large celestial objects that do not fit the criteria to be considered an actual planet. Pluto, which was once called the ninth planet, had its status downgraded to that of a dwarf planet in 2006 and belongs to the outer solar system. Yet Pluto is not always so distant from the sun, and its elliptical orbit at times places it closer to the sun than Neptune, the farthest from the sun of the eight planets. Besides Pluto and Eris, the other dwarf planets are Ceres, Haumea, and Makemake. Ceres actually resides in the asteroid belt between Mars and Jupiter. Haumea, meanwhile, is approximately forty-three AU from the sun and completes a single orbit in 285 years while Makemake is around forty-six AU from the sun and takes 310 years to orbit it. Every distant dwarf planet is small, rocky, and cold and is covered in frozen substances, most likely methane.

ACTUAL TEST **05**

151

26 The author's description of the Kuiper Belt in paragraph 4 mentions which of the following?

Ⓐ How the comets that are found there tend to move around

Ⓑ The total volume of material that can be found there

Ⓒ The precise number of objects orbiting the sun from there

Ⓓ What materials comets that are formed there are comprised of

27 The word diverted in the passage is closest in meaning to

Ⓐ extended

Ⓑ reconsidered

Ⓒ redirected

Ⓓ distracted

28 In paragraph 6, the author discusses the Oort Cloud in order to

Ⓐ argue that it is the outer limit of the solar system

Ⓑ propose the possibility that it does not exist

Ⓒ claim that humans have not been able to visit it

Ⓓ explain that very little is known about it yet

4→ Pluto, Haumea, and Makemake are all located within the Kuiper Belt. The Kuiper Belt, astronomers theorize, is a donut-shaped region between thirty and fifty AU from the sun. It contains around 70,000 objects, many of which are merely small icy bodies. Astronomers believe that they are the remains of the materials that were used during the creation of the solar system billions of years ago. Comets continually move into and out of the Kuiper Belt as they orbit the sun. Some of their orbits are very long and irregular, but others, such as Halley's Comet, engage in relatively short orbits that can be predicted with some regularity.

As for Eris, it exists slightly outside the Kuiper Belt although some astronomers claim it is located inside that area. Others, however, believe that Eris is located in the Oort Cloud. This is a region that theoretically extends up to 50,000 AU from the sun. Its existence was first proposed by Dutch astronomer Jan Oort in the 1950s. Oort believed that all comets had to have originated from somewhere, so he theorized a region where they formed. Later, they were diverted from their courses by gravitational forces and then moved into the inner solar system. The majority of objects that may be in the Oort Cloud are too small and distant to be seen with modern telescopes.

6→ In fact, the actual existence of the Oort Cloud is mostly based upon a theoretical belief since the long-term comets that orbit the sun must come from somewhere. Beyond the Oort Cloud lies the vast emptiness of space that leads to other stars located light years away from the solar system. How far past the Oort Cloud the sun's gravitational pull extends is uncertain though. It is a question that cannot be answered until modern science makes more technological advances.

29 Look at the four squares [ ■ ] that indicate where the following sentence could be added to the passage.

**For example, Halley's Comet takes seventy-five years to orbit the sun.**

Where would the sentence best fit?

Click on a square [ ■ ] to add the sentence to the passage.

Pluto, Haumea, and Makemake are all located within the Kuiper Belt. The Kuiper Belt, astronomers theorize, is a donut-shaped region between thirty and fifty AU from the sun. It contains around 70,000 objects, many of which are merely small icy bodies. ■ Astronomers believe that they are the remains of the materials that were used during the creation of the solar system billions of years ago. ■ Comets continually move into and out of the Kuiper Belt as they orbit the sun. ■ Some of their orbits are very long and irregular, but others, such as Halley's Comet, engage in relatively short orbits that can be predicted with some regularity. ■

ACTUAL TEST 05

**30 Directions:** Select the appropriate statements from the answer choices and match them to the region of the outer solar system to which they relate. TWO of the answer choices will NOT be used. **This question is worth 3 points.**

> Drag your answer choices to the spaces where they belong.
> To remove an answer choice, click on it. To review the passage, click on **View Text**.

### Answer Choices

1. Lies adjacent to the inner solar system

2. Contains the eight planets as well as their moons

3. Is a theoretical place where comets are formed

4. Holds unused material from when the solar system formed

5. May extend tens of thousands of AU from the sun

6. Is the location of the asteroid belt

7. Presently contains three dwarf planets

### REGION OF THE OUTER SOLAR SYSTEM

**Kuiper Belt**

- 
- 
- 

**Oort Cloud**

- 
-

TOEFL® MAP

# ACTUAL
# TEST  Reading 1

06

# Reading Section Directions

This section measures your ability to understand academic passages in English. You will have **72 minutes** to read and answer questions about **4 passages**. A clock at the top of the screen will show you how much time is remaining.

Most questions are worth 1 point but the last question for each passage is worth more than 1 point. The directions for the last question indicate how many points you may receive.

Some passages include a word or phrase that is <u>underlined</u> in blue. Click on the word or phrase to see a definition or an explanation.

When you want to move to the next question, click on **Next**. You may skip questions and go back to them later. If you want to return to previous questions, click on **Back**. You can click on **Review** at any time, and the review screen will show you which questions you have answered and which you have not answered. From this review screen, you may go directly to any question you have already seen in the Reading section.

Click on **Continue** to go on.

# Whitetail Deer Antlers

A whitetail deer with antlers in Oklahoma

One of the most common large mammals in the Americas is the whitetail deer. Although it lives primarily in the United States, its territory covers parts of Canada, Mexico, and Central America and even some regions in South America. The North American whitetail deer population stands at approximately twenty-five million while it exists in lesser numbers in other places. Males of the species can grow to around 120 kilograms in weight and frequently stand about 1.3 meters high at the shoulder. In addition to the long white tail that gives the animal its name, the whitetail deer is also known for the antlers found on its head.

The whitetail deer belongs to the Cervidae family of animals, which includes the elk, the moose, and the caribou. Like all other species of deer except for the musk deer and the Chinese water deer, the whitetail deer has antlers. These are sometimes mistakenly referred to as horns, such as those found on cows, sheep, and goats, but deer antlers are different from them. The antlers that grow on deer's heads are made of bone and are comprised mostly of calcium and phosphorous. Interestingly, the antlers are deciduous, so they grow during the spring and the summer and are subsequently shed during the winter, leaving the deer bereft of antlers until they begin to grow once more in the spring of the following year.

Not all whitetail deer have antlers however. For instance, female whitetail deer rarely possess them. There have been some documented cases of female whitetail deer with antlers, but these have all been anomalies. Indeed, of all the members of the Cervidae family, only female caribou regularly develop antlers. One likely reason that females lack antlers is evolutionary in nature: Bucks regularly use their antlers to attract females and to fight other bucks when they compete for mates.

Neither of those is an activity that females engage in, so without a demonstrated need for antlers, female whitetail deer virtually never develop them.

Some male whitetail deer may occasionally lack antlers themselves. As a general rule, the antlers on a male whitetail deer begin growing when it is ten months old. Every following year, the deer will grow a new set of antlers which it sheds during the winter; however, sometimes, the region in which a deer is living may have an insufficient supply of food. In that case, its antlers may develop either extremely slowly or perhaps not at all. Starting in April, a buck requires a larger-than-normal amount of nutrition since its antlers can grow about 0.6 centimeters per day. After a month, its antlers split apart and develop individual tines. For most deer, their antlers become fully developed within four months of the onset of growth. Nevertheless, in areas suffering from droughts, famines, or other problems that decrease the food supply, an inordinate number of bucks may not grow antlers.

When deer suffer harm to their legs, the growth of their antlers may likewise be affected. For most bucks, an injury to a back leg will cause the antler on the opposite side to develop in a deformed manner. Hence a back right leg injury will result in the antler on the deer's left-hand side to appear unusual. These deformations typically appear every year even after the deer's wound heals. Additionally, deer that incur injuries to their heads may experience stunted antler growth, so their antlers will be much shorter than those of healthy bucks. Finally, deer sometimes suffer damage to their antlers, which can break off, for instance, when they are fighting one another. On those occasions, the antlers almost always grow again the following year.

Finally, there is a period of time during which all deer are without antlers. Female deer commonly go into heat sometime in November, and the mating season lasts for several weeks after that. Upon ending, the testosterone levels in male deer decrease, so during the middle of January, they begin to lose their antlers. It takes about two or three weeks for the antlers to fall off. From that time until April, when the bucks' antlers regenerate, it becomes more difficult to differentiate between males and females as none of them has any antlers.

---

**Glossary**

**tine:** a projecting point on a deer's antler; a prong
**go into heat:** to experience a time when the female of a species is fertile and ready to reproduce

1 According to paragraph 1, which of the following is true of the whitetail deer?

(A) There are a number of different countries in which it makes its home.

(B) People tend to notice its antlers more often than its long white tail.

(C) Both males and females can weigh more than 100 kilograms at times.

(D) It is the largest North American land mammal that is not a predator.

**Whitetail Deer Antlers**

[1] → One of the most common large mammals in the Americas is the whitetail deer. Although it lives primarily in the United States, its territory covers parts of Canada, Mexico, and Central America and even some regions in South America. The North American whitetail deer population stands at approximately twenty-five million while it exists in lesser numbers in other places. Males of the species can grow to around 120 kilograms in weight and frequently stand about 1.3 meters high at the shoulder. In addition to the long white tail that gives the animal its name, the whitetail deer is also known for the antlers found on its head.

**2** The word them in the passage refers to

Ⓐ the whitetail deer

Ⓑ horns

Ⓒ cows, sheep, and goats

Ⓓ deer antlers

**3** Which of the sentences below best expresses the essential information in the highlighted sentence in the passage? *Incorrect* answer choices change the meaning in important ways or leave out essential information.

Ⓐ Deer have antlers that develop during two seasons and fall off in another, so deer do not have any antlers for a while until they grow back again.

Ⓑ It takes two entire seasons for a deer's antlers to grow, but they may fall off somewhat rapidly as soon as winter starts.

Ⓒ Because deer do not have any antlers on their heads from winter to spring, they have no way to protect themselves from predators in the winter.

Ⓓ Some deer keep their antlers all year round, but most deer shed their antlers during winter and regrow them during spring.

The whitetail deer belongs to the Cervidae family of animals, which includes the elk, the moose, and the caribou. Like all other species of deer except for the musk deer and the Chinese water deer, the whitetail deer has antlers. These are sometimes mistakenly referred to as horns, such as those found on cows, sheep, and goats, but deer antlers are different from them. The antlers that grow on deer's heads are made of bone and are comprised mostly of calcium and phosphorous. Interestingly, the antlers are deciduous, so they grow during the spring and the summer and are subsequently shed during the winter, leaving the deer bereft of antlers until they begin to grow once more in the spring of the following year.

**4** The word anomalies in the passage is closest in meaning to

Ⓐ protuberances

Ⓑ irregularities

Ⓒ transformations

Ⓓ appearances

**5** According to paragraph 3, female deer lack antlers because

Ⓐ they have no particular need to develop them

Ⓑ female deer with antlers cannot attract mates

Ⓒ they are rarely forced to fight other deer

Ⓓ the antlers weigh too much for them to handle

**6** Which of the following can be inferred from paragraph 4 about deer antlers?

Ⓐ Most of the antlers deer have fall off after growing for eleven months.

Ⓑ Deer that are older develop fairly large sets of antlers.

Ⓒ It is possible for some antlers to grow more than one meter long.

Ⓓ They often begin growing during the month of April.

³➡ Not all whitetail deer have antlers however. For instance, female whitetail deer rarely possess them. There have been some documented cases of female whitetail deer with antlers, but these have all been anomalies. Indeed, of all the members of the Cervidae family, only female caribou regularly develop antlers. One likely reason that females lack antlers is evolutionary in nature: Bucks regularly use their antlers to attract females and to fight other bucks when they compete for mates. Neither of those is an activity that females engage in, so without a demonstrated need for antlers, female whitetail deer virtually never develop them.

⁴➡ Some male whitetail deer may occasionally lack antlers themselves. As a general rule, the antlers on a male whitetail deer begin growing when it is ten months old. Every following year, the deer will grow a new set of antlers which it sheds during the winter; however, sometimes, the region in which a deer is living may have an insufficient supply of food. In that case, its antlers may develop either extremely slowly or perhaps not at all. Starting in April, a buck requires a larger-than-normal amount of nutrition since its antlers can grow about 0.6 centimeters per day. After a month, its antlers split apart and develop individual tines. For most deer, their antlers become fully developed within four months of the onset of growth. Nevertheless, in areas suffering from droughts, famines, or other problems that decrease the food supply, an inordinate number of bucks may not grow antlers.

**Glossary**   ⊖

**tine:** a projecting point on a deer's antler; a prong

**7** According to paragraph 5, why do some deer's antlers look misshapen?

   Ⓐ Their antlers started to grow too late in the year.

   Ⓑ The deer failed to get enough nutrition at some point.

   Ⓒ Parts of their antlers may have broken in a fight.

   Ⓓ Sometimes their back legs may get hurt.

**8** In paragraph 6, the author implies that testosterone

   Ⓐ is closely related to the development of antlers in deer

   Ⓑ exists in higher quantities in females than in males

   Ⓒ can prevent a deer's antlers from becoming deformed

   Ⓓ is an effective substitute for some types of nutrition for deer

⁵➡ When deer suffer harm to their legs, the growth of their antlers may likewise be affected. For most bucks, an injury to a back leg will cause the antler on the opposite side to develop in a deformed manner. Hence a back right leg injury will result in the antler on the deer's left-hand side to appear unusual. These deformations typically appear every year even after the deer's wound heals. Additionally, deer that incur injuries to their heads may experience stunted antler growth, so their antlers will be much shorter than those of healthy bucks. Finally, deer sometimes suffer damage to their antlers, which can break off, for instance, when they are fighting one another. On those occasions, the antlers almost always grow again the following year.

⁶➡ Finally, there is a period of time during which all deer are without antlers. Female deer commonly go into heat sometime in November, and the mating season lasts for several weeks after that. Upon ending, the testosterone levels in male deer decrease, so during the middle of January, they begin to lose their antlers. It takes about two or three weeks for the antlers to fall off. From that time until April, when the bucks' antlers regenerate, it becomes more difficult to differentiate between males and females as none of them has any antlers.

**Glossary** ⊖

**go into heat:** to experience a time when the female of a species is fertile and ready to reproduce

9 Look at the four squares [ ■ ] that indicate where the following sentence could be added to the passage.

**In addition, bucks may use them to protect themselves from wolves, coyotes, and other predators.**

Where would the sentence best fit?

Click on a square [ ■ ] to add the sentence to the passage.

Not all whitetail deer have antlers however. For instance, female whitetail deer rarely possess them. **1** There have been some documented cases of female whitetail deer with antlers, but these have all been anomalies. **2** Indeed, of all the members of the Cervidae family, only female caribou regularly develop antlers. **3** One likely reason that females lack antlers is evolutionary in nature: Bucks regularly use their antlers to attract females and to fight other bucks when they compete for mates. **4** Neither of those is an activity that females engage in, so without a demonstrated need for antlers, female whitetail deer virtually never develop them.

10  **Directions:** An introductory sentence for a brief summary of the passage is provided below. Complete the summary by selecting the THREE answer choices that express the most important ideas of the passage. Some sentences do not belong because they express ideas that are not presented in the passage or are minor ideas in the passage. **This question is worth 2 points.**

> Drag your answer choices to the spaces where they belong.
> To remove an answer choice, click on it. To review the passage, click on **View Text**.

**Though most male whitetail deer grow antlers, they may sometimes experience problems with the development of their antlers.**

- 
- 
- 

**Answer Choices**

1  Bucks with a large number of tines, or points, on their antlers are highly prized by sportsmen and hunters.

2  Most bucks begin to develop their antlers during spring, and they can grow at a fairly rapid rate each day.

3  The antlers that whitetail deer grow are actually bone and thus are different from the horns found on some other animals.

4  If a deer experiences some kind of an injury, as a result, its antlers may not grow well in the following years.

5  Female caribou frequently grow antlers, but female whitetail deer almost never have antlers on their heads.

6  If a deer fails to eat enough during the spring, its antlers may not grow or may simply be much smaller than is typical.

# The Helicopter

A Bell UH-1 helicopter used during the Vietnam War

Helicopters are different from the vast majority of airplanes in that they have vertical takeoff and landing capabilities and can hover in the air over a fixed point. These features enable them to play significant roles in certain aspects of civilian and military life. Helicopters are used to transport people and things into tight, congested spots where heavy-lifting power and stability are required. In wartime, they provide platforms for weapons and swiftly bring soldiers to battlefields, resupply them, and extract wounded individuals. They also serve as search-and-rescue vehicles and save people from certain death in rough terrain, in burning buildings, and on sinking ships. These unique machines owe their capabilities to their design and special features, which took years to perfect.

Man has dreamed of flying since ancient times, but it was not until the modern era that practical machines were built to enable this. The helicopter was one of the last flying devices developed. It followed balloons, gliders, and airplanes primarily due to the difficulty involved in creating a machine that could take off and land vertically, fly straight, and hover. Many inventors—mostly in the United States and Europe—strived to develop practical helicopters throughout the twentieth century. Several models managed to get off the ground and fly for a few minutes, but most were unstable, and crashes were more common than instances of sustained flight.

Nevertheless, by the mid-1930s, the stability issues had been overcome. In 1936, German aviation engineer Heinrich Focke built the first practical helicopter, which saw limited service in the 1940s during World War II. Russian-American aircraft designer Igor Sikorsky, however, is credited with inventing the first large-scale helicopter in 1942. His machine utilized the single main rotor and the smaller tail rotor common in most helicopters today. The helicopter Sikorsky developed was for the American military, so initially, most helicopters had military roles rather than civilian ones.

The helicopter first gained prominence during the Korean War, which lasted from 1950 to 1953. In Korea, helicopters were regularly used for observation, the search and rescue of downed fliers, and the ferrying of wounded soldiers quickly from the battlefield to medical care centers. It was in this last task that helicopters played their most significant role in Korea as they greatly reduced the time it took for wounded soldiers to receive proper treatment. The transportation time decreased even further from 1965 to 1973, which was the period when the United States participated in the Vietnam War. During that conflict, casualties were often speedily plucked from the battlefield and transported to modern hospitals in thirty minutes or fewer.

The helicopter assumed another role in the Vietnam War. It was most frequently utilized as a troop and equipment carrier, so it airlifted men, weapons, and equipment rapidly to anywhere they were needed. But the helicopters were noisy, so the enemy typically heard them long before they saw them, and helicopters were vulnerable to antiaircraft fire. The American military lost an enormous number of helicopters during the war. This weakness is still a significant problem for helicopters employed in war, but more modern machines have stronger protection in the form of armor as well as a greater array of weapons to deal with enemy air and ground forces.

While military helicopters dominated the early years of the helicopter industry, civilian helicopters were slowly developed by companies, most particularly Bell Aviation in the United States. These early helicopters were mainly two-seaters with limited carrying capacities. Most early helicopters—both military and civilian—relied on gasoline-powered internal combustion engines. Then, in the 1950s, engineers developed turbine engines for helicopters that were lighter and stronger than internal combustion engines. This enabled designers to create larger, more powerful helicopters.

Over time, a wide variety of extremely versatile helicopters, including massive ones capable of carrying huge loads and ones able to fly in adverse weather conditions, started being manufactured around the world. Today, these helicopters are used for numerous civilian purposes. Some are building skyscrapers, fighting forest fires, rescuing people in dangerous situations, finding and apprehending criminals, and reporting on traffic conditions and news events. At present, the helicopter is a vital part of human life and does jobs that were virtually impossible prior to its development.

---

### Glossary

**hover:** to remain suspended in the air under one's own power

**casualty:** a person who is killed or injured in battle or in an accident

**11** The word extract in the passage is closest in meaning to

  (A) locate

  (B) assist

  (C) eliminate

  (D) remove

**12** Which of the following can be inferred from paragraph 1 about airplanes?

  (A) Some of them are able to take off and land vertically.

  (B) The majority of them are larger than the average helicopter.

  (C) They have more limited uses than most helicopters.

  (D) The cost of purchasing one is greater than that of a helicopter.

**13** The author uses balloons, gliders, and airplanes as examples of

  (A) machines that employ similar mechanisms as the helicopter

  (B) inventions that were created at times during the modern era

  (C) aircraft that were utilized in times prior to the helicopter's invention

  (D) the most advanced flying machines that have been made by humans

### The Helicopter

[1] ➙ Helicopters are different from the vast majority of airplanes in that they have vertical takeoff and landing capabilities and can hover in the air over a fixed point. These features enable them to play significant roles in certain aspects of civilian and military life. Helicopters are used to transport people and things into tight, congested spots where heavy-lifting power and stability are required. In wartime, they provide platforms for weapons and swiftly bring soldiers to battlefields, resupply them, and extract wounded individuals. They also serve as search-and-rescue vehicles and save people from certain death in rough terrain, in burning buildings, and on sinking ships. These unique machines owe their capabilities to their design and special features, which took years to perfect.

Man has dreamed of flying since ancient times, but it was not until the modern era that practical machines were built to enable this. The helicopter was one of the last flying devices developed. It followed balloons, gliders, and airplanes primarily due to the difficulty involved in creating a machine that could take off and land vertically, fly straight, and hover. Many inventors—mostly in the United States and Europe—strived to develop practical helicopters throughout the twentieth century. Several models managed to get off the ground and fly for a few minutes, but most were unstable, and crashes were more common than instances of sustained flight.

| **Glossary** ⊖ |
| --- |
| **hover:** to remain suspended in the air under one's own power |

ACTUAL TEST **06**

14  According to paragraph 3, which of the following is true of the first helicopters?

   Ⓐ Their civilian roles were more important than their military ones.

   Ⓑ Some of them had two rotors that were different in size.

   Ⓒ Heinrich Focke and Igor Sikorsky worked together to invent them.

   Ⓓ They were widely used in a war that was fought during the 1940s.

15  According to paragraph 4, during the Korean War, the primary use of helicopters was to

   Ⓐ engage enemy targets in order to eliminate them from the field of battle

   Ⓑ transport large numbers of troops to places where they were needed to fight

   Ⓒ search for invading enemy soldiers to watch for their movements

   Ⓓ carry injured soldiers away from harm and take them to places of safety

³→ Nevertheless, by the mid-1930s, the stability issues had been overcome. In 1936, German aviation engineer Heinrich Focke built the first practical helicopter, which saw limited service in the 1940s during World War II. Russian-American aircraft designer Igor Sikorsky, however, is credited with inventing the first large-scale helicopter in 1942. His machine utilized the single main rotor and the smaller tail rotor common in most helicopters today. The helicopter Sikorsky developed was for the American military, so initially, most helicopters had military roles rather than civilian ones.

⁴→ The helicopter first gained prominence during the Korean War, which lasted from 1950 to 1953. In Korea, helicopters were regularly used for observation, the search and rescue of downed fliers, and the ferrying of wounded soldiers quickly from the battlefield to medical care centers. It was in this last task that helicopters played their most significant role in Korea as they greatly reduced the time it took for wounded soldiers to receive proper treatment. The transportation time decreased even further from 1965 to 1973, which was the period when the United States participated in the Vietnam War. During that conflict, casualties were often speedily plucked from the battlefield and transported to modern hospitals in thirty minutes or fewer.

**Glossary**                              ⊖

**casualty:** a person who is killed or injured in battle or in an accident

**16** The phrase vulnerable to in the passage is closest in meaning to

(A) attacked by

(B) destroyed by

(C) exposed to

(D) responsible for

**17** According to paragraph 6, people began building stronger helicopters because

(A) they were made with composite materials reducing their overall weight

(B) they were constructed with turbine engines that gave them more power

(C) they were designed to be able to carry more than two people at one time

(D) they were manufactured with civilian rather than military uses in mind

**18** Which of the sentences below best expresses the essential information in the highlighted sentence in the passage? *Incorrect* answer choices change the meaning in important ways or leave out essential information.

(A) Companies in many of the world's countries began to manufacture helicopters.

(B) Some of the most unique helicopters can bear a lot of weight and fly in the worst possible weather.

(C) By making creative designs, the helicopter industry has expanded and popularized the flying machines.

(D) All types of helicopters with various functions were eventually made in many countries.

The helicopter assumed another role in the Vietnam War. It was most frequently utilized as a troop and equipment carrier, so it airlifted men, weapons, and equipment rapidly to anywhere they were needed. But the helicopters were noisy, so the enemy typically heard them long before they saw them, and helicopters were vulnerable to antiaircraft fire. The American military lost an enormous number of helicopters during the war. This weakness is still a significant problem for helicopters employed in war, but more modern machines have stronger protection in the form of armor as well as a greater array of weapons to deal with enemy air and ground forces.

**6**→ While military helicopters dominated the early years of the helicopter industry, civilian helicopters were slowly developed by companies, most particularly Bell Aviation in the United States. These early helicopters were mainly two-seaters with limited carrying capacities. Most early helicopters—both military and civilian—relied on gasoline-powered internal combustion engines. Then, in the 1950s, engineers developed turbine engines for helicopters that were lighter and stronger than internal combustion engines. This enabled designers to create larger, more powerful helicopters.

Over time, a wide variety of extremely versatile helicopters, including massive ones capable of carrying huge loads and ones able to fly in adverse weather conditions, started being manufactured around the world. Today, these helicopters are used for numerous civilian purposes. Some are building skyscrapers, fighting forest fires, rescuing people in dangerous situations, finding and apprehending criminals, and reporting on traffic conditions and news events. At present, the helicopter is a vital part of human life and does jobs that were virtually impossible prior to its development.

ACTUAL TEST **06**

**19** Look at the four squares [ ■ ] that indicate where the following sentence could be added to the passage.

**In fact, research has shown that more than 5,000 of the roughly 12,000 helicopters used in Vietnam by the United States military were destroyed.**

Where would the sentence best fit?

Click on a square [ ■ ] to add the sentence to the passage.

The helicopter assumed another role in the Vietnam War. It was most frequently utilized as a troop and equipment carrier, so it airlifted men, weapons, and equipment rapidly to anywhere they were needed. **1** But the helicopters were noisy, so the enemy typically heard them long before they saw them, and helicopters were vulnerable to antiaircraft fire. **2** The American military lost an enormous number of helicopters during the war. **3** This weakness is still a significant problem for helicopters employed in war, but more modern machines have stronger protection in the form of armor as well as a greater array of weapons to deal with enemy air and ground forces. **4**

**20** **Directions:** An introductory sentence for a brief summary of the passage is provided below. Complete the summary by selecting the THREE answer choices that express the most important ideas of the passage. Some sentences do not belong because they express ideas that are not presented in the passage or are minor ideas in the passage. **This question is worth 2 points.**

> Drag your answer choices to the spaces where they belong.
> To remove an answer choice, click on it. To review the passage, click on **View Text**.

**The helicopter is a multipurpose flying machine that has both military and civilian applications.**

- 
- 
- 

### Answer Choices

1. While the first helicopters were almost exclusively military vehicles, their functions expanded to the civilian world over time.

2. Armies utilize helicopters to ferry troops to places and also to evacuate wounded soldiers from battle.

3. Thousands of helicopters were destroyed during events such as the Korean and Vietnam wars.

4. It took many decades of designing and redesigning before the first helicopters could actually fly.

5. Igor Sikorsky and Heinrich Focke are two of the most notable names in the field of helicopter design.

6. Helicopters today are frequently seen engaging in the search and rescue of people in precarious situations.

# Competing Theories of Evolution

A statue of Jean Lamarck in Paris, France

In 1859, Charles Darwin published his seminal work *On the Origin of Species*, which detailed his theories about how living organisms gradually evolve. Due to his observations as a naturalist, Darwin was certain what he had written was correct, yet he had trouble explaining the actual process through which species changed. This lack of an explanation and the absence of solid evidence suggested that, instead of gradual evolution occurring, there was instead an instantaneous leap from one species to another. Prior to Darwin's time, another evolutionary theorist, Jean-Baptiste Lamarck, postulated that species were created by spontaneous generation and evolved through a series of steps. Eventually, it was thanks to scientific inquiry that the process of genetic inheritance, which explains how evolution works, was discovered.

Darwin's theory of evolution centers on natural selection. It posits that all species are designed to survive by producing offspring. In an environment with limited resources, only offspring with the abilities which allow them to survive will live long enough to produce offspring themselves. Therefore, in each succeeding generation, the survivors are the strongest members of the species, and they pass on their abilities to the following generations. Over time, a new species—one better able to adapt and survive—evolves. This is especially true if the environment changes since only those organisms that can adapt to new conditions will survive. Due to the slow and steady process of change, this theory of natural selection is sometimes referred to as gradualism.

Darwin based his theory of natural selection on both observations and inferences since he had no solid evidence to explain how it actually took place. This left Darwin open to attack. For instance, some critics pointed out that in the fossil record, there are periods during which entire species disappeared, but then similar—yet in some ways different—species emerged later despite there being no fossils suggesting any links between the two. One example was the lack of fossils linking land animals and whales. Darwin himself was positive that whales had evolved from some land animal yet could not prove it through the fossil record.

Darwin's inability to prove his theory of gradualism lent weight to a competing theory, one stating that all living things derive from spontaneous generation and are created from the elements of the Earth through a mystical force. This theory dates back as far as Aristotle, who lived more than two thousand years ago in ancient Greece, and has had supporters throughout history. One of its strongest enthusiasts was Frenchman Jean-Baptiste Lamarck, who lived from 1744 to 1829.

Lamarck believed in spontaneous generation yet also felt that species evolved through a series of planned steps. According to Lamarck, species began as simple lifeforms through spontaneous generation, but natural life-enhancing fluids in their bodies pushed them to transform into more complex creatures. These fluids created new organs, and, as time passed, they became more complex, which allowed for even further evolution of the organisms. Lamarck's theories additionally stated that a second force influenced living species. This was the adaptive force, which enabled a species to adjust so that it could survive changes in its environment. Some species were able to adapt and therefore survived while others lacked this adaptive force—or had it but used it improperly—so they failed to change and accordingly died out.

Lamarck's support of spontaneous generation as the creative force in life was the major weak point in his theory. However, his thoughts on the mechanism of change were not so erroneous as to result in the outright dismissal of his theories. What was missing from both his and Darwin's theories was an understanding of how organisms operate at the genetic level. There is a life force inside all living things that causes them to change: genes. Genes determine the traits of organisms and are passed from parent to offspring. Organisms evolve by inheriting these genetic traits from their parents and by passing them on to successive generations of offspring. Over time, a species will change its characteristics, particularly if it must adapt to a new environment. But without any knowledge of genes, which were not discovered until after both Lamarck's and Darwin's times, each man's theory was flawed.

**Glossary**

**naturalist:** a person who studies natural history, especially biology or zoology
**fossil record:** all of the fossils ever discovered and the information that has been learned from them

**Competing Theories of Evolution**

In 1859, Charles Darwin published his seminal work *On the Origin of Species*, which detailed his theories about how living organisms gradually evolve. Due to his observations as a naturalist, Darwin was certain what he had written was correct, yet he had trouble explaining the actual process through which species changed. This lack of an explanation and the absence of solid evidence suggested that, instead of gradual evolution occurring, there was instead an instantaneous leap from one species to another. Prior to Darwin's time, another evolutionary theorist, Jean-Baptiste Lamarck, postulated that species were created by spontaneous generation and evolved through a series of steps. Eventually, it was thanks to scientific inquiry that the process of genetic inheritance, which explains how evolution works, was discovered.

2 → Darwin's theory of evolution centers on natural selection. It posits that all species are designed to survive by producing offspring. In an environment with limited resources, only offspring with the abilities which allow them to survive will live long enough to produce offspring themselves. Therefore, in each succeeding generation, the survivors are the strongest members of the species, and they pass on their abilities to the following generations. Over time, a new species— one better able to adapt and survive—evolves. This is especially true if the environment changes since only those organisms that can adapt to new conditions will survive. Due to the slow and steady process of change, this theory of natural selection is sometimes referred to as gradualism.

**21** The word seminal in the passage is closest in meaning to

- Ⓐ well-researched
- Ⓑ extensive
- Ⓒ influential
- Ⓓ groundbreaking

**22** In paragraph 2, why does the author mention gradualism?

- Ⓐ To provide an alternative name for natural selection
- Ⓑ To emphasize how slowly it happens in most organisms
- Ⓒ To claim that Darwin spent most of his life studying it
- Ⓓ To point out that Darwin was not a great believer in it

**23** The author's description of natural selection in paragraph 2 mentions all of the following EXCEPT:

- Ⓐ the manner in which species manage to reproduce
- Ⓑ the speed with which the process of evolution takes place
- Ⓒ the effect that a changing environment can have on evolution
- Ⓓ the organisms that have evolved the most over time

---

**Glossary**                                            ⊖

**naturalist:** a person who studies natural history, especially biology or zoology

---

**24** According to paragraph 3, some people criticized Darwin's theory of natural selection because

   Ⓐ the fossil record proved that most animals had never evolved

   Ⓑ Darwin was never able to prove how evolution happened

   Ⓒ many of them supported the theories of Jean-Baptiste Lamarck instead

   Ⓓ some fossils were found that disproved Darwin's ideas

**25** In stating that Darwin's inability to prove his theory of gradualism lent weight to a competing theory, the author means that the competing theory was

   Ⓐ revised

   Ⓑ supported

   Ⓒ accepted

   Ⓓ proved

**26** In paragraph 4, the author implies that spontaneous generation

   Ⓐ is much more likely to be true than gradualism is

   Ⓑ was considered plausible by Darwin for some time

   Ⓒ has been believed in much longer than natural selection

   Ⓓ was proven to be true by Aristotle many centuries ago

**3** ➡ Darwin based his theory of natural selection on both observations and inferences since he had no solid evidence to explain how it actually took place. This left Darwin open to attack. For instance, some critics pointed out that in the fossil record, there are periods during which entire species disappeared, but then similar—yet in some ways different—species emerged later despite there being no fossils suggesting any links between the two. One example was the lack of fossils linking land animals and whales. Darwin himself was positive that whales had evolved from some land animal yet could not prove it through the fossil record.

**4** ➡ Darwin's inability to prove his theory of gradualism lent weight to a competing theory, one stating that all living things derive from spontaneous generation and are created from the elements of the Earth through a mystical force. This theory dates back as far as Aristotle, who lived more than two thousand years ago in ancient Greece, and has had supporters throughout history. One of its strongest enthusiasts was Frenchman Jean-Baptiste Lamarck, who lived from 1744 to 1829.

ACTUAL TEST **06**

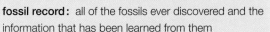

**Glossary** ⊖

**fossil record :** all of the fossils ever discovered and the information that has been learned from them

**27** Which of the sentences below best expresses the essential information in the highlighted sentence in the passage? *Incorrect* answer choices change the meaning in important ways or leave out essential information.

Ⓐ Every species that had the adaptive force managed to evolve, so they did not die out but changed instead.

Ⓑ While some organisms changed, for various reasons, others did not, so they never evolved but instead went extinct.

Ⓒ A lot of animals evolved in improper ways or simply failed to evolve at all, so they quickly disappeared from the Earth.

Ⓓ Some species adapted, yet others did not because their environments remained the same, so there was no need to change.

**28** According to paragraph 6, which of the following is true of genes?

Ⓐ They are responsible for the various traits that organisms possess.

Ⓑ They were discovered by Darwin but remained unknown to Lamarck.

Ⓒ Without genes, organisms are unable to undergo any kind of evolution.

Ⓓ Darwin mentioned genes in his work but had little understanding of them.

Lamarck believed in spontaneous generation yet also felt that species evolved through a series of planned steps. According to Lamarck, species began as simple lifeforms through spontaneous generation, but natural life-enhancing fluids in their bodies pushed them to transform into more complex creatures. These fluids created new organs, and, as time passed, they became more complex, which allowed for even further evolution of the organisms. Lamarck's theories additionally stated that a second force influenced living species. This was the adaptive force, which enabled a species to adjust so that it could survive changes in its environment. Some species were able to adapt and therefore survived while others lacked this adaptive force—or had it but used it improperly—so they failed to change and accordingly died out.

[6] ➡ Lamarck's support of spontaneous generation as the creative force in life was the major weak point in his theory. However, his thoughts on the mechanism of change were not so erroneous as to result in the outright dismissal of his theories. What was missing from both his and Darwin's theories was an understanding of how organisms operate at the genetic level. There is a life force inside all living things that causes them to change: genes. Genes determine the traits of organisms and are passed from parent to offspring. Organisms evolve by inheriting these genetic traits from their parents and by passing them on to successive generations of offspring. Over time, a species will change its characteristics, particularly if it must adapt to a new environment. But without any knowledge of genes, which were not discovered until after both Lamarck's and Darwin's times, each man's theory was flawed.

29 Look at the four squares [ ■ ] that indicate where the following sentence could be added to the passage.

**It was not until decades later that advanced scientific methods proved whales had an ancestor that had once walked on land.**

Where would the sentence best fit?

Click on a square [ ■ ] to add the sentence to the passage.

Darwin based his theory of natural selection on both observations and inferences since he had no solid evidence to explain how it actually took place. This left Darwin open to attack. **1** For instance, some critics pointed out that in the fossil record, there are periods during which entire species disappeared, but then similar—yet in some ways different—species emerged later despite there being no fossils suggesting any links between the two. **2** One example was the lack of fossils linking land animals and whales. **3** Darwin himself was positive that whales had evolved from some land animal yet could not prove it through the fossil record. **4**

---

**Glossary**

**fossil record:** all of the fossils ever discovered and the information that has been learned from them

**30** **Directions:** Select the appropriate statements from the answer choices and match them to the scientist to which they relate. TWO of the answer choices will NOT be used. **This question is worth 3 points.**

Drag your answer choices to the spaces where they belong.
To remove an answer choice, click on it. To review the passage, click on **View Text**.

### Answer Choices

1. Was supported by many leading scientists of his time

2. Believed in a theory that had been proposed in ancient Greece

3. Was attacked because his work was not supported by the fossil record

4. Felt that organisms took a long time to change

5. Had trouble explaining the process of evolution

6. Incorporated information about genes into his work

7. Thought that fluids in organisms made them change

### SCIENTIST

**Charles Darwin**

•

•

•

**Jean-Baptiste Lamark**

•

•

# Economic Success in Southeast Asia

One of the world's most vibrant economic zones is in Southeast Asia in the region that includes Hong Kong, Macau, Vietnam, Cambodia, Laos, Myanmar, Singapore, Malaysia, Thailand, the Philippines, and Indonesia. While they were once providers of wealth for European colonial empires, several of these nations have developed strong economies during the past fifty years. Buoyed by low-cost labor, abundant natural resources, and access to global markets, they are poised to enjoy continued growth in future decades.

Southeast Asia was first explored by Europeans during the sixteenth century, and many remained there to build trading ports to export valuable spices and other exotic goods to their homelands. By the nineteenth century, the Dutch, Portuguese, British, Spanish, and French had all founded colonies there. The Dutch occupied the Indonesian archipelago, the Portuguese set up a trading port in Macau, the British did the same in Singapore and Hong Kong, the Spanish occupied the Philippines, and the French established a large colony in the modern-day states of Vietnam, Laos, and Cambodia. With the exception of the Philippines, which became an American possession in the late nineteenth century, these lands remained firmly in European hands until after World War II ended in 1945. Thailand alone remained independent of foreign control. However, like most of the region, it was occupied by Japanese troops during World War II.

Economically, these colonies were vital cogs in the Europeans' empires since they served as sources of raw materials such as spices, rubber, and oil and also provided cheap sources of labor. Singapore and Hong Kong became Southeast Asia's greatest ports and served as entry points for products from around the world to reach the interior of the continent. Locally, most economies were based on agriculture as the majority of the population lived off the land. Each colony had different experiences depending upon its rulers, but the foreign colonizers clearly exploited the lands for as much wealth as possible.

One result of what was widely regarded by the natives as oppression by their colonial masters was that independence movements sprang up almost everywhere. The majority were successful as, after World War II, the colonies became independent states one by one. The sole exceptions were Hong Kong and Macau, which remained European possessions until being returned to China at the end of the twentieth century. In most places, the transfer of power from colonizer to colony was peaceful. Democracy was practiced in these newly independent nations except for in Vietnam, which turned to communism after a long, bloody struggle.

All of the nations remained poor after gaining their independence, but they maintained strong ties to their former colonial masters, which served as trading partners. While Southeast Asian countries continued relying heavily on agriculture, they improved their economies by engaging in various industries. As a result, they became major centers of manufacturing for electronics, textiles, and automobiles. Many also successfully marketed themselves as tourist destinations, thereby earning millions or billions of dollars annually from tourists coming to see their beautiful landscapes, sandy beaches, and religious and historical sites.

These various industries combined to create robust economies in several nations. More confident in their economic power, many Southeast Asian countries organized themselves into the economic bloc called the Association of Southeast Asian Nations (ASEAN). One of ASEAN's primary goals is to stimulate regional economic growth. Of its members, Indonesia has the largest economy and is the only ASEAN country that belongs to the international G-20 group of top economic nations in the world.

One troubling aspect of the economic growth in Southeast Asia concerns how workers there are treated. Most employees receive significantly lower wages than workers in European and North American nations. For example, American factory workers typically make three times as much per hour as Singaporean factory workers and over twenty times more than Filipino factory workers. Thus numerous foreign companies have moved their manufacturing operations to Southeast Asia. This lets them reduce their manufacturing costs and increase their profits. Unfortunately, some products made there are the result of child labor. Many workers also endure long shifts in poor working conditions. Yet many countries are making concerted efforts to reduce these negative aspects and to make working safer and more profitable for their people.

**Glossary**

**archipelago:** a large chain of islands

**bloc:** a group of people, businesses, or countries that are united for a certain purpose

**31** According to paragraph 1, the economies of countries in Southeast Asia improved because

Ⓐ the nations that colonized them provided them with economic assistance

Ⓑ they were able to sell their products to places all around the world

Ⓒ the laborers who worked in them proved to be very efficient

Ⓓ they utilized advanced technology to improve their manufacturing base

**32** In paragraph 2, the author implies that Thailand

Ⓐ resisted invasions by both the French and Spanish

Ⓑ fought against and lost to the Japanese in World War II

Ⓒ became the most powerful country in Southeast Asia

Ⓓ built ports from which it exported many exotic goods

## Economic Success in Southeast Asia

¹➜ One of the world's most vibrant economic zones is in Southeast Asia in the region that includes Hong Kong, Macau, Vietnam, Cambodia, Laos, Myanmar, Singapore, Malaysia, Thailand, the Philippines, and Indonesia. While they were once providers of wealth for European colonial empires, several of these nations have developed strong economies during the past fifty years. Buoyed by low-cost labor, abundant natural resources, and access to global markets, they are poised to enjoy continued growth in future decades.

²➜ Southeast Asia was first explored by Europeans during the sixteenth century, and many remained there to build trading ports to export valuable spices and other exotic goods to their homelands. By the nineteenth century, the Dutch, Portuguese, British, Spanish, and French had all founded colonies there. The Dutch occupied the Indonesian archipelago, the Portuguese set up a trading port in Macau, the British did the same in Singapore and Hong Kong, the Spanish occupied the Philippines, and the French established a large colony in the modern-day states of Vietnam, Laos, and Cambodia. With the exception of the Philippines, which became an American possession in the late nineteenth century, these lands remained firmly in European hands until after World War II ended in 1945. Thailand alone remained independent of foreign control. However, like most of the region, it was occupied by Japanese troops during World War II.

ACTUAL TEST **06**

---

| **Glossary** | ⊖ |

**archipelago :** a large chain of islands

**33** Which of the sentences below best expresses the essential information in the highlighted sentence in the passage? *Incorrect* answer choices change the meaning in important ways or leave out essential information.

Ⓐ The colonies were important sources of materials and labor for the Europeans.

Ⓑ The Europeans needed more colonies to get free raw materials and workers.

Ⓒ It was cheaper for the Europeans to import raw materials from their colonies.

Ⓓ Most of the colonists in Southeast Asia acquired raw materials and laborers.

**34** The author discusses Hong Kong and Macau in paragraph 4 in order to

Ⓐ mention that they are currently economic colonies of the Chinese

Ⓑ point out that they serve as invaluable ports in Southeast Asia

Ⓒ contrast their post-World War II history with that of other colonies

Ⓓ describe the types of governments that they currently have

**35** According to paragraph 4, Vietnam failed to become a democracy because

Ⓐ the Vietnamese people were more interested in being ruled by a monarchy

Ⓑ it began practicing another form of government after it had a civil war

Ⓒ the European colonizers, particularly France, did not permit that to happen

Ⓓ there was no tradition of democracy for the Vietnamese to draw upon

Economically, these colonies were vital cogs in the Europeans' empires since they served as sources of raw materials such as spices, rubber, and oil and also provided cheap sources of labor. Singapore and Hong Kong became Southeast Asia's greatest ports and served as entry points for products from around the world to reach the interior of the continent. Locally, most economies were based on agriculture as the majority of the population lived off the land. Each colony had different experiences depending upon its rulers, but the foreign colonizers clearly exploited the lands for as much wealth as possible.

⁴→ One result of what was widely regarded by the natives as oppression by their colonial masters was that independence movements sprang up almost everywhere. The majority were successful as, after World War II, the colonies became independent states one by one. The sole exceptions were Hong Kong and Macau, which remained European possessions until being returned to China at the end of the twentieth century. In most places, the transfer of power from colonizer to colony was peaceful. Democracy was practiced in these newly independent nations except for in Vietnam, which turned to communism after a long, bloody struggle.

**36** According to paragraph 5, which of the following is NOT true of how Southeast Asian countries improved their economies?

ⓐ They each focused on a single major industry to make money.

ⓑ They manufactured a number of different types of products.

ⓒ They made money from people visiting them from other countries.

ⓓ The majority of their people continued to farm the land.

**37** The word robust in the passage is closest in meaning to

ⓐ adequate

ⓑ improving

ⓒ dominant

ⓓ strong

⁵➡ All of the nations remained poor after gaining their independence, but they maintained strong ties to their former colonial masters, which served as trading partners. While Southeast Asian countries continued relying heavily on agriculture, they improved their economies by engaging in various industries. As a result, they became major centers of manufacturing for electronics, textiles, and automobiles. Many also successfully marketed themselves as tourist destinations, thereby earning millions or billions of dollars annually from tourists coming to see their beautiful landscapes, sandy beaches, and religious and historical sites.

These various industries combined to create robust economies in several nations. More confident in their economic power, many Southeast Asian countries organized themselves into the economic bloc called the Association of Southeast Asian Nations (ASEAN). One of ASEAN's primary goals is to stimulate regional economic growth. Of its members, Indonesia has the largest economy and is the only ASEAN country that belongs to the international G-20 group of top economic nations in the world.

ACTUAL TEST 06

---

**Glossary** ⊖

**bloc:** a group of people, businesses, or countries that are united for a certain purpose

**38** The word significantly in the passage is closest in meaning to

Ⓐ primarily

Ⓑ considerably

Ⓒ appropriately

Ⓓ reputably

One troubling aspect of the economic growth in Southeast Asia concerns how workers there are treated. Most employees receive significantly lower wages than workers in European and North American nations. For example, American factory workers typically make three times as much per hour as Singaporean factory workers and over twenty times more than Filipino factory workers. Thus numerous foreign companies have moved their manufacturing operations to Southeast Asia. This lets them reduce their manufacturing costs and increase their profits. Unfortunately, some products made there are the result of child labor. Many workers also endure long shifts in poor working conditions. Yet many countries are making concerted efforts to reduce these negative aspects and to make working safer and more profitable for their people.

**39** Look at the four squares [ ■ ] that indicate where the following sentence could be added to the passage.

**Some of their largest manufacturers have even managed to become global suppliers.**

Where would the sentence best fit?

Click on a square [ ■ ] to add the sentence to the passage.

All of the nations remained poor after gaining their independence, but they maintained strong ties to their former colonial masters, which served as trading partners. **1** While Southeast Asian countries continued relying heavily on agriculture, they improved their economies by engaging in various industries. **2** As a result, they became major centers of manufacturing for electronics, textiles, and automobiles. **3** Many also successfully marketed themselves as tourist destinations, thereby earning millions or billions of dollars annually from tourists coming to see their beautiful landscapes, sandy beaches, and religious and historical sites. **4**

**40** **Directions:** An introductory sentence for a brief summary of the passage is provided below. Complete the summary by selecting the THREE answer choices that express the most important ideas of the passage. Some sentences do not belong because they express ideas that are not presented in the passage or are minor ideas in the passage. **This question is worth 2 points.**

Drag your answer choices to the spaces where they belong.
To remove an answer choice, click on it. To review the passage, click on **View Text**.

**Many of the nations in Southeast Asia have become independent and have improved their economies in the past fifty years.**

- 
- 
- 

## Answer Choices

1. Countries in the region have profited by diversifying their economies, which has earned them more money.

2. Following World War II, most of the countries in Southeast Asia were granted their independence.

3. The plight of workers in Southeast Asia is a source of concern for people all over the world.

4. While agriculture is still important in Southeast Asia, manufacturing and tourism are lucrative as well.

5. England, France, and other European countries had colonies of their own in Southeast Asia.

6. Many of the raw materials found in the region were taken by colonizers in order to make into manufactured products.

TOEFL® MAP

# ACTUAL
# TEST Reading 1

07

CONTINUE

# Reading Section Directions

This section measures your ability to understand academic passages in English. You will have **54 minutes** to read and answer questions about **3 passages**. A clock at the top of the screen will show you how much time is remaining.

Most questions are worth 1 point but the last question for each passage is worth more than 1 point. The directions for the last question indicate how many points you may receive.

Some passages include a word or phrase that is underlined in blue. Click on the word or phrase to see a definition or an explanation.

When you want to move to the next question, click on **Next**. You may skip questions and go back to them later. If you want to return to previous questions, click on **Back**. You can click on **Review** at any time, and the review screen will show you which questions you have answered and which you have not answered. From this review screen, you may go directly to any question you have already seen in the Reading section.

Click on **Continue** to go on.

# The Great Plains

The grasslands of the Great Plains in South Dakota

Across western North America, an enormous area of land lies flat beneath the blue sky and blazing sun. This is the Great Plains, one of the world's largest flatlands. The Great Plains stretches from the north in Canada and goes south through the United States and down into Mexico. It starts at the Mississippi River and stretches westward to the Rocky Mountains. Once home to numerous tribes of Native Americans and millions of buffalo, the Great Plains today is one of the world's largest sources of grain; however, this cultivation has left the Great Plains ecosystem in a precarious state as it annually faces the threat of a long-term drought.

Millions of years ago, the Great Plains was the floor of a large inland sea. Over time, the sea disappeared, leaving behind a fertile plain. The Great Plains are not entirely flat though; instead, there are distinct rolling fields, plateaus, occasional hills, and stands of trees. For the most part, the Great Plains is too dry to sustain large forests, and it is also speculated that, in the past, wildfires destroyed any large clusters of trees that once existed. Rivers and streams cut through the land, but it is devoid of large lakes.

There are three distinct regions in the Great Plains. They are divided according to the amount of rainfall they receive and the height of the wild grasses growing in them. In the western part of the Great Plains in the shadow of the Rocky Mountains, there is less rainfall, so, consequently, the grasses grow shorter, and the soil is looser. Some areas there get so little rainfall that they are suitable only for grazing animals, not for cultivating crops. Moving away from the Rockies further east, the amount of rainfall increases in the central region, which has a combination of short and long grasses. Finally, the eastern section of the Great Plains is the wettest and has the tallest

ACTUAL TEST **07**

grasses and the strongest soil.

Prior to the arrival of humans approximately twelve thousand years ago, the Great Plains was home to many large types of fauna, including giant sloths, woolly mammoths, and saber-toothed tigers. The first humans, however, eliminated most large beasts, leaving behind no trace of them except for their bones. For thousands of years, these Native Americans lived as hunter-gatherers on the Great Plains and had much of their needs provided for by the vast herds of buffalo wandering there. These Native Americans therefore never developed farming like the tribes to the east and the south did. But when European explorers and, later, American hunters, ranchers, and farmers, arrived, the face of the Great Plains changed. The buffalo were hunted almost to extinction while the land itself began to be cultivated.

During the 1800s, tens of thousands of immigrants began making their way to the western United States and Canada, where they broke ground and started new lives. During times when rain frequently fell, they thrived, but rain was not always common on the Great Plains. Occasional years with little rain caused the soil to harden, dry up, and get blown away by the wind. Since there are few obstacles to deflect it, the wind tends to blow longer and stronger on the Great Plains. The worst drought lasted almost a decade during the 1920s and 1930s and reduced much of the southern Great Plains to a virtual desert. Huge dust storms ravaged farms and forced many to abandon farming and to move away. Slowly, the land recovered, but it constantly exists in a fragile state because it is at the mercy of the forces of nature.

Since that extended period of drought—referred to as the Dust Bowl—the number of people engaged in farming in the Great Plains has decreased. Nevertheless, it is estimated that a quarter of the world's wheat, corn, barley, oats, sorghum, and rye are cultivated there. This is on account of modern farming methods, improved farming equipment, and the extensive use of irrigation. Much of the water for these irrigation systems comes from groundwater located far beneath the surface. This has some people worried, though, as they fear that using too much groundwater will cause the next extended drought to be even worse than the Dust Bowl was.

---

### Glossary

**plateau:** a stretch of land that is relatively flat but higher in altitude than the surrounding land

**fauna:** the animals that live in a particular region

**The Great Plains**

¹➡ Across western North America, an enormous area of land lies flat beneath the blue sky and blazing sun. This is the Great Plains, one of the world's largest flatlands. The Great Plains stretches from the north in Canada and goes south through the United States and down into Mexico. It starts at the Mississippi River and stretches westward to the Rocky Mountains. Once home to numerous tribes of Native Americans and millions of buffalo, the Great Plains today is one of the world's largest sources of grain; however, this cultivation has left the Great Plains ecosystem in a precarious state as it annually faces the threat of a long-term drought.

²➡ Millions of years ago, the Great Plains was the floor of a large inland sea. Over time, the sea disappeared, leaving behind a fertile plain. The Great Plains are not entirely flat though; instead, there are distinct rolling fields, plateaus, occasional hills, and stands of trees. For the most part, the Great Plains is too dry to sustain large forests, and it is also speculated that, in the past, wildfires destroyed any large clusters of trees that once existed. Rivers and streams cut through the land, but it is devoid of large lakes.

1   The word precarious in the passage is closest in meaning to

   Ⓐ damaged

   Ⓑ unstable

   Ⓒ dynamic

   Ⓓ altered

2   In paragraph 1, the author's description of the Great Plains mentions all of the following EXCEPT:

   Ⓐ an ecological problem that it currently faces

   Ⓑ the locations of its eastern and western boundaries

   Ⓒ the countries in which it can be found

   Ⓓ the crops that are grown there by farmers

3   According to paragraph 2, the Great Plains lacks forests because

   Ⓐ they were destroyed by fires that completely burned them

   Ⓑ the area lacks enough rainfall to support entire forests

   Ⓒ most of the land there is not fertile enough for forests

   Ⓓ large parts of it were once covered by a saltwater sea

**Glossary** ⊖

**plateau:** a stretch of land that is relatively flat but higher in altitude than the surrounding land

**4**  According to paragraph 3, which of the following is true of the Great Plains?

  Ⓐ The easternmost part of it receives the greatest amount of rainfall.

  Ⓑ The best cropland to be found in it is located in the central region.

  Ⓒ The weather in its eastern and western parts is fairly similar.

  Ⓓ Most of the animals raised there live near the Rocky Mountains.

**5**  According to paragraph 4, when Europeans and Americans moved to the Great Plains, the region changed in that

  Ⓐ many Native Americans living there sought new homes elsewhere

  Ⓑ large areas of land began to be farmed by people

  Ⓒ most of the animals on the Great Plains were killed

  Ⓓ the buffalo were wiped out by the hunters who arrived

³➔ There are three distinct regions in the Great Plains. They are divided according to the amount of rainfall they receive and the height of the wild grasses growing in them. In the western part of the Great Plains in the shadow of the Rocky Mountains, there is less rainfall, so, consequently, the grasses grow shorter, and the soil is looser. Some areas there get so little rainfall that they are suitable only for grazing animals, not for cultivating crops. Moving away from the Rockies further east, the amount of rainfall increases in the central region, which has a combination of short and long grasses. Finally, the eastern section of the Great Plains is the wettest and has the tallest grasses and the strongest soil.

⁴➔ Prior to the arrival of humans approximately twelve thousand years ago, the Great Plains was home to many large types of fauna, including giant sloths, woolly mammoths, and saber-toothed tigers. The first humans, however, eliminated most large beasts, leaving behind no trace of them except for their bones. For thousands of years, these Native Americans lived as hunter-gatherers on the Great Plains and had much of their needs provided for by the vast herds of buffalo wandering there. These Native Americans therefore never developed farming like the tribes to the east and the south did. But when European explorers and, later, American hunters, ranchers, and farmers, arrived, the face of the Great Plains changed. The buffalo were hunted almost to extinction while the land itself began to be cultivated.

---

**Glossary**                                                    ⊖

**fauna:** the animals that live in a particular region

**6** The word deflect in the passage is closest in meaning to

Ⓐ exhaust

Ⓑ reduce

Ⓒ advance

Ⓓ avert

**7** In paragraph 6, why does the author mention the Dust Bowl?

Ⓐ To remark about its effects on the Great Plains once it ended

Ⓑ To name a period in history when a drought affected the Great Plains

Ⓒ To explain the specific regions in which it primarily took place

Ⓓ To comment on how it made farmers in the Great Plains modernize their methods

**8** According to paragraph 6, which of the following is NOT true of the reasons why so many crops are grown in the Great Plains?

Ⓐ The farmers there are able to utilize water that is located beneath the surface.

Ⓑ Farming methods that are sophisticated are used by the farmers living there.

Ⓒ Farmers in the Great Plains have advanced machinery that they can use.

Ⓓ Water from the numerous rivers and streams there is used for plants.

During the 1800s, tens of thousands of immigrants began making their way to the western United States and Canada, where they broke ground and started new lives. During times when rain frequently fell, they thrived, but rain was not always common on the Great Plains. Occasional years with little rain caused the soil to harden, dry up, and get blown away by the wind. Since there are few obstacles to deflect it, the wind tends to blow longer and stronger on the Great Plains. The worst drought lasted almost a decade during the 1920s and 1930s and reduced much of the southern Great Plains to a virtual desert. Huge dust storms ravaged farms and forced many to abandon farming and to move away. Slowly, the land recovered, but it constantly exists in a fragile state because it is at the mercy of the forces of nature.

⁶➡ Since that extended period of drought—referred to as the Dust Bowl—the number of people engaged in farming in the Great Plains has decreased. Nevertheless, it is estimated that a quarter of the world's wheat, corn, barley, oats, sorghum, and rye are cultivated there. This is on account of modern farming methods, improved farming equipment, and the extensive use of irrigation. Much of the water for these irrigation systems comes from groundwater located far beneath the surface. This has some people worried, though, as they fear that using too much groundwater will cause the next extended drought to be even worse than the Dust Bowl was.

ACTUAL TEST **07**

TOEFL® MAP **ACTUAL TEST**

Q
REVIEW

?
HELP

◀◀
BACK

▶▶
NEXT

**READING** | Question 9 of 30

00:54:00 ⊖ HIDE TIME

**9** Look at the four squares [ ■ ] that indicate where the following sentence could be added to the passage.

**These were also the years when the Great Depression happened in the United States, so the amount of suffering in that region was enormous.**

Where would the sentence best fit?

Click on a square [ ■ ] to add the sentence to the passage.

During the 1800s, tens of thousands of immigrants began making their way to the western United States and Canada, where they broke ground and started new lives. During times when rain frequently fell, they thrived, but rain was not always common on the Great Plains. Occasional years with little rain caused the soil to harden, dry up, and get blown away by the wind. Since there are few obstacles to deflect it, the wind tends to blow longer and stronger on the Great Plains. **1** The worst drought lasted almost a decade during the 1920s and 1930s and reduced much of the southern Great Plains to a virtual desert. **2** Huge dust storms ravaged farms and forced many to abandon farming and to move away. **3** Slowly, the land recovered, but it constantly exists in a fragile state because it is at the mercy of the forces of nature. **4**

10 **Directions:** An introductory sentence for a brief summary of the passage is provided below. Complete the summary by selecting the THREE answer choices that express the most important ideas of the passage. Some sentences do not belong because they express ideas that are not presented in the passage or are minor ideas in the passage. **This question is worth 2 points.**

Drag your answer choices to the spaces where they belong.
To remove an answer choice, click on it. To review the passage, click on **View Text**.

**The Great Plains is an enormous area of relatively flat grasslands that serves as an important farming region.**

- 
- 
- 

**Answer Choices**

1. The first inhabitants of the Great Plains were Native Americans, who mostly hunted on the land.

2. The Dust Bowl was a period of time when the Great Plains suffered from a decade-long drought.

3. Approximately a quarter of the world's supply of various grains is cultivated in the Great Plains.

4. The Great Plains sits on an area of land that was once submerged because of the presence of an inland sea.

5. Large parts of the Great Plains are suitable for agriculture thanks to modern irrigation methods.

6. The Great Plains covers a large amount of land in Canada, the United States, and Mexico.

ACTUAL TEST 07

195

# The Economics of Education

The Great Dome at the Massachusetts Institute of Technology

There is a great disparity in the economies of the world's nations. The strongest, such as those found in North America, Europe, and parts of Asia, tend to be those with the best-educated workforces. Meanwhile, the countries whose economies lag behind the others typically have educational systems in which the majority of their citizens fail to advance beyond the elementary level. While there are many forces that combine to determine whether or not national economies are successful, having a well-educated workforce is clearly one of the most important of them.

In most cases, the government of a nation determines its educational policies and also invests in education. Decisions on education made at the top trickle down to the lowest levels of society, where they have a pronounced influence on a country's people and economy. By looking at one country—the United States—it is easy to recognize several factors in its educational policy during the past century that benefitted the entire nation and enabled it to develop the world's largest economy. Among these factors are the expansion of high school education, the implementation of the GI Bill, and the explosion of secondary education that took place during the late twentieth century.

In the early years of the twentieth century, the United States was already an economic powerhouse, but had the country maintained its educational system at that time, its growth ultimately would have been restricted. In the early 1900s, most people were engaged in agriculture, and their children only received an elementary education. In 1900, for instance, seventy-one percent of children ages five to seventeen were enrolled in school. The majority never advanced past elementary school. In 1900, only 62,000 students graduated from American high schools.

Two decades later, in the 1920s, a movement to establish new high schools across the country and to ensure that children attended them began. This push for more high schools came primarily from national, state, and local governments, which also provided funds to build the schools and to train and pay the teachers. By 1940, twenty-six percent of all American children were enrolled in high school, and by the 1980s, that number had increased to thirty-two percent. Additionally, those numbers only take into account students in public schools and not the thousands of others attending private schools and getting homeschooled.

The same trend has occurred in university education. Few Americans attended college in the early twentieth century. In 1940, American universities had a total enrollment of fewer than 200,000 students. But after World War II in the 1940s, the American government introduced the GI Bill. It permitted servicemen and women to attend university while the government paid their tuition. Suddenly, by 1940, there were almost 400,000 students enrolled in American universities. During the latter half of the twentieth century, the numbers continued to rise until by 2000, more than one million American students matriculated to universities each year. A construction explosion took place around the country during the latter half of the 1900s. Hundreds of new campuses were built while existing ones were expanded. Today, American universities are widely considered the world's best in terms of students, faculty, and facilities, and tens of thousands of foreigners come to study at them every year.

The economical impact of this educational explosion has been felt in many areas. First, many high school and university graduates became managers, engineers, teachers, doctors, and business leaders. They paid taxes, and the increased tax revenues helped further expand the country's educational facilities. The rise in the number of people with a higher education paved the way for the United States to become the global leader in many fields, including engineering, medicine, aerospace technology, and business. Without these educated masses, the American economy would not have expanded to such a level. The same is true for other nations that have also heavily emphasized higher education. These countries, particularly ones in Europe and Northeast Asia, have found that having a highly educated populace has led to increased economic prosperity. At the other extreme, poorer nations, such as many of those in Africa, have trouble providing their young with an elementary education. It should come as no surprise that many of them are facing bleak economic conditions.

ACTUAL TEST 07

## Glossary

**GI:** a member of the American military, especially an enlisted soldier
**serviceman:** a member of the military; a soldier

**11** The word them in the passage refers to

- Ⓐ their citizens
- Ⓑ many forces
- Ⓒ national economies
- Ⓓ a well-educated workforce

**12** The word pronounced in the passage is closest in meaning to

- Ⓐ spoken
- Ⓑ arguable
- Ⓒ noticeable
- Ⓓ solitary

**13** According to paragraph 2, the United States managed to become the world's largest economy because

- Ⓐ its people worked much harder than those in other countries
- Ⓑ the country's schools produced a highly educated workforce
- Ⓒ a number of different factors combined to enable this to happen
- Ⓓ the GI Bill permitted everyone to attend universities for free

---

**The Economics of Education**

There is a great disparity in the economies of the world's nations. The strongest, such as those found in North America, Europe, and parts of Asia, tend to be those with the best-educated workforces. Meanwhile, the countries whose economies lag behind the others typically have educational systems in which the majority of their citizens fail to advance beyond the elementary level. While there are many forces that combine to determine whether or not national economies are successful, having a well-educated workforce is clearly one of the most important of them.

² ➔ In most cases, the government of a nation determines its educational policies and also invests in education. Decisions on education made at the top trickle down to the lowest levels of society, where they have a pronounced influence on a country's people and economy. By looking at one country—the United States—it is easy to recognize several factors in its educational policy during the past century that benefitted the entire nation and enabled it to develop the world's largest economy. Among these factors are the expansion of high school education, the implementation of the GI Bill, and the explosion of secondary education that took place during the late twentieth century.

---

| **Glossary** | ⊖ |
|---|---|

**GI:** a member of the American military, especially an enlisted soldier

**14** Which of the sentences below best expresses the essential information in the highlighted sentence in the passage? *Incorrect* answer choices change the meaning in important ways or leave out essential information.

Ⓐ The U.S. economy was strong in the early 1900s, but it would not have grown much more unless its educational system changed.

Ⓑ Because the U.S. kept teaching students in the same manner, it became an economic powerhouse in the early 1900s.

Ⓒ In the twentieth century, the U.S. went from being a country with a strong economy to one with the world's largest economy.

Ⓓ It was due solely to improvements in the American educational system that it was able to have such a powerful economy.

**15** According to paragraph 3, which of the following is NOT true of education in the United States around 1900?

Ⓐ Most American students only attended elementary school.

Ⓑ There was a movement to establish more high schools then.

Ⓒ The majority of children who were of school age attended schools.

Ⓓ Fewer than 100,000 students graduated from high school.

³→ In the early years of the twentieth century, the United States was already an economic powerhouse, but had the country maintained its educational system at that time, its growth ultimately would have been restricted. In the early 1900s, most people were engaged in agriculture, and their children only received an elementary education. In 1900, for instance, seventy-one percent of children ages five to seventeen were enrolled in school. The majority never advanced past elementary school. In 1900, only 62,000 students graduated from American high schools. Two decades later, in the 1920s, a movement to establish new high schools across the country and to ensure that children attended them began. This push for more high schools came primarily from national, state, and local governments, which also provided funds to build the schools and to train and pay the teachers. By 1940, twenty-six percent of all American children were enrolled in high school, and by the 1980s, that number had increased to thirty-two percent. Additionally, those numbers only take into account students in public schools and not the thousands of others attending private schools and getting homeschooled.

**16** Which of the following can be inferred from paragraph 3 about American education in the 1980s?

    Ⓐ The quality of private schools enabled more students to get accepted to colleges.

    Ⓑ The number of students in high school was larger than what statistics showed.

    Ⓒ The salaries of teachers decreased in some states yet increased in others.

    Ⓓ The homeschooling movement began to attract a large number of students.

³➙ In the early years of the twentieth century, the United States was already an economic powerhouse, but had the country maintained its educational system at that time, its growth ultimately would have been restricted. In the early 1900s, most people were engaged in agriculture, and their children only received an elementary education. In 1900, for instance, seventy-one percent of children ages five to seventeen were enrolled in school. The majority never advanced past elementary school. In 1900, only 62,000 students graduated from American high schools. Two decades later, in the 1920s, a movement to establish new high schools across the country and to ensure that children attended them began. This push for more high schools came primarily from national, state, and local governments, which also provided funds to build the schools and to train and pay the teachers. By 1940, twenty-six percent of all American children were enrolled in high school, and by the 1980s, that number had increased to thirty-two percent. Additionally, those numbers only take into account students in public schools and not the thousands of others attending private schools and getting homeschooled.

**17** According to paragraph 4, more universities were built in the United States because

  Ⓐ they were required in order to attract students from other countries

  Ⓑ the number of students getting a higher education rose dramatically

  Ⓒ more people were interested in becoming university faculty members

  Ⓓ governments needed to spend the money they had budgeted for education

⁴➡ The same trend has occurred in university education. Few Americans attended college in the early twentieth century. In 1940, American universities had a total enrollment of fewer than 200,000 students. But after World War II in the 1940s, the American government introduced the GI Bill. It permitted servicemen and women to attend university while the government paid their tuition. Suddenly, by 1940, there were almost 400,000 students enrolled in American universities. During the latter half of the twentieth century, the numbers continued to rise until by 2000, more than one million American students matriculated to universities each year. A construction explosion took place around the country during the latter half of the 1900s. Hundreds of new campuses were built while existing ones were expanded. Today, American universities are widely considered the world's best in terms of students, faculty, and facilities, and tens of thousands of foreigners come to study at them every year.

**Glossary** ⊖

**serviceman:** a member of the military; a soldier

ACTUAL TEST **07**

201

**18** In paragraph 5, the author's description of the results of the increase in American education mentions which of the following?

Ⓐ Why the increasing number of university graduates led to more tax revenues

Ⓑ Which subjects the majority of universities focused on teaching their students

Ⓒ How many universities were founded in the United States in the 1900s

Ⓓ What percentage of American high school students went on to study at universities

⁵➜ The economical impact of this educational explosion has been felt in many areas. First, many high school and university graduates became managers, engineers, teachers, doctors, and business leaders. They paid taxes, and the increased tax revenues helped further expand the country's educational facilities. The rise in the number of people with a higher education paved the way for the United States to become the global leader in many fields, including engineering, medicine, aerospace technology, and business. Without these educated masses, the American economy would not have expanded to such a level. The same is true for other nations that have also heavily emphasized higher education. These countries, particularly ones in Europe and Northeast Asia, have found that having a highly educated populace has led to increased economic prosperity. At the other extreme, poorer nations, such as many of those in Africa, have trouble providing their young with an elementary education. It should come as no surprise that many of them are facing bleak economic conditions.

19 Look at the four squares [ ■ ] that indicate where the following sentence could be added to the passage.

**Many of these countries are found in Africa, parts of Asia, and Central America.**

Where would the sentence best fit?

Click on a square [ ■ ] to add the sentence to the passage.

There is a great disparity in the economies of the world's nations. **1** The strongest, such as those found in North America, Europe, and parts of Asia, tend to be those with the best-educated workforces. **2** Meanwhile, the countries whose economies lag behind the others typically have educational systems in which the majority of their citizens fail to advance beyond the elementary level. **3** While there are many forces that combine to determine whether or not national economies are successful, having a well-educated workforce is clearly one of the most important of them. **4**

**20** **Directions:** An introductory sentence for a brief summary of the passage is provided below. Complete the summary by selecting the THREE answer choices that express the most important ideas of the passage. Some sentences do not belong because they express ideas that are not presented in the passage or are minor ideas in the passage. **This question is worth 2 points.**

Drag your answer choices to the spaces where they belong.
To remove an answer choice, click on it. To review the passage, click on **View Text**.

**In the 1900s, the economy of the United States became the world's largest thanks in part to the focus on education in the country.**

- 
- 
- 

## Answer Choices

1. As more Americans attended colleges, the people trained at them got high-paying jobs and paid more taxes.

2. Governments in the United States started opening more schools and paying for teachers in the 1920s.

3. People in countries in both Europe and Asia stress education, so their national economies have improved.

4. The GI Bill enabled a large number of soldiers to attend college for free starting in the 1940s.

5. Many people from countries all around the world go to the United States to enroll in the country's colleges and universities.

6. Few Americans got more than an elementary school education during the early years of the 1900s.

# Plant Adaptations

An Ohia Lehua tree growing on lava rocks in Hawaii

The Earth contains a wide variety of plant species, virtually all of which require three things to survive: sunlight, a sufficient supply of water, and soil with nutrients. Regrettably, these three necessities—quality soil in particular—are not available everywhere. For instance, soil can be too wet, dry, rocky, or frozen to allow many plants to grow. Nevertheless, some plants have managed to adapt to these adverse conditions by developing root systems which enable them to survive in harsh, difficult terrain.

All plants are either vascular or nonvascular. The majority are vascular, so they have internal systems that channel water, nutrients, and other necessities throughout their various parts. The roots belong to these internal systems and are typically found underground although they may be exposed to the air, particularly in exceptionally wet environments. The size and the depth of a plant's roots depend on the plant and the soil conditions. In dry regions, a plant's roots may extend far underground as they search for water and nutrients. Some plants have roots extending more than sixty meters beneath the surface. However, in tundra zones, where only the soil's upper layer remains unfrozen, a plant's roots may descend a few centimeters. Besides facing freezing conditions, the roots of plants growing in tundra may be restrained from descending far by the presence of rocky layers beneath the ground.

Because plants can face a wide variety of unique environments, many have developed specialized root systems. In deserts, tree roots often grow far beneath the surface. For instance, the mesquite tree has a single long, straight root, called a taproot, which descends around thirty meters belowground. Other desert plants, including numerous cactus species, have shallow yet extensive root systems that stretch horizontally to absorb moisture from as wide an area as possible. In watery areas, including bogs, swamps, marshes, and places near lakes and seashores, some plants have roots that grow above the ground. Botanists call these aerating roots. Some species with them, such as mangrove and cypress trees, seem able to absorb the gases plants need to survive from the atmosphere itself. Finally, in cases where plants grow in soil with a rich upper layer, their roots typically grow along the surface or just beneath it. Even in environments with fertile soil and adequate water, some plants have adapted in unusual ways. Mistletoe, for instance, is a parasitic plant with a root system that attaches to other plants to absorb their water and nutrients.

One of the harshest places where plants grow is the Arctic tundra. In tundra conditions, the ground is frequently entirely frozen to a great depth. The unfrozen soil also contains few nutrients since bacteria that help produce nitrogen in the soil exist in low numbers. Furthermore, strong winds make it difficult for plants to remain attached to the ground. Resultantly, plants growing in tundra are small, grow low to the ground, and have shallow roots. Nevertheless, their roots are quite strong and can anchor plants in windy conditions. They are also excellent at drawing moisture and nutrients from poor soil. During the summer months, when the ground thaws to a greater depth, the roots grow deeper, which grants them access to more nutrients. Thanks to their root systems, plants in tundra can survive even in freezing conditions.

Occasionally, the root systems of some plants can modify an environment to make it more suitable for other plants. When the Hawaiian Islands first formed, they were mostly covered by hard volcanic rock. In those harsh conditions, few plants could grow. But strong winds carried the seeds of plants great distances over water and deposited them on the islands. One of these plants, the ohia lehua tree, has a unique root system that gives it the ability to burrow deep into lava rocks, where there are nutrients and moisture in lava tubes, which are hollow spaces created by fast-flowing lava during a volcanic eruption. Inside these lava tubes, moisture gathered, which the roots used to enable the trees to survive. Over time, these roots began breaking down the lava rocks. As more trees grew, the hard lava further transformed into rich soil, thereby allowing the Hawaiian Islands to become the lush tropical paradise they are today.

---

## Glossary

**aerating:** exposed to the air

**parasitic:** relating to an organism that lives on or inside another organism and gets nutrients from its host

**21** The word adverse in the passage is closest in meaning to

  Ⓐ surprising

  Ⓑ inappropriate

  Ⓒ unfavorable

  Ⓓ diverse

**22** In paragraph 1, the author's description of plants mentions all of the following EXCEPT:

  Ⓐ how the soil may be poor for plants to grow in

  Ⓑ what soil must have for plants to be able to survive

  Ⓒ what most plants need in order to live

  Ⓓ how plants' roots have adapted through evolution

**23** According to paragraph 2, plants have deep roots in dry places because

  Ⓐ there are usually abundant supplies of water deep underground

  Ⓑ this allows them to search large areas for water as well as nutrients

  Ⓒ the rocky soil at the top is poor and does not let the plants grow well

  Ⓓ they must have strong taproots to keep them anchored in the ground

## Plant Adaptations

[1] → The Earth contains a wide variety of plant species, virtually all of which require three things to survive: sunlight, a sufficient supply of water, and soil with nutrients. Regrettably, these three necessities—quality soil in particular—are not available everywhere. For instance, soil can be too wet, dry, rocky, or frozen to allow many plants to grow. Nevertheless, some plants have managed to adapt to these adverse conditions by developing root systems which enable them to survive in harsh, difficult terrain.

[2] → All plants are either vascular or nonvascular. The majority are vascular, so they have internal systems that channel water, nutrients, and other necessities throughout their various parts. The roots belong to these internal systems and are typically found underground although they may be exposed to the air, particularly in exceptionally wet environments. The size and the depth of a plant's roots depend on the plant and the soil conditions. In dry regions, a plant's roots may extend far underground as they search for water and nutrients. Some plants have roots extending more than sixty meters beneath the surface. However, in tundra zones, where only the soil's upper layer remains unfrozen, a plant's roots may descend a few centimeters. Besides facing freezing conditions, the roots of plants growing in tundra may be restrained from descending far by the presence of rocky layers beneath the ground.

ACTUAL TEST **07**

**24** According to paragraph 3, which of the following is NOT true of tree roots?

- Ⓐ They may sometimes grow above the ground rather than beneath it.
- Ⓑ The roots of plants in watery areas may grow horizontally close to the surface.
- Ⓒ Some use parasitic methods to extract nutrients from other organisms.
- Ⓓ It is possible for a single root to grow straight down for many meters.

³➡ Because plants can face a wide variety of unique environments, many have developed specialized root systems. In deserts, tree roots often grow far beneath the surface. For instance, the mesquite tree has a single long, straight root, called a taproot, which descends around thirty meters belowground. Other desert plants, including numerous cactus species, have shallow yet extensive root systems that stretch horizontally to absorb moisture from as wide an area as possible. In watery areas, including bogs, swamps, marshes, and places near lakes and seashores, some plants have roots that grow above the ground. Botanists call these aerating roots. Some species with them, such as mangrove and cypress trees, seem able to absorb the gases plants need to survive from the atmosphere itself. Finally, in cases where plants grow in soil with a rich upper layer, their roots typically grow along the surface or just beneath it. Even in environments with fertile soil and adequate water, some plants have adapted in unusual ways. Mistletoe, for instance, is a parasitic plant with a root system that attaches to other plants to absorb their water and nutrients.

| Glossary | ⊖ |
|---|---|

**aerating:** exposed to the air

**parasitic:** relating to an organism that lives on or inside another organism and gets nutrients from its host

**25** The word drawing in the passage is closest in meaning to

Ⓐ extracting

Ⓑ transforming

Ⓒ identifying

Ⓓ attracting

**26** According to paragraph 4, which of the following is true of plants in tundra conditions?

Ⓐ Some of their roots grow deep underground to gain access to more nutrients.

Ⓑ They develop more rapidly in the winter months than in the summer months.

Ⓒ Their strong roots prevent the wind from ripping them out of the ground.

Ⓓ It is possible for some of them to grow to heights of a few meters above the ground.

⁴➡ One of the harshest places where plants grow is the Arctic tundra. In tundra conditions, the ground is frequently entirely frozen to a great depth. The unfrozen soil also contains few nutrients since bacteria that help produce nitrogen in the soil exist in low numbers. Furthermore, strong winds make it difficult for plants to remain attached to the ground. Resultantly, plants growing in tundra are small, grow low to the ground, and have shallow roots. Nevertheless, their roots are quite strong and can anchor plants in windy conditions. They are also excellent at drawing moisture and nutrients from poor soil. During the summer months, when the ground thaws to a greater depth, the roots grow deeper, which grants them access to more nutrients. Thanks to their root systems, plants in tundra can survive even in freezing conditions.

ACTUAL TEST **07**

**27** The author uses the ohia lehua tree as an example of

Ⓐ a unique plant that has the ability to grow inside lava tubes

Ⓑ one of the plants that transformed Hawaii into a place filled with life

Ⓒ a plant whose seeds are often transported by birds from place to place

Ⓓ the only plant that is able to grow quickly on volcanic land

**28** According to paragraph 5, lava tubes help some plants grow because

Ⓐ they contain water that some plants' roots can utilize

Ⓑ many of the nutrients that plants require are found in them

Ⓒ they have more fertile soil than other areas near volcanoes

Ⓓ they enable plants with aerating roots to grow swiftly

⁵➡ Occasionally, the root systems of some plants can modify an environment to make it more suitable for other plants. When the Hawaiian Islands first formed, they were mostly covered by hard volcanic rock. In those harsh conditions, few plants could grow. But strong winds carried the seeds of plants great distances over water and deposited them on the islands. One of these plants, the ohia lehua tree, has a unique root system that gives it the ability to burrow deep into lava rocks, where there are nutrients and moisture in lava tubes, which are hollow spaces created by fast-flowing lava during a volcanic eruption. Inside these lava tubes, moisture gathered, which the roots used to enable the trees to survive. Over time, these roots began breaking down the lava rocks. As more trees grew, the hard lava further transformed into rich soil, thereby allowing the Hawaiian Islands to become the lush tropical paradise they are today.

29 Look at the four squares [ ■ ] that indicate where the following sentence could be added to the passage.

**Sugar maples, silver maples, and several others species of maples are all trees which have shallow root systems.**

Where would the sentence best fit?

Click on a square [ ■ ] to add the sentence to the passage.

Because plants can face a wide variety of unique environments, many have developed specialized root systems. In deserts, tree roots often grow far beneath the surface. For instance, the mesquite tree has a single long, straight root, called a taproot, which descends around thirty meters belowground. Other desert plants, including numerous cactus species, have shallow yet extensive root systems that stretch horizontally to absorb moisture from as wide an area as possible. In watery areas, including bogs, swamps, marshes, and places near lakes and seashores, some plants have roots that grow above the ground. Botanists call these aerating roots. Some species with them, such as mangrove and cypress trees, seem able to absorb the gases plants need to survive from the atmosphere itself. **1** Finally, in cases where plants grow in soil with a rich upper layer, their roots typically grow along the surface or just beneath it. **2** Even in environments with fertile soil and adequate water, some plants have adapted in unusual ways. **3** Mistletoe, for instance, is a parasitic plant with a root system that attaches to other plants to absorb their water and nutrients. **4**

**Glossary** ⊖

**aerating:** exposed to the air
**parasitic:** relating to an organism that lives on or inside another organism and gets nutrients from its host

ACTUAL TEST **07**

**30** **Directions:** Select the appropriate sentences from the answer choices and match the plant adaptations to the locations to which they relate. TWO of the answer choices will NOT be used. **This question is worth 4 points.**

> Drag your answer choices to the spaces where they belong.
> To remove an answer choice, click on it. To review the passage, click on **View Text**.

| Answer Choices | LOCATION |
|---|---|
| | **Desert** |
| ① Plants have shallow roots that extend very far horizontally. | • |
| ② Some plants can cause an entire environment to change. | • |
| ③ Plants may have strong roots that are very shallow. | • |
| ④ The roots of some plants can take in gases from the air. | **Watery Area** |
| ⑤ A few plants can transform hard ground into rich soil. | • |
| ⑥ Some plants develop taproots that grow straight down. | • |
| ⑦ The roots of some plants grow deeper during the summer. | **Tundra** |
| ⑧ A few plants are able to absorb water from a large area. | • |
| ⑨ Some of the roots of plants may grow above the ground. | • |

# TOEFL® MAP

# ACTUAL
# TEST Reading 1

Answers and
Explanations

## Answers

| | | | | |
|---|---|---|---|---|
| 1 Ⓒ | 2 Ⓓ | 3 Ⓑ | 4 Ⓑ | 5 Ⓐ |
| 6 Ⓐ | 7 Ⓒ | 8 Ⓐ | 9 **2** | |

10 ②, ③, ④

| | | | | |
|---|---|---|---|---|
| 11 Ⓓ | 12 Ⓑ | 13 Ⓐ | 14 Ⓑ | 15 Ⓓ |
| 16 Ⓒ | 17 Ⓐ | 18 Ⓐ | 19 **2** | |

20 ③, ⑤, ⑥

| | | | | |
|---|---|---|---|---|
| 21 Ⓓ | 22 Ⓑ | 23 Ⓑ | 24 Ⓐ | 25 Ⓓ |
| 26 Ⓑ | 27 Ⓑ | 28 Ⓓ | 29 **1** | |

30 Cause: ③, ⑤, ⑦   Effect: ②, ④

## Explanations

### Passage 1
p.15

1 **Factual Question** | The author mentions, "A close examination of these fossils has proven that an ancient species of whales once had both legs and numerous similarities to the modern-day hippopotamus. As a result, scientists today accept that a hippopotamus-like creature moved into the ocean around fifty million years ago and, over the course of millions of years, evolved into the modern whale."

2 **Vocabulary Question** | When something comes to light, it means that it appears or is discovered.

3 **Rhetorical Purpose Question** | The author discusses fossils of whales being discovered on land when writing, "In the 1980s, American paleontologists working in Pakistan and Egypt found some fossils of whales with legs. They unearthed these fossils on ancient sea beds. Previously in the past, the area that is Pakistan and Egypt today was covered by a body of water called the Tethys Ocean."

4 **Factual Question** | It is written, "Paleontologists digging in Egypt unearthed more than 1,000 whale fossils in Wadi Hitan."

5 **Negative Factual Question** | The author writes, "Finally, in 2000, some paleontologists noticed that the ankle bones of the fossilized whale were practically identical to those of animals in the family of mammals which hippopotamuses belong to." But this refers to fossilized whales, not modern-day whales. There is no mention in the passage about whales presently having ankle bones.

6 **Inference Question** | In the paragraph, the author writes about paleontologists and molecular biologists studying whales. In addition, other scientists conducted studies of whale blood. So it can be inferred that whales are studied by scientists in a wide range of fields.

7 **Vocabulary Question** | When food sources are abundant, they are ample or plentiful.

8 **Sentence Simplification Question** | The sentence points out that changes in the environment brought nutrients up to the surface of the water, which provided a lot of food for whales. As a result, they did not need to live on land anymore. This thought is best expressed by the sentence in answer choice Ⓐ.

9 **Insert Text Question** | The sentence before the second square reads, "Interestingly, years earlier in the 1950s, some scientists learned that whale blood possesses similar properties to the blood of animals in the mammalian order that includes pigs, deer, camels, and hippopotamuses." The sentences to be added notes how all of "these animals" look similar to one another in various ways. Thus the two sentences go well together.

10 **Prose Summary Question** | The summary sentence notes that whales evolved over millions of years to change from animals that dwelled on land to animals that lived in the ocean. This thought is best described in answer choices ②, ③, and ④. Answer choices ① and ⑤ are minor points, so they are incorrect answers. Answer choice ⑥ contains wrong information, so it is also incorrect.

### Passage 2
p.23

11 **Vocabulary Question** | When an event is in its heyday, it is at its peak.

12 **Factual Question** | According to the author, "English pirates were the scourges of the oceans as they seized cargoes from countless ships. This frequently brought them into conflict with others, especially the Spanish Empire, and it was even a principal cause of a war between England and Spain."

13 **Vocabulary Question** | When privateering captains were searching for Spanish treasure to plunder, they were looking to rob the Spanish of their valuables.

14 **Rhetorical Purpose Question** | About the immense Spanish Armada, the author writes, "Yet in the sixteenth century, first under King Henry VIII and then under his daughter Elizabeth, the English navy became better established. Its defeat of the immense Spanish Armada in 1588 enhanced its reputation." So the author mentions it to note how the defeat of the Spanish Armada made the English navy improve in status.

15 **Sentence Simplification Question** | The sentence points out that English monarchs became less interested in using privateers as they came to rely more on the navy to fight for them. This thought is best explained by the sentence in answer choice Ⓓ.

16 **Inference Question** | About the English navy, the author mentions, "In previous centuries, the English navy had expanded during times of war but subsequently disappeared during times of peace. Yet in the sixteenth century, first under King Henry VIII and then under his daughter Elizabeth, the English navy became better established." So it can be inferred that the English navy was not permanent prior to the sixteenth century.

17 **Negative Factual Question** | About the Barbary pirates, the author comments, "The Barbary Coast pirates were different from European pirates in one major way: They enslaved the people they captured. They typically sailed in galleys, which used sails and oars and were mostly rowed by slaves. There were also slave markets in the Middle East that the pirates filled by capturing people from ships and on coastal raids." So the pirates seemed to prefer to capture people rather than to kill them since they could sell captured individuals as slaves.

18 **Factual Question** | The author notes, "By the time the nineteenth century arrived, the use of sanctioned privateers in warfare had been abolished, and English piracy and privateering disappeared for good."

19 **Insert Text Question** | The sentence before the second square reads, "For centuries, the southwestern English counties of Devon and Cornwall were home to many pirate-controlled harbors." The sentence to be added notes that the harbors were located on two major bodies of water, so pirate ships could get to open water easily. Thus the two sentences go well together.

20 **Prose Summary Question** | The summary sentence notes that English kings and queens once allowed piracy to exist, but piracy later declined and then disappeared. This thought is best described in answer choices ③, ⑤, and ⑥. Answer choices ① and ② are minor points, so they are incorrect answers. Answer choice ④ contains

information not mentioned in the passage, so it is also incorrect.

## Passage 3 p.32

21 **Inference Question** | The author describes many different ways in which children role-play. So it can be inferred that they may do so in a wide variety of manners.

22 **Vocabulary Question** | When role-playing situations are elaborate, they are complicated.

23 **Vocabulary Question** | When a person devises plans, that individual creates or comes up with new plans or ideas.

24 **Factual Question** | It is written, "Sometimes they must solve puzzles, work out steps that need to be taken to complete a task, and devise plans to act out an adventure or story. In order to do these activities, children may need to make costumes, gather materials, decide on colors and decorations, and put everything together in a cohesive manner."

25 **Negative Factual Question** | There is no mention in the paragraph about what children think the best ways to utilize their resources are.

26 **Factual Question** | The author notes, "They can enhance their vocabulary, develop their sentence structure, and gradually improve other verbal skills."

27 **Sentence Simplification Question** | The sentence points out that role-playing activities let children overcome their fears of various encounters that could possibly cause them emotional pain. This thought is best explained by the sentence in answer choice Ⓑ.

28 **Vocabulary Question** | When children master their fears, they are able to overcome them so that they are no longer afraid.

29 **Insert Text Question** | The sentence before the first square reads, "For instance, boys may pretend to shave like their fathers or may perform various chores inside and outside their homes." The sentence to be added notes that some pretend activities may be doing yardwork, which is outside the home, and repairing something broken, which is inside the home. Thus the two sentences go well together.

30 **Fill in a Table Question** | Regarding causes, the author writes, "Many children try imitating their parents in one

common form of role-playing," and, "Other types of role-playing involve more elaborate situations. Children may imagine that to belong to a group of superheroes on an adventure. In doing so, they might dress up in costumes and assume different roles. Sometimes, children imitate real-life situations, such as when they act as if they are cowboys on the range or police officers apprehending criminals." The author then adds, "One final beneficial aspect of role-playing is that it can help children deal with certain actions that may cause them emotional distress, such as the fear they face when going to school for the first time or making a visit to the doctor." As for effects, the author notes, "All of these actions stimulate children's curiosity about the world and encourage them to learn as much as they can," and, "At times, children will disagree, so they must learn to negotiate and compromise with one another."

# Actual Test 02

## Answers

| | | | | |
|---|---|---|---|---|
| 1 Ⓐ | 2 Ⓓ | 3 Ⓒ | 4 Ⓑ | 5 Ⓓ |
| 6 Ⓑ | 7 Ⓓ | 8 Ⓒ | 9 **2** | |
| 10 ①, ②, ⑤ | | | | |
| 11 Ⓑ | 12 Ⓐ | 13 Ⓓ | 14 Ⓑ | 15 Ⓑ |
| 16 Ⓑ | 17 Ⓒ | 18 Ⓒ | 19 **4** | |
| 20 ②, ⑤, ⑥ | | | | |
| 21 Ⓐ | 22 Ⓒ | 23 Ⓓ | 24 Ⓑ | 25 Ⓑ |
| 26 Ⓐ | 27 Ⓐ | 28 Ⓓ | 29 **3** | |
| 30 Cold: ①, ②, ④  Heat: ③, ⑥ | | | | |
| 31 Ⓑ | 32 Ⓓ | 33 Ⓐ | 34 Ⓐ | 35 Ⓒ |
| 36 Ⓓ | 37 Ⓐ | 38 Ⓒ | 39 **4** | |
| 40 ①, ④, ⑤ | | | | |

## Explanations

### Passage 1

1 **Negative Factual Question** | The paragraph contains no information about when 3D printers started being utilized by large numbers of people in the field of medicine.

2 **Vocabulary Question** | Crude methods are ones that are clumsy.

3 **Factual Question** | The passage reads, "Surgeons make an MRI or CAT scan of the region affected and then construct a three-dimensional drawing of the body part requiring replacement. After that, the surgical team uses a 3D printer to make the part from plastic and finally performs the surgery to insert the implant."

4 **Reference Question** | The "it" that has blood vessels inside itself is the liver.

5 **Factual Question** | The author writes, "To reduce surgery time and to improve the chances of a successful operation, surgical teams build and train on 3D models of organs. Perhaps a patient requires liver surgery. The surgical team will conduct scans of the patient's liver and then create an accurate model of it with a 3D printer. The model will be clear and show the internal structure of the liver, including the placement of every blood vessel inside it. If there are any cancerous tumors in the liver, the 3D printer will include them in the model. Prior to the actual operation, the surgical team trains on the model of the liver, thereby ensuring that the patient has the best chance of having a successful surgery."

6 **Sentence Simplification Question** | The sentence points out that the softer materials have elastic properties letting them resemble real organs, so doctors can know how to perform the operations better. This thought is best explained by the sentence in answer choice Ⓑ.

7 **Inference Question** | The passage reads, "As 3D-printed organ model technology advances and models become more realistic, the hope is that one day, 3D printers can be used to construct artificial organs to replace malfunctioning ones." The author therefore implies that 3D printers are not unable to make organs that can be used by human bodies.

8 **Vocabulary Question** | A feasible option is one that is practical.

9 **Insert Text Question** | The sentence before the second square reads, "While every human body has the same general internal structure, there are often unique differences between patients." The sentence to be added notes that heart disease and cancer can make the organs of sick people larger than those of healthy people, which shows some differences between patients. Thus the two sentences go well together.

**10 Prose Summary Question** | The summary sentence notes that the medical industry is using 3D printers now and that the printers will likely be more valuable in the future. This thought is best described in answer choices ①, ②, and ⑤. Answer choices ③ and ④ are minor points, so they are incorrect answers. Answer choice ⑥ contains information not mentioned in the passage, so it is also incorrect.

---

## Passage 2                                                      p.50

**11 Inference Question** | The passage reads, "Initially, who made the artwork and why were mysteries that baffled experts. Over time, however, thanks to archaeological methods and scientific analysis, many answers have progressively been revealed." The author notes, "Many answers have progressively been revealed." However, there is no mention that all of the answers have been revealed. So it can be inferred that experts in cave art still need to learn more about it.

**12 Vocabulary Question** | When people believed that cave art was an elaborate hoax, they thought that it was a deception. They did not truly believe that cave art had been painted thousands of years ago.

**13 Factual Question** | The author writes, "Radiocarbon dating of the materials used in the artwork and organic material found in the caves established the time of its creation to have been between 40,000 and 10,000 B.C. The majority of the art was determined to have been made from 18,000 to 10,000 B.C."

**14 Reference Question** | The "them" that were enabled to shape harder rocks thanks to the flint-based tools were early men.

**15 Negative Factual Question** | The passage mentions that tools were used to cut into rock, but there is nothing mentioned about using hard rocks to cut into softer rocks.

**16 Rhetorical Purpose Question** | The passage includes, "What has survived, however, are hollow bone tubes through which paint was blown onto rock in a fine spray to make it spread evenly." So the author is writing about tools that artists used to make cave art.

**17 Factual Question** | The passage reads, "The artists then utilized vegetable and animal oils to make the paint bind to their rocky canvases."

**18 Vocabulary Question** | When some facts lend credence

to a theory, then the theory is supported, so it becomes believable.

**19 Insert Text Question** | The sentence before the fourth square reads, "For instance, red was derived from iron oxide, black from magnesium dioxide or burned pine or juniper, and white from mica." The sentence to be added names an additional material—blood—that was also used to make paint. Thus the two sentences go well together.

**20 Prose Summary Question** | The summary sentence notes that many caves in Europe feature various types of artwork that were made by primitive tools or paints. This thought is best described in answer choices ②, ⑤, and ⑥. Answer choices ①, ③, and ④ are all minor points, so they are incorrect answers.

---

## Passage 3                                                      p.58

**21 Vocabulary Question** | When people's bodies employ coping mechanisms, they are using methods that will ensure the survival of their bodies.

**22 Rhetorical Purpose Question** | When the author writes, "Thermoregulation is the term used to describe the human body's ability to control its internal temperature," the author is defining a term.

**23 Factual Question** | The passage reads, "Although a human's average body temperature is around thirty-seven degrees Celsius, various parts of the body maintain different temperatures. At the body's core—the head, the chest, and the abdomen—the temperature is slightly higher than in the extremities—the arms and the legs."

**24 Inference Question** | The author remarks, "The reason is that people's most vital organs are in their head, chest, and abdomen. The three most important organs for human survival are the brain, the heart, and the liver, so the body attempts to ensure that these organs function as well as possible." In noting that the "most important organs for human survival are the brain, the heart, and the liver" and mentioning that they are in the "head, chest, and abdomen," the author implies that organs critical to an individual's survival are not found in a person's arms and legs.

**25 Sentence Simplification Question** | The sentence points out that when the weather is cold, more warm blood stays around certain organs, so blood vessels closer to the skin get less blood. This thought is best expressed by the sentence in answer choice Ⓑ.

26 **Vocabulary Question** | When the body pools warm blood into certain areas, it is collecting the blood so that it can protect the body's vital organs.

27 **Factual Question** | The author notes, "Body hairs lie flat to prevent heat from being trapped. The flowing of blood toward the surface of the skin increases, which thereby transfers more heat out of the body."

28 **Negative Factual Question** | There is no mention in the paragraph about a person vomiting due either to extremely hot or cold weather.

29 **Insert Text Question** | The sentence before the third square reads, "Unless these fluids are replaced, dehydration will result if the body's internal level of fluids becomes too low." The sentence to be added notes that people who are taking part in athletic events are advised to drink a lot of liquids. Thus the two sentences go well together.

30 **Fill in a Table Question** | Regarding cold as an extreme weather condition, the author writes, "This can result in a person developing pale skin and frostbite once the moisture in the skin and the outer flesh freezes," and, "If a person's core body temperature falls beneath thirty-two degrees Celsius, unconsciousness will ensue." The author then adds, "Second, the brain sends signals to other muscles to begin contracting rapidly, causing the person to shiver, which produces more body heat." As for heat as an extreme weather condition, the author notes, "The body also produces sweat to keep its temperature from rising too much," and, "Body hairs lie flat to prevent heat from being trapped."

## Passage 4                                        p.65

31 **Factual Question** | The author points out, "Vasari is famed for coining the term *renaissance* to describe the new style of art which existed during his lifetime and of which he was also a practitioner."

32 **Factual Question** | It is written, "Tragedy struck when Vasari was sixteen as his father died of the plague, and being the oldest son, Vasari took over the family's affairs. Due to that event, he developed a lifelong desire for financial security for himself and his family, which he successfully attained through his friendship with and the patronage of the Medici family."

33 **Negative Factual Question** | There is no mention in the paragraph about the number and types of paintings that Giorgio Vasari created during his entire art career.

34 **Inference Question** | The passage reads, "However, modern-day critics believe that Vasari's style was largely copied from the masters who preceded him, especially his friend Michelangelo." The author therefore implies that Giorgio Vasari is not considered an original artist by modern-day experts.

35 **Rhetorical Purpose Question** | In writing, "Vasari was well versed in Latin and ancient literature, and thus, when he wrote his biography of artists, he may have been influenced by the works of ancient Roman writers such as Plutarch and Vitruvius," the author is naming two individuals whose writing positively affected Giorgio Vasari.

36 **Vocabulary Question** | When Giorgio Vasari attempted to salvage his reputation, he was trying to rescue it.

37 **Rhetorical Purpose Question** | About Titian, the author comments, "The majority, however, were from the Florence region, and Vasari gave little space to artists in other areas until the second edition in 1568, when he included some Venetian artists such as Titian."

38 **Vocabulary Question** | When Giorgio Vasari was accused of embellishing certain events, he was accused of exaggerating what happened during them.

39 **Insert Text Question** | The sentence before the fourth square reads, "Vasari's family had connections with the famed Medici banking family." The sentence to be added notes that some of the people in the Medici family were powerful not just in Florence but also in all of Italy. Thus the two sentences go well together.

40 **Prose Summary Question** | The summary sentence notes that Giorgio Vasari was both an important artist and influential writer. This thought is best described in answer choices ①, ④, and ⑤. Answer choices ③ and ⑥ are minor points, so they are incorrect answers. Answer choice ② contains wrong information, so it is also incorrect.

# Answers

| | | | | |
|---|---|---|---|---|
| 1 Ⓐ | 2 Ⓒ | 3 Ⓐ | 4 Ⓑ | 5 Ⓒ |
| 6 Ⓓ | 7 Ⓓ | 8 Ⓐ | 9 **1** | |
| 10 ②, ④, ⑥ | | | | |

| | | | | |
|---|---|---|---|---|
| 11 Ⓑ | 12 Ⓒ | 13 Ⓐ | 14 Ⓐ | 15 Ⓑ |
| 16 Ⓓ | 17 Ⓑ | 18 Ⓒ | 19 **2** | |
| 20 Roman Republic: ③, ⑥  Roman Empire: ②, ④, ⑦ | | | | |

| | | | | |
|---|---|---|---|---|
| 21 Ⓒ | 22 Ⓐ | 23 Ⓑ | 24 Ⓒ | 25 Ⓒ |
| 26 Ⓐ | 27 Ⓓ | 28 Ⓒ | 29 **3** | |
| 30 ①, ④, ⑥ | | | | |

# Explanations

## Passage 1                                                        p.75

1   **Factual Question** | The passage reads, "Clouds themselves are primarily comprised of water vapor."

2   **Vocabulary Question** | When water vapor droplets converge, they unite, which then enables them to form clouds.

3   **Inference Question** | The author writes, "Over time, as more and more water vapor droplets come together, they increase the size of their cloud until it reaches a point that it is so heavy that it releases its water, which falls to the ground as precipitation." This implies that clouds filled with water are likely to cause rain to fall.

4   **Reference Question** | The "It" that is often invisible is common dust.

5   **Rhetorical Purpose Question** | The author notes, "There is a massive amount of dust in the atmosphere. It is often invisible, but, at times, it may be observed as smoke, smog, and haze."

6   **Negative Factual Question** | The author points out, "In addition, they are responsible for much of the electrical transference between clouds that causes lightning." Thus it is not true that ice nuclei have little to do with the creation of lightning in clouds.

7   **Vocabulary Question** | A farfetched idea is an unbelievable one.

8   **Factual Question** | It is written, "Scientists have also learned that bacteria may be a part of cloud formations. More than twenty-five years ago, it was proposed that bacteria could form ice nuclei and then spread to other parts of the world by falling to the ground along with rain and snow. While this theory was at first disregarded, there is a growing body of evidence that this, in fact, happens. Various forms of bacteria common to plants have been collected from ice samples in many different places, even in the Earth's Polar Regions in places where there are no plants. It seems that the bacteria are blown into the atmosphere, form ice nuclei, which then become ice crystals, and later fall as rain or snow and land in new areas."

9   **Insert Text Question** | The sentence before the first square reads, "The human sources can be anything that puts dust into the atmosphere, including farming, forestry, mining, and manufacturing." The sentence to be added points out that smoke from factories, which are made by humans, are also major sources of dust. Thus the two sentences go well together.

10  **Prose Summary Question** | The summary sentence notes that clouds are formed by water vapor and other substances. This thought is best described in answer choices ②, ④, and ⑥. Answer choices ① and ③ are minor points, so they are incorrect answers. Answer choice ⑤ contains wrong information, so it is also incorrect.

## Passage 2                                                        p.83

11  **Sentence Simplification Question** | The sentence points out that the Roman Senate was unable to stop powerful Roman families from engaging in various intrigues, and this would lead to its eventual downfall. This thought is best expressed by the sentence in answer choice Ⓑ.

12  **Rhetorical Purpose Question** | About Julius Caesar, the author first notes, "Julius Caesar was at the center of this period of conflict." Then, the author focuses on the actions that Caesar took that brought about the downfall of the Roman Republic.

13  **Vocabulary Question** | A virtual dictator is a person who is practically one even though he might not be called a dictator.

14  **Factual Question** | It is written, "After a short civil war, Caesar defeated his enemies and became the ruler of Rome. He invested the power of many political offices

in his own person and ruled as a virtual dictator for five years. Caesar's acts deprived the Senate of much of its authority and set in motion the process for all of Rome's power to be held by a single individual."

**15 Rhetorical Purpose Question** | About Actium, the author notes, "At the great naval battle of Actium in 31 B.C., Octavian's forces defeated Anthony and Cleopatra."

**16 Factual Question** | The passage includes, "Having expected to be named Caesar's heir instead of the young Octavian, Anthony managed to hold his jealousy in check while the two men worked together to defeat those who had been responsible for Caesar's assassination. Once this was accomplished, Anthony came out against Octavian by joining forces with the Egyptian queen Cleopatra, who had been romantically involved with Caesar prior to his death."

**17 Vocabulary Question** | Something that is characteristic of others is distinctive of them.

**18 Negative Factual Question** | There is no mention in the passage of Augustus's son, nor is there any mention of any training that he did for his heir in order to become the emperor.

**19 Insert Text Question** | The sentence before the second square reads, "At the great naval battle of Actium in 31 B.C., Octavian's forces defeated Anthony and Cleopatra." The sentence to be added points out that Anthony and Cleopatra lost both the battle and their lives. Thus the two sentences go well together.

**20 Fill in a Table Question** | Regarding the Roman Republic, the author writes, "Rome emerged as a center of power on the Italian peninsula by the banks of the Tiber River sometime around 500 B.C. After an early period of monarchy, the Roman people overthrew their leaders, established a culture that employed a system of democratic beliefs, and created an entity that would become known as the Roman Republic." As for the Roman Empire, the author notes, "The emperors who immediately followed Augustus imitated his custom of adopting heirs and training them well. Eventually, the position became hereditary though, and too many later emperors were weak and poorly trained," and, "Second, he maintained the respect of the citizens of Rome, which provided him with a strong power base." The author also writes, "The emperors who immediately followed Augustus imitated his custom of adopting heirs and training them well."

Passage 3                                                                p.91

**21 Factual Question** | The passage reads, "Nevertheless, some plants are carnivorous, so they devour small creatures such as insects to get the nourishment they need to sustain them."

**22 Rhetorical Purpose Question** | About protocarnivorous plants, the author writes, "Yet one class of plants traps insects and uses bacteria that the plants themselves do not produce when they digest their prey, so some botanists insist that they are not actually carnivorous plants. There are more than 300 of these types of borderline carnivorous plants, which have been termed protocarnivorous plants." So the author is giving the name used for plants that are not truly carnivorous.

**23 Factual Question** | The author mentions, "Botanists also disagree on the mechanism of digestion. Some think that a plant must utilize enzymes which it produces to digest insects to be considered carnivorous."

**24 Vocabulary Question** | An enticing smell is an appealing one.

**25 Negative Factual Question** | The Venus flytrap has no connection to the pitfall trap since the plant relies upon a different method to trap insects.

**26 Inference Question** | It is written, "While the Venus flytrap is a relatively well-known carnivorous plant, it is in fact one of only two plants that utilize the snapping-trap mechanism." So the author implies that snapping traps, which are possessed by only two plants, are the least common entrapment method used.

**27 Factual Question** | The author writes, "Suction traps are frequently utilized by plants growing near water."

**28 Factual Question** | The passage reads, "Other carnivorous plants have specialized cell structures that open temporarily to permit the nutrients to pass through the cuticle."

**29 Insert Text Question** | The sentence before the third square reads, "Tiny hairs on the plants' surfaces point only in one direction, which allows insects to enter, but when they try to leave, the hairs prevent them from escaping." The sentence to be added notes that the hairs force the insects to go backward into a chamber, where they can then be digested. Thus the two sentences go well together.

**30 Prose Summary Question** | The summary sentence

notes that carnivorous plants have various methods to trap insects and then digest them to use their nutrients. This thought is best described in answer choices [1], [4], and [6]. Answer choices [2] and [3] are minor points, so they are incorrect answers. Answer choice [5] contains wrong information, so it is also incorrect.

## Actual Test 04

p.97

## Answers

| | | | | |
|---|---|---|---|---|
| 1 Ⓑ | 2 Ⓓ | 3 Ⓐ | 4 Ⓒ | 5 Ⓐ |
| 6 Ⓓ | 7 Ⓒ | 8 Ⓑ | 9 **1** | |
| 10 [4], [5], [6] | | | | |
| 11 Ⓓ | 12 Ⓑ | 13 Ⓐ | 14 Ⓐ | 15 Ⓒ |
| 16 Ⓐ | 17 Ⓓ | 18 Ⓐ | 19 **3** | |
| 20 [1], [2], [6] | | | | |
| 21 Ⓑ | 22 Ⓓ | 23 Ⓓ | 24 Ⓐ | 25 Ⓒ |
| 26 Ⓒ | 27 Ⓓ | 28 Ⓒ | 29 **1** | |
| 30 Water Clock: [1], [2], [6] Spring-Powered Clock: [4], [5] | | | | |
| 31 Ⓒ | 32 Ⓒ | 33 Ⓒ | 34 Ⓓ | 35 Ⓒ |
| 36 Ⓒ | 37 Ⓑ | 38 Ⓒ | 39 **4** | |
| 40 [1], [5], [6] | | | | |

## Explanations

### Passage 1

p.99

1  **Rhetorical Purpose Question** | In writing, "One time when there were significant climate differences from modern times was the Cambrian Period. It lasted from 541 to 285 million years ago and was a part of a longer geological time period called the Paleozoic Era," the author mentions the Paleozoic Era in order to state that the Cambrian Period took place during a part of it.

2  **Vocabulary Question** | Because the Cambrian Period was more amenable to newer life forms than previous periods, it was more agreeable to them.

3  **Factual Question** | The passage reads, "Scientists theorize that the average global temperature during the Cambrian Period was approximately twenty-two degrees Celsius. This compares to the present-day average of

fourteen degrees Celsius. The temperature was thought to have been so high due to the greenhouse effect caused by the sun's heat being trapped near the Earth's surface for an extended period of time."

4  **Factual Question** | The author notes, "In order to discover temperatures during the Cambrian Period, the British team of scientists studied oxygen levels in fossils. They examined two oxygen isotopes, oxygen-16, which is very common on the Earth, and the rarer isotope oxygen-18."

5  **Rhetorical Purpose Question** | The author points out that the conodont was found to have absorbed oxygen into its shell and bones in writing, "The use of fossils was necessary in this study due to the properties of calcium carbonate and calcium phosphate, which can absorb oxygen, in shells and bones. However, the researchers initially found only one set of fossils for which this technique managed to yield the desired results. This was an early form of vertebrate called a conodont."

6  **Vocabulary Question** | When the method yielded data, it provided data for the scientists.

7  **Inference Question** | The author mentions, "Furthermore, the theory of a greenhouse climate was bolstered when the temperature data was compared and found to be similar to better known periods of greenhouse-like effects during the Mesozoic and Cenozoic eras." In writing that, the author implies that scientists do not know as much about the Cambrian Period as they do the Mesozoic and Cenozoic eras.

8  **Negative Factual Question** | There is no mention in the passage about what parts of the world scientists have found fossils from the Cambrian Period in.

9  **Insert Text Question** | The sentence before the first square reads, "However, with the rise in global temperatures, conditions became more favorable, so a greater number of multi-cellular organisms, including shellfish and vertebrates, developed during the Cambrian Period." The sentence to be added notes that this time was called the Cambrian Explosion and that it is considered important because so many new organisms that are the ancestors of modern-day ones appeared during it. Thus the two sentences go well together.

10  **Prose Summary Question** | The summary sentence notes the Cambrian Period was very warm, so many new organisms developed during it. This thought is best described in answer choices [4], [5], and [6]. Answer choices [1] and [2] are minor points, so they are incorrect

answers. Answer choice ③ contains information not mentioned in the passage, so it is also incorrect.

## Passage 2

p.106

**11 Vocabulary Question** | People who are susceptible to maladies are vulnerable to them. So it is easy for them to get these maladies.

**12 Rhetorical Purpose Question** | About the cause of progeria, the author writes, "The disease is caused by a defect in a person's genetic code in the protein Lamin A."

**13 Inference Question** | The passage reads, "Likewise, there is no ethnicity or nation that has many more cases than others; this is unlike other rare diseases, which frequently affect a particular ethnic or racial group more than others." So it can be inferred that progeria acts differently from other rare diseases.

**14 Rhetorical Purpose Question** | The author notes, "Common health issues for children with progeria are hip dislocations, heart disease, and strokes."

**15 Negative Factual Question** | There is no mention in the paragraph about how much or how little pain people with progeria must endure.

**16 Vocabulary Question** | A viable cure is one that is feasible, so it might work.

**17 Factual Question** | The author writes, "These tests are only in their initial stages though, so it will likely take at least several more years before a viable cure exists."

**18 Inference Question** | The author remarks, "Nevertheless, progeria has recently attracted the interest of some members of the medical community because research on it may offer clues into why people age. Some speculate that if researchers find a way to cure progeria, they might also learn how to slow advanced aging in adults." So it can be inferred that, as more researchers begin to study progeria, larger amounts of money will be spent on it in the future.

**19 Insert Text Question** | The sentence before the third square reads, "Doctors estimate that progeria sufferers age at a rate eight to ten times faster than healthy children." The sentence to be added notes that a child with progeria would resemble a person several decades older in some ways. Thus the two sentences go well together.

**20 Prose Summary Question** | The summary sentence

notes that progeria is a rare and incurable disease that makes children age rapidly. This thought is best described in answer choices ①, ②, and ⑥. Answer choices ④ and ⑤ are minor points, so they are incorrect answers. Answer choice ③ contains wrong information, so it is also incorrect.

## Passage 3

p.113

**21 Factual Question** | The author writes, "Early men frequently relied upon the movements of heavenly bodies and the passing of the seasons to measure time."

**22 Inference Question** | The passage reads, "But stargazing and keeping track of the seasons were employed to measure large units of time—months and years." The author mentions that stargazing can be used to measure months and years. However, it includes nothing about keeping track of short periods of time, such as what hour of the day it is. So the author implies that stores are not useful for telling what time it is during the day.

**23 Rhetorical Purpose Question** | About sundials, the author writes, "Among the earliest clocks made by humans were sundials. They were limited in that they could not be used after the sun had set and the shadows that sundials cast depend upon the latitude at which a person is. Resultantly, sundials could only be utilized to keep track of the local time during daylight hours, which made them unreliable and relatively ineffective." Much of the information about sundials in the paragraph focuses upon their disadvantages.

**24 Sentence Simplification Question** | The sentence points out that water clocks were either invented by people in ancient civilizations, such as Egypt, or the people were taught about the clocks by others. This thought is best expressed by the sentence in answer choice Ⓐ.

**25 Negative Factual Question** | About water clocks, the author writes, "It was a relatively simple device that measured the passage of time with flowing water." So water clocks were simple and did not have several intricate parts.

**26 Factual Question** | The author remarks, "Spring-powered clocks had several advantages over water clocks. First, by employing spring power, smaller clocks—even those that people could carry—were able to be made."

**27 Factual Question** | The author mentions, "Pendulum clocks proved to be so accurate that minute hands—and eventually second hands—were added to clock faces."

**28 Vocabulary Question** | When something such as a watch is too cumbersome, it is bulky, so it is difficult to carry around.

**29 Insert Text Question** | The sentence before the first square reads, "It was not until the 1400s that a new type of clock, one which used spring power, was developed." The sentence to be added notes that this time—the 1400s—was during the Renaissance, which was when there were many advances in different fields made by Europeans. Thus the two sentences go well together.

**30 Fill in a Table Question** | Regarding water clocks, the author writes, "A water clock was either an inflow or outflow type," and, "Water clocks were created by the ancient Egyptians thousands of years ago, and many other early societies either independently invented them or learned about them from other civilizations." The author then adds, "The first dependable mechanical clock was the water clock." As for spring-powered clocks, the author notes, "First, spring-powered clocks had to be rewound once the spring unwound," and, "Eventually, by the late 1800s, small watches with a strap on them were being worn by women on their wrists whereas most men refused to wear them."

## Passage 4                                                    p.122

**31 Rhetorical Purpose Question** | The author discusses the location of the Aztec Empire in writing, "The Aztec Empire, which was centered on the land occupied by present-day Mexico City, was by far the most violent of the three."

**32 Inference Question** | First, the author mentions that Templo Mayor was in Tenochtitlan. Then, the author writes, "Over time, its foundation and many artifacts were covered up, and Mexico City eventually rose around it."

**33 Vocabulary Question** | When the Spanish razed the Templo Mayor, they demolished it. That is, they destroyed it.

**34 Factual Question** | The author notes, "The first temple was constructed around 1325, and later Aztec rulers sought to show off their power and prestige by rebuilding and expanding Templo Mayor."

**35 Vocabulary Question** | When something is bedecked in luxurious jewels, it is decorated with them.

**36 Factual Question** | The passage reads, "Underneath the stone was a multilayered chamber where each layer had several items placed on it as offerings to the gods. Included in these items were animal carcasses, gold and jade jewelry, and seashells. The sacrificed animals were birds and mammals, particularly eagles and dogs. In one of the lowest levels, archaeologists found a dog bedecked in luxurious jewels, which prompted them to dub the beast Aristo-Dog." So there were a variety of sacrificial items found in the chamber's levels.

**37 Factual Question** | The author mentions, "In 1978, when the decision was made to unearth the temple, thirteen modern buildings stood on the site. The Mexican government paid off the owners and knocked the buildings down, which cleared the site."

**38 Factual Question** | It is written, "One reason for this is the mystical attachment many Mexicans feel toward their Aztec ancestors. To them, the Aztecs represent a connection to the past prior to the arrival of the Spanish."

**39 Insert Text Question** | The sentence before the fourth square reads, "At first, the archaeologists thought that they had discovered a royal tomb and that the dog had been placed there to serve as a companion and guide for its dead master on his journey in the afterlife; however, no human remains were found there, so the purpose of Aristo-Dog remains a mystery." The sentence to be added points out that there are some theories about Aristo-Dog's purpose, but nothing has been proven to be true yet. Thus the two sentences go well together.

**40 Prose Summary Question** | The summary sentence notes that Templo Mayor, an important place in the Aztec Empire, has been undergoing excavations since 1978. This thought is best described in answer choices ①, ⑤, and ⑥. Answer choices ③ and ④ are minor points, so they are incorrect answers. Answer choice ② contains wrong information, so it is also incorrect.

# Actual Test 05

p.131

## Answers

| | | | | |
|---|---|---|---|---|
| 1 ⓒ | 2 ⓓ | 3 ⓒ | 4 ⓓ | 5 ⓐ |
| 6 ⓒ | 7 ⓒ | 8 ⓓ | 9 **2** | |
| 10 ②, ③, ④ | | | | |
| 11 ⓓ | 12 ⓒ | 13 ⓐ | 14 ⓓ | 15 ⓐ |
| 16 ⓒ | 17 ⓐ | 18 ⓒ | 19 **1** | |
| 20 ③, ④, ⑥ | | | | |
| 21 ⓓ | 22 ⓑ | 23 ⓑ | 24 ⓒ | 25 ⓒ |
| 26 ⓐ | 27 ⓒ | 28 ⓓ | 29 **4** | |
| 30 Kuiper Belt: ①, ④, ⑦   Oort Cloud: ③, ⑤ | | | | |

## Explanations

### Passage 1

p.133

1 **Vocabulary Question** | When blue holes are mentioned as being perilous, they are being described as dangerous. Notice the use of the word "risks" in the sentence following the one with "perilous" in it.

2 **Inference Question** | The passage reads, "Nevertheless, dive teams willingly accept these risks as they hurry to investigate the depths of blue holes since the holes may not be around for much longer." In writing that blue holes "may not be around for much longer," the author implies that they are temporary rather than permanent.

3 **Negative Factual Question** | The passage reads, "Meanwhile, the middle layer, which is between ten and thirty meters, is composed of a mixture of fresh and salt water while the bottom layer, which can be a few meters or tens of meters deep, is pure salt water." Therefore, it is not always true that the lowest of the three layers is always the largest.

4 **Sentence Simplification Question** | The sentence points out that the layer of hydrogen sulfide gas forms a layer that can cause problems—including death— for divers, so divers always move quickly through this layer. This thought is best expressed by the sentence in answer choice ⓓ.

5 **Inference Question** | About the bacteria in blue holes, the author writes, "These bacteria need light from the sun but cannot tolerate oxygen." So the author implies that the bacteria will be harmed if they are exposed to oxygen.

6 **Factual Question** | The passage notes that blue holes' "unique ecosystems can provide scientists with knowledge of how life formed on the Earth billions of years ago. Their oxygen-deprived environments are similar to what the Earth was like when it formed."

7 **Vocabulary Question** | A delicate balance of fresh and salt water is a fragile one that can be upset easily.

8 **Factual Question** | It is written, "When the level of the ocean rises, blue holes become subjected to an influx of sea water from the top. Many are located near the sea, so they will soon be underwater. When this occurs, the delicate balance of fresh and salt water, which creates the conditions required for the blue hole ecosystem, will be destroyed."

9 **Insert Text Question** | The sentence before the second square reads, "Additionally, by examining blue hole ecosystems, scientists may be able to learn how life could evolve on planets lacking oxygen." The sentence to be added points out that blues holes could be of interest to people who study astronomy, which includes the study of other planets. Thus the two sentences go well together.

10 **Prose Summary Question** | The summary sentences notes that Bahamian blue holes have unique ecosystems but that they may disappear soon. This thought is best described in answer choices ②, ③, and ④. Answer choices ①, ⑤, and ⑥ are minor points, so they are incorrect answers.

### Passage 2

p.140

11 **Rhetorical Purpose Question** | About Herodotus, the author writes, "Greek historian Herodotus, who lived from 484 to 430 B.C., wrote about the ancient Egyptians, and countless others have emulated him over the years." The focus of the sentence is that Herodotus wrote about the ancient Egyptians in his works.

12 **Factual Question** | It is written, "Its myriad monuments, temples, pyramids, and tombs have attracted explorers, treasure hunters, and tourists since ancient times."

13 **Vocabulary Question** | When the early conquerors of Egypt exploited ancient Egypt's remains, they utilized them.

14 **Sentence Simplification Question** | The sentence points out that grave robbers have looted Egyptian tombs for centuries to make money rather than to improve knowledge of ancient Egypt. This thought is best expressed by the sentence in answer choice Ⓓ.

15 **Factual Question** | The passage mentions, "The team's greatest find was the Rosetta Stone, a stone slab that was inscribed with three languages: ancient Greek, demotic, and hieroglyphics. The writing on the Rosetta Stone contained the same message composed in all three languages."

16 **Vocabulary Question** | When a person is meticulous in his explorations, he is precise.

17 **Inference Question** | The author writes, "He spent most of his later years in Egypt and was the mentor of Howard Carter, who discovered the most renowned of Egyptian sites, the tomb of King Tutankhamen, in 1922." Since King Tutankhamen's tomb became the most renowned Egyptian site upon its discovery, it can be inferred that Howard Carter, the man who discovered it, became famous after doing so.

18 **Factual Question** | The passage reads, "Now that Egypt is free of foreign occupiers, the Egyptians have begun to reassert their rights over their ancient ancestors. While foreign archaeologists are still permitted to dig, the Egyptians are applying pressure to foreign museums and collectors to return many of their artifacts. Some have been returned, but many remain in other countries. The Egyptians have responded by refusing permits for some foreign archaeologists who want to dig in the country."

19 **Insert Text Question** | The sentence before the first square reads, "He refused to rush, and he taught the workers at his sites to dig carefully and to uncover remains without causing damage." The sentence to be added notes that Flinders Petrie's methods let him preserve the places he excavated, which therefore helped improve the field of Egyptology. Thus the two sentences go well together.

20 **Prose Summary Question** | The summary sentence notes that Egyptology is the study of ancient Egypt and is often done through archaeological excavations. This thought is best described in answer choices ③, ④, and ⑥. Answer choices ① and ⑤ are minor points, so they are incorrect answers. Answer choice ② contains wrong information, so it is also incorrect.

21 **Vocabulary Question** | An innumerable number of objects is a countless number of them.

22 **Factual Question** | The author writes, "Astronomers refer to the region of space where the majority of these faraway objects orbit the sun as the Kuiper Belt."

23 **Rhetorical Purpose Question** | About Eris, the author notes, "The most distant visible object that is still a part of the solar system is Eris, the largest dwarf planet, which is sixty-three AU from the sun."

24 **Factual Question** | It is written, "Yet Pluto is not always so distant from the sun, and its elliptical orbit at times places it closer to the sun than Neptune, the farthest from the sun of the eight planets."

25 **Inference Question** | The author remarks, "Besides Pluto and Eris, the other dwarf planets are Ceres, Haumea, and Makemake. Ceres actually resides in the asteroid belt between Mars and Jupiter. Haumea, meanwhile, is approximately forty-three AU from the sun and completes a single orbit in 285 years while Makemake is around forty-six AU from the sun and takes 310 years to orbit it. Every distant dwarf planet is small, rocky, cold, and covered in frozen substances, most likely methane." First, the author mentions that Ceres is in the asteroid belt. Then, the author writes, "Every distant dwarf planet is small, rocky, and cold and is covered in frozen substances, most likely methane." So it can be inferred that Ceres, which is not a distant dwarf planet, is different from the others.

26 **Factual Question** | It is written, "Comets continually move into and out of the Kuiper Belt as they orbit the sun."

27 **Vocabulary Question** | When comets are diverted from their courses, they are redirected by various forces, such as gravity.

28 **Rhetorical Purpose Question** | The paragraph about the Oort Cloud reads, "In fact, the actual existence of the Oort Cloud is mostly based upon a theoretical belief since the long-term comets that orbit the sun must come from somewhere. Beyond the Oort Cloud lies the vast emptiness of space that leads to other stars located light years away from the solar system. How far past the Oort Cloud the sun's gravitational pull extends is uncertain though. It is a question that cannot be answered until modern science makes more technological advances." In the passage, the author stresses that the Oort Cloud

is "theoretical" and that much about it is "uncertain." So the author is explaining that little is known about it yet.

29 **Insert Text Question** | The sentence before the fourth square reads, "Some of their orbits are very long and irregular, but others, such as Halley's Comet, engage in relatively short orbits that can be predicted with some regularity." The sentence to be added points out that Halley's Comet takes seventy-five years to orbit the sun. Thus the two sentences go well together.

30 **Fill in a Table Question** | Regarding the Kuiper Belt, the author writes, "The boundary of the solar system is the limit of the sun's gravitational pull since any objects that get caught by its gravity will begin to orbit the sun. So far, the most distant object discovered that orbits the sun is approximately sixty-eight astronomical units (AU) from the sun, yet some astronomers believe that the sun's pull may extend even further than that. One AU is equivalent to the distance of Earth from the sun— roughly 150 million kilometers. Astronomers refer to the region of space where the majority of these faraway objects orbit the sun as the Kuiper Belt," and, "Pluto, Haumea, and Makemake are all located within the Kuiper Belt. The Kuiper Belt, astronomers theorize, is a donut-shaped region between thirty and fifty AU from the sun. It contains around 70,000 objects, many of which are merely small icy bodies. Astronomers believe that they are the remains of the materials that were used during the creation of the solar system billions of years ago." As for the Oort Cloud, the author notes, "In fact, the actual existence of the Oort Cloud is mostly based upon a theoretical belief since the long-term comets that orbit the sun must come from somewhere," and, "Others, however, believe that Eris is located in the Oort Cloud. This is a region that theoretically extends up to 50,000 AU from the sun."

## Answers

| | | | | |
|---|---|---|---|---|
| 1 Ⓐ | 2 Ⓑ | 3 Ⓐ | 4 Ⓑ | 5 Ⓐ |
| 6 Ⓓ | 7 Ⓓ | 8 Ⓐ | 9 **4** | |
| 10 ②, ④, ⑥ | | | | |
| 11 Ⓓ | 12 Ⓐ | 13 Ⓒ | 14 Ⓑ | 15 Ⓓ |
| 16 Ⓒ | 17 Ⓑ | 18 Ⓓ | 19 **3** | |
| 20 ①, ②, ⑥ | | | | |
| 21 Ⓒ | 22 Ⓐ | 23 Ⓓ | 24 Ⓑ | 25 Ⓑ |
| 26 Ⓒ | 27 Ⓑ | 28 Ⓐ | 29 **4** | |

30 Charles Darwin: ③, ④, ⑤   Jean-Baptiste Lamark: ②, ⑦

| | | | | |
|---|---|---|---|---|
| 31 Ⓑ | 32 Ⓑ | 33 Ⓐ | 34 Ⓒ | 35 Ⓑ |
| 36 Ⓐ | 37 Ⓓ | 38 Ⓑ | 39 **3** | |
| 40 ①, ②, ④ | | | | |

## Explanations

### Passage 1
p.157

1 **Factual Question** | The author writes, "Although it lives primarily in the United States, its territory covers parts of Canada, Mexico, and Central America and even some regions in South America."

2 **Reference Question** | The "them" that deer antlers are different from are horns.

3 **Sentence Simplification Question** | The sentence points out that it takes deer two seasons to grow their antlers, which then fall off in another season. After that, deer lack antlers until the time when they grow back the following year. This thought is best expressed by the sentence in answer choice Ⓐ.

4 **Vocabulary Question** | Anomalies are irregularities.

5 **Factual Question** | The author remarks, "Neither of those is an activity that females engage in, so without a demonstrated need for antlers, female whitetail deer virtually never develop them."

6 **Inference Question** | The author writes, "Starting in April, a buck requires a larger-than-normal amount of nutrition since its antlers can grow about 0.6 centimeters

per day." Since deer need more nutrition starting in April, it can be inferred that their antlers begin to grow in April as well.

**7  Factual Question** | The passage includes, "When deer suffer harm to their legs, the growth of their antlers may likewise be affected. For most bucks, an injury to a back leg will cause the antler on the opposite side to develop in a deformed manner. Hence a back right leg injury will result in the antler on the deer's left-hand side to appear unusual."

**8  Inference Question** | The author notes, "Upon ending, the testosterone levels in male deer decrease, so during the middle of January, they begin to lose their antlers." Since the author mentions the decrease of testosterone levels and the losing of antlers in the same sentence, it can be inferred that the two are closely related.

**9  Insert Text Question** | The sentence before the fourth square reads, "One likely reason that females lack antlers is evolutionary in nature: Bucks regularly use their antlers to attract females and to fight other bucks when they compete for mates" The sentence to be added points out an additional reason why bucks have antlers. Here, the phrase "in addition" is a key phrase in the sentence. Thus the two sentences go well together.

**10  Prose Summary Question** | The summary sentence notes that whitetail deer grow antlers but that their antlers may have problems developing at times. This thought is best described in answer choices ②, ④, and ⑥. Answer choices ③ and ⑤ are minor points, so they are incorrect answers. Answer choice ① contains information not found in the passage, so it is also incorrect.

---

## Passage 2                                                          p.165

**11  Vocabulary Question** | When helicopters extract wounded individuals from battlefields, they remove them from the places where people are fighting.

**12  Inference Question** | The passage reads, "Helicopters differ from the vast majority of airplanes in that they have vertical takeoff and landing capabilities and can also hover in the air over a fixed point." In noting that helicopters are different from "the vast majority of airplanes" because of their ability to take off and land vertically, it can be inferred that some airplanes are able to take off and land vertically.

**13  Rhetorical Purpose Question** | The passage reads,

"The helicopter was one of the last flying devices developed. It followed balloons, gliders, and airplanes primarily due to the difficulty involved in creating a machine that could take off and land vertically, fly straight, and hover."

**14  Factual Question** | The author notes, "His machine utilized the single main rotor and the smaller tail rotor common in most helicopters today."

**15  Factual Question** | The author writes, "In Korea, helicopters were regularly used for observation, the search and rescue of downed fliers, and the ferrying of wounded soldiers quickly from the battlefield to medical care centers. It was in this last task that helicopters played their most significant role in Korea as they greatly reduced the time it took for wounded soldiers to receive proper treatment."

**16  Vocabulary Question** | As helicopters are vulnerable to antiaircraft fire, they are susceptible to being shot down by it.

**17  Factual Question** | It is written, "Then, in the 1950s, engineers developed turbine engines for helicopters that were lighter and stronger than internal combustion engines. This enabled designers to create larger, more powerful helicopters."

**18  Sentence Simplification Question** | The sentence points out that helicopters with varying functions were made in many different countries. This thought is best expressed by the sentence in answer choice Ⓓ.

**19  Insert Text Question** | The sentence before the third square reads, "The American military lost an enormous number of helicopters during the war." The sentence to be added notes that more than 5,000 helicopters out of 12,000 used by the United States military were destroyed during the Vietnam War. Thus the two sentences go well together.

**20  Prose Summary Question** | The summary sentence notes that the helicopter can be used for a variety of purposes by civilians and the military. This thought is best described in answer choices ①, ②, and ⑥. Answer choices ④ and ⑤ are minor points, so they are incorrect answers. Answer choice ③ contains information not mentioned in the passage, so it is also incorrect.

---

## Passage 3                                                          p.172

**21  Vocabulary Question** | A seminal work is one that is

**22 Rhetorical Purpose Question** | The author remarks, "Due to the slow and steady process of change, this theory of natural selection is sometimes referred to as gradualism."

**23 Negative Factual Question** | The author does not note any organisms that have undergone the most changes due to evolution. In fact, there is no mention of the names of any organisms in the entire paragraph.

**24 Factual Question** | The author writes, "Darwin based his theory of natural selection on both observations and inferences since he had no solid evidence to explain how it actually took place. This left Darwin open to attack."

**25 Vocabulary Question** | When something lends weight to a theory, it supports that theory.

**26 Inference Question** | About spontaneous generation, the author notes, "Darwin's inability to prove his theory of gradualism lent weight to a competing theory, one stating that all living things derive from spontaneous generation and are created from the elements of the Earth through a mystical force. This theory dates back as far as Aristotle, who lived more than two thousand years ago in ancient Greece, and has had supporters throughout history." Since Charles Darwin came up with the theory of natural selection and he lived in the 1800s, it can be inferred that spontaneous generation has been believed in for a much longer period of time.

**27 Sentence Simplification Question** | The sentence points out that some organisms changed, but as for the ones that did not evolve for various reasons, they went extinct. This thought is best expressed by the sentence in answer choice Ⓑ.

**28 Factual Question** | The passage includes, "There is a life force inside all living things that causes them to change: genes. Genes determine the traits of organisms and are passed from parent to offspring. Organisms evolve by inheriting these genetic traits from their parents and by passing them on to successive generations of offspring."

**29 Insert Text Question** | The sentence before the fourth square reads, "Darwin himself was positive that whales had evolved from some land animal yet could not prove it through the fossil record." The sentence to be added points out that this proof was provided decades later thanks to advanced scientific methods. Thus the two sentences go well together.

**30 Fill in a Table Question** | Regarding Charles Darwin, the author writes, "This left Darwin open to attack. For instance, some critics pointed out that in the fossil record, there are periods during which entire species disappeared, but then similar—yet in some ways different—species emerged later despite there being no fossils suggesting any links between the two," and, "Darwin's theory of evolution centers on natural selection. It posits that all species are designed to survive by producing offspring. In an environment with limited resources, only offspring with the abilities which allow them to survive will live long enough to produce offspring themselves. Therefore, in each succeeding generation, the survivors are the strongest members of the species, and they pass on their abilities to the following generations. Over time, a new species—one better able to adapt and survive—evolves." The author then adds, "Due to his observations as a naturalist, Darwin was certain what he had written was correct, yet he had trouble explaining the actual process through which species changed." As for Jean-Baptiste Lamark, the author notes, "Darwin's inability to prove his theory of gradualism lent weight to a competing theory, one stating that all living things derive from spontaneous generation and are created from the elements of the Earth through a mystical force. This theory dates back as far as Aristotle, who lived more than two thousand years ago in ancient Greece, and has had supporters throughout history. One of its strongest enthusiasts was Frenchman Jean-Baptiste Lamarck, who lived from 1744 to 1829," and, "According to Lamarck, species began as simple lifeforms through spontaneous generation, but natural life-enhancing fluids in their bodies pushed them to transform into more complex creatures. These fluids created new organs, and, as time passed, they became more complex, which allowed for even further evolution of the organisms."

## Passage 4                                              p.179

**31 Factual Question** | The passage reads, "Buoyed by low-cost labor, abundant natural resources, and access to global markets, they are poised to enjoy continued growth in future decades."

**32 Inference Question** | The author writes, "Thailand alone remained independent of foreign control. However, like most of the region, it was occupied by Japanese troops during World War II." Since Thailand was "occupied by Japanese troops during World War II," it can be inferred that the Thais fought against and lost to the Japanese then.

highly influential.

**33 Sentence Simplification Question** | The sentence points out that the Europeans' colonies provided them with both raw materials and labor. This thought is best expressed by the sentence in answer choice Ⓐ.

**34 Rhetorical Purpose Question** | The author focuses on the contrast of status in writing, "The majority of them were successful as, after World War II, the colonies became independent states one by one. The sole exceptions were Hong Kong and Macau, which remained European possessions until being returned to China at the end of the twentieth century."

**35 Factual Question** | About Vietnam, the author writes, "Democracy was practiced in these newly independent nations except for in Vietnam, which turned to communism after a long, bloody struggle."

**36 Negative Factual Question** | The author notes, "While Southeast Asian countries continued relying heavily on agriculture, they improved their economies by engaging in various industries." So it is not true that each country focused on a single major industry.

**37 Vocabulary Question** | A robust economy is very strong.

**38 Vocabulary Question** | When wages are significantly lower, they are considerably lower than they are in other countries.

**39 Insert Text Question** | The sentence before the third square reads, "As a result, they became major centers of manufacturing for electronics, textiles, and automobiles." The sentence to be added points out that some of the manufacturers in these countries became global suppliers. Thus the two sentences go well together.

**40 Prose Summary Question** | The summary sentence notes that the past fifty years have seen many countries in Southeast Asia gain their independence and improve their economies. This thought is best described in answer choices ①, ②, and ④. Answer choices ⑤ and ⑥ are minor points, so they are incorrect answers. Answer choice ③ contains information that is not mentioned in the passage, so it is also incorrect.

## Actual Test 07

p.187

### Answers

| | | | | |
|---|---|---|---|---|
| 1 Ⓑ | 2 Ⓓ | 3 Ⓐ | 4 Ⓐ | 5 Ⓑ |
| 6 Ⓓ | 7 Ⓑ | 8 Ⓓ | 9 **2** | |
| 10 ③, ⑤, ⑥ | | | | |
| 11 Ⓑ | 12 Ⓒ | 13 Ⓒ | 14 Ⓐ | 15 Ⓑ |
| 16 Ⓑ | 17 Ⓑ | 18 Ⓐ | 19 **3** | |
| 20 ①, ②, ④ | | | | |
| 21 Ⓒ | 22 Ⓓ | 23 Ⓑ | 24 Ⓑ | 25 Ⓐ |
| 26 Ⓒ | 27 Ⓑ | 28 Ⓐ | 29 **2** | |
| 30 Desert: ①, ⑥, ⑧  Watery Area: ④, ⑨  Tundra: ③, ⑦ | | | | |

### Explanations

#### Passage 1

p.189

**1 Vocabulary Question** | When an ecosystem is a precarious state, it is unstable, so it may face various threats to its stability.

**2 Negative Factual Question** | In the first paragraph, the author notes that grains are grown in the Great Plains, but the exact crops that are grown there are not named.

**3 Factual Question** | It is written, "For the most part, the Great Plains is too dry to sustain large forests, and it is also speculated that, in the past, wildfires destroyed any large clusters of trees that once existed."

**4 Factual Question** | The author writes, "Finally, the eastern section of the Great Plains is the wettest and has the tallest grasses and the strongest soil."

**5 Factual Question** | It is written, "But when European explorers and, later, American hunters, ranchers, and farmers, arrived, the face of the Great Plains changed. The buffalo were hunted almost to extinction while the land itself began to be cultivated."

**6 Vocabulary Question** | When the wind gets deflected, it is averted.

**7 Rhetorical Purpose Question** | The author describes how a drought in the 1920s and 1930s affected the Great Plains. Then, the author writes, "Since that extended period of drought—referred to as the Dust Bowl—the number of people engaged in farming in the Great Plains has decreased." So the author mentions the Dust Bowl to give the name of that period of history.

8  **Negative Factual Question** | The water used to irrigate crops comes from groundwater sources, not from rivers and streams.

9  **Insert Text Question** | The sentence before the second square reads, "The worst drought lasted almost a decade during the 1920s and 1930s and reduced much of the southern Great Plains to a virtual desert." The sentence to be added notes that those years were when the Great Depression took place, so there was a lot of suffering in the area. Thus the two sentences go well together.

10  **Prose Summary Question** | The summary sentence notes that the Great Plains is a large grasslands that is an important farming region. This thought is best described in answer choices ③, ⑤, and ⑥. Answer choices ①, ②, and ④ are minor points, so they are incorrect answers.

---

## Passage 2

11  **Reference Question** | The "them" that are very important are many forces.

12  **Vocabulary Question** | When something has a pronounced influence, it is noticeable.

13  **Factual Question** | The passage reads, "By looking at one country—the United States—it is easy to recognize several factors in its educational policy during the past century that benefitted the entire nation and enabled it to develop the world's largest economy."

14  **Sentence Simplification Question** | The sentence points out that while the United States' economy as strong in the early 1900s, without changes in its educational system, it would not have grown much more. This thought is best expressed by the sentence in answer choice Ⓐ.

15  **Negative Factual Question** | The passage reads, "Two decades later, in the 1920s, a movement to establish new high schools across the country and to ensure that children attended them began." This happened in the 1920s, not around 1900.

16  **Inference Question** | The passage notes, "By 1940, twenty-six percent of all American children were enrolled in high school, and, by the 1980s, that number had increased to thirty-two percent. Additionally, those

numbers only take into account students in public schools and not the thousands of others attending private schools and getting homeschooled." By mentioning that the statistics omitted private school students and homeschooled students, the author implies that the number of students in high school was larger than what was reported.

17  **Factual Question** | The author writes, "During the latter half of the twentieth century, the numbers continued to rise until by 2000, more than one million American students matriculated to universities each year. A construction explosion took place around the country during the latter half of the 1900s. Hundreds of new campuses were built while existing ones were expanded."

18  **Factual Question** | The author notes, "First, many of these high school and university graduates became managers, engineers, teachers, doctors, and business leaders. They paid taxes, and the increased tax revenues helped further expand the country's educational facilities."

19  **Insert Text Question** | The sentence before the third square reads, "Meanwhile, the countries whose economies lag behind the others typically have educational systems in which the majority of their citizens fail to advance beyond the elementary level." The sentence to be added names some of the continents in which countries with poor educational systems are found. Thus the two sentences go well together.

20  **Prose Summary Question** | The summary sentence notes that the United States became the world's largest economy in the 1900s thanks to its focus on education. This thought is best described in answer choices ①, ②, and ④. Answer choices ③, ⑤, and ⑥ minor points, so they are incorrect answers.

---

## Passage 3

21  **Vocabulary Question** | Adverse conditions are unfavorable ones.

22  **Negative Factual Question** | In the paragraph, there is no mention of evolution.

23  **Factual Question** | The author writes, "In dry regions, a plant's roots may extend far underground as they search for water and nutrients."

24  **Negative Factual Question** | The passage reads,

"Other desert plants, including numerous cactus species, have shallow yet extensive root systems that stretch horizontally to absorb moisture from as wide an area as possible. In watery areas, including bogs, swamps, marshes, and places near lakes and seashores, some plants have roots that grow above the ground." So desert plants—not plants growing in watery areas—have roots that grow horizontally close to the surface.

25 **Vocabulary Question** | Something that can draw moisture and nutrients from poor soil can extract them.

26 **Factual Question** | The author writes, "Furthermore, strong winds make it difficult for plants to remain attached to the ground. Resultantly, plants growing in tundra are small, grow low to the ground, and have shallow roots. Nevertheless, their roots are quite strong and can anchor plants in windy conditions."

27 **Rhetorical Purpose Question** | About the ohia lehua tree, the author notes, "One of these plants, the ohia lehua tree, has a unique root system that gives it the ability to burrow deep into lava rocks, where there are nutrients and moisture in lava tubes, which are hollow spaces created by fast-flowing lava during a volcanic eruption. Inside these lava tubes, moisture gathered, which the roots used to enable the trees to survive. Over time, these roots began breaking down the lava rocks. As more trees grew, the hard lava further transformed into rich soil, thereby allowing the Hawaiian Islands to become the lush tropical paradise they are today." So the author focuses on how these plants helped transform Hawaii.

28 **Factual Question** | It is written, "Inside these lava tubes, moisture gathered, which the roots used to enable the trees to survive."

29 **Insert Text Question** | The sentence before the second square reads, "Finally, in cases where plants grow in soil with a rich upper layer, their roots typically grow along the surface or just beneath it." The sentence to be added notes that several species of maple trees have shallow root systems. Thus the two sentences go well together.

30 **Fill in a Table Question** | Regarding plants that grow in the desert, the author writes, "In deserts, tree roots often grow far beneath the surface. For instance, the mesquite tree has a single long, straight root, called a taproot, which descends around thirty meters belowground. Other desert plants, including numerous cactus species, have shallow yet extensive root systems that stretch horizontally to absorb moisture from as wide an area as possible." As for plants that grow in watery areas, the author notes, "In watery areas, including bogs, swamps, marshes, and places near lakes and seashores, some plants have roots that grow above the ground. Botanists call these aerating roots. Some species with them, such as mangrove and cypress trees, seem able to absorb the gases plants need to survive from the atmosphere itself. Finally, in cases where plants grow in soil with a rich upper layer, their roots typically grow along the surface or just beneath it." Finally, about plants that grow in tundra, the author mentions, "Resultantly, plants growing in tundra are small, grow low to the ground, and have shallow roots. Nevertheless, their roots are quite strong and can anchor plants in windy conditions. They are also excellent at drawing moisture and nutrients from poor soil. During the summer months, when the ground thaws to a greater depth, the roots grow deeper, which grants them access to more nutrients."

# TOEFL MAP ACTUAL TEST

New TOEFL Edition

**Reading 1**

Translations

DARAKWON

# Actual Test 01

## Passage 1 • Marine Biology ───────────────── p.15

### 고래의 진화

고래는 세상에서 가장 거대한 동물로 수중 환경에 적합한 동물이지만, 고래가 처음부터 수중 생물은 아니었으며 약 5천만 년 전에 육상 생물로부터 진화했다는 증거가 존재한다. 이러한 증거는 고생물학자들이 이집트와 파키스탄 등의 장소에서 발굴한 화석에서 나왔는데, 이들 지역은 예전에 물속에 잠겨 있었다. 이러한 화석들을 면밀히 조사한 결과, 고대의 고래 종들에게는 두 다리가 있었으며, 이들은 현재의 하마와 유사한 점들을 많이 가지고 있었다는 점이 입증되었다. 따라서 오늘날 과학자들은 약 5천만 년 전 하마와 비슷하게 생긴 동물이 바다로 이동을 했고, 이들이 수백만 년에 걸쳐 현재의 고래로 진화했다는 점을 인정하고 있다.

1800년대 중반 찰스 다윈이 진화에 관한 자신의 이론을 제시한 이후로 고래가 육상 동물로부터 진화했다는 주장은 터무니없는 것으로 생각되었다. 다윈 자신은 고래가 어떠한 방식으로 진화를 했을 것이라고 믿었지만, 이를 증명하지는 못했다. 실제로 20세기 후반이 되기 전까지는 어떠한 증거도 나타나지 않았다. 1980년대에 파키스탄과 이집트에서 발굴 작업을 하던 미국의 고생물학자들이 다리가 달린 고래의 화석들을 발견했다. 그들은 고대에 해저였던 곳에서 이 화석을 발굴했다. 현재의 파키스탄과 이집트에 해당하는 지역은 오래 전 테티스 해라는 수역에 잠겨 있었다. 이 바다는 지중해뿐만 아니라 중동의 여러 지역에 걸쳐 있었다. 이집트에서 발굴 작업 중이던 고생물학자들은 와디 히탄에서 1,000개가 넘는 화석을 발굴했다. 1989년 바로 이곳에서 뒷다리, 발목, 발, 그리고 발가락이 달려 있는 고대의 고래 종을 발견해 냈다.

고래의 다리가 발견됨으로써 조사 중이던 고생물학자들은 고래가 한때 땅 위를 걸어 다녔을 것이라고 추측했다. 하지만 발견된 특정 종은 결코 그런 적이 없었다. 그들은 고래의 다리가 너무 작고 약해서 고래가 걷지 못했을 것이라는 결론을 내렸다. 게다가 화석에서 발견된 몇몇 다른 특징들로 인해 고생물학자들은 고래가 물속에서만 살았을 것이라고 생각했다. 발견 후 조사 팀은 발이 달린 고래의 조상, 즉 한때 육지에 살았지만 결국 바다로 간 동물의 화석 기록을 찾기 시작했다. 흥미롭게도 1950년대 전반에 몇몇 과학자들이 고래의 혈액에 돼지, 사슴, 낙타, 그리고 하마가 속해 있는 포유류 동물의 혈액과 유사한 특성이 포함되어 있다는 점을 알게 되었다. (이 동물들은 모두 신체적인 유사성을 가지고 있다.) 이후 1990년대에 한 분자생물학자팀이 현재 살아 있는 고래의 가장 가까운 친척은 하마라는 점을 밝혀냈다. 마침내 2000년 몇몇 고생물학자들이 화석화된 고래의 발목뼈가 하마를 포함하는 포유류과 동물들의 발목뼈와 사실상 동일하다는 점을 알아냈다.

그럼에도 불구하고 전문가들은 어떤 종이 고래의 진정한 조상이었는지에 관해 확신을 갖지 못하고 있다. 지금까지는, 고래로 보이는 가장 오래된 화석이 5천만 년 전의 것으로 생각되기 때문에, 현재 고래의 조상은 모두 그 이후에 살면서 진화했을 것이다. 몇몇 과학자들은 하마와 비슷하게 생긴 고래의 조상이 테티스 해의 수심이 낮은 해안 지역에서 서식했을 것이라는 이론을 제시했다. 그곳에서 이 동물은 풍부한 먹이를 찾으며 육지에 있는 포식자들로부터 자신을 보호했다. 점차적으로 육상보다 수중에 자주 머무르기 시작했다. 몸의 형태도 수중 생활에 적합하도록 변했을 것이다. 예를 들어 이 동물의 콧구멍은 머리의 위쪽으로 이동해 물을 뿜는 구멍이 되었고, 다리는 점차적으로 진화하여 물갈퀴가 달린 지느러미로 변했으며, 꼬리는 갈라진 형태로 바뀌었다. 이 새로운 종은 담수를 마시기 위해, 혹은 짝짓기를 해서 새끼를 낳기 위해 가끔씩 육지로 되돌아왔을지도 모르지만, 수백만 년이 흐른 뒤에는 영구적으로 물속에서 살게 되었다.

진화의 마지막 단계는 지구에 전 세계적인 냉각기가 진행 중이던 3천 5백만 년 전쯤에 일어났을 가능성이 높다. 수온이 낮아짐으로써 바다 속 깊은 곳에 있던 영양분들이 해수면으로 올라오게 되었고, 이로써 고래에게 먹이가 풍부한 환경이 조성되어 고래는 육지에서 사는 것보다 바다에서 사는 것이 더 매력적이게 되었다. 따라서 바다에 사는 포유류로의 고래의 진화가 완성되었다. 오늘날 고래는 찰스 다윈의 진화론을 입증하는 완벽한 사례로서 간주되고 있다: 생물은 새로운 환경에 적응하며, 시간이 지나면 그곳에서 번성하게 된다.

---

**WORD REMINDER**

**well-suited** 잘 어울리는, 적합한   **paleontologist** 고생물학자
**hippopotamus** 하마   **ludicrous** 우스꽝스러운, 터무니없는
**blowhole** 고래의 물 뿜는 구멍   **fluke** 고래의 갈라진 꼬리

---

## Passage 2 • History ───────────────── p.23

### 영국 해적의 몰락

영국에서 해적의 전성기는 16세기에서 17세기까지 지속되었다. 이 기간은 범선이 크게 유행했던 시기로, 탐험과 무역으로 인해 항해 중인 선박의 수와 운송되던 화물의 가치가 증가했다. 16세기 대부분의 기간 동안 영국 해적들은 수많은 선박의 화물을 약탈함으로써 바다의 재앙과 같은 존재였다. 이로 인해 해적은 다른 이들, 특히 스페인 제국과 종종 충돌하게 되었고, 이는 영국과 스페인 간 전쟁의 주요 원인이 되기도 했다. 하지만 17세기 중반, 유럽 해역에서 영국 해적의 행위는 몇 가지 이유로 위축되기 시작했다. 1800년대까지 계속되기는 했지만, 영국 해적의 행위는 1500년대만큼 강력한 위력을 보이지 못했다.

수 세기 동안, 영국 남부의 데본 주와 콘월 주에는 해적들이 지배하던 항구가 많았다. (대서양 및 영국 해협 모두와 접해 있기 때문에 이곳에서는 해적선들이 쉽게 공해로 나갈 수 있었다.) 런던의 중앙 권력으로부터 멀리 떨어져 지방 당국의 암묵적인 동의 하에 활동을 하는 경우가 많았던 해적들은 대부분 제재를 받지 않으면서 활동했다. 실제로 영국의 왕과 여왕들은 합법적인 해적 행위를 하는, 사략선 기능을 할 수 있는 해적선에 종종 의지했는데, 이는 당시 전쟁에서 필요한 부분이자 적법한 것이었다. 영국의 사략선들은 전시에 군주로부터 그들의 행동을 합법화시켜 주는 편지를 받는 경우가 많았다. 영국 주변의 해역에서 선박을 공격하는 것과 나포하는 것이 허용되었기 때문에 적국의 항로가 봉쇄될 수 있었다. 프랜시스 드레이크와 같은 몇몇 대담한 사략선 선장들은 스페인의 보물을 약탈하기 위해 자신의 배를 이끌고 대서양을 건너 카리브 해까지 항해하기도 했다. 이러한 활동들로 인해 영국과 스페인 간에는 거의 20년 동안 전쟁이 계속되었다.

전쟁의 한 가지 결과로서 영국 해군의 힘과 명성이 모두 증가했다. 수 세기 전 영국 해군은 전시에 규모가 확대되었지만, 이후 평시에는 해산되었다. 하지만 16세기에, 처음에는 헨리 8세가 통치했고 그 후에는 그의 딸인 엘리자베스가 통치를 했는데, 영국 해군의 위상이 보다 확고해졌다. 1588년 대규모의 스페인 무적 함대를 패배시킴으로써 영국 해군의 명성이 높아졌다. 해군 복무가 명예로운 일로 생각되었기 때문에, 17세기 초반 영국 해군은 상비군이 되었다. 이후 영국의 군주들은 더 이상 과거에 그랬던 것처럼 해적선

을 사력선으로 전환하는 것이 불필요하다고 생각하게 되었고, 대신 영국 해군이 단독으로 해전을 수행해야 한다고 생각했다. 이와 동시에 많은 위대한 해적선 선장들이 더 이상 활동을 하지 않게 되었는데, 일부는 사망을 했고, 나이가 들어 은퇴를 한 후 자신의 부를 향유한 사람들도 있었으며, 해군에 입대해 왕실 선박이나 함대 전체를 지휘한 사람도 있었다.

영국 해군은 초창기에 너무나 약해서 새로운 위협이었던 바바리 해적으로부터 영국의 선박과 해안 도시들을 방어할 수 없었다. 이 무자비한 뱃사람들은 북아프리카의 알제를 자신들의 모항으로 삼고 있었다. 16세기 초반, 규모가 커지고 활동 범위도 넓어짐에 따라 바바리 해적들은 지중해를 벗어나 대서양으로 항행을 하여 서유럽과 북아메리카 지역까지 진출했다. 바바리 해적들은 한 가지 중요한 측면에서 유럽 해적들과 차이를 보였다. 그들은 자신이 붙잡은 사람들을 노예로 삼았다. 그들은 보통 갤리선으로 항해를 했는데, 이 배에서는 돛과 노가 사용되었고 주로 노예들이 노를 저었다. 또한 중동 지역에는 선상 납치와 해안가 습격으로 사람들을 포획하여 만들어진, 해적들로 분비는 노예 시장이 존재했다. 17세기 초반 이들은 대담하게도 영국 남서부 해안가를 습격하기 시작했는데, 여기에는 한때 영국 해적들의 안전한 피난처였던 곳들도 포함되어 있었다. 이러한 습격으로 수십 명의 — 때로는 수백 명의 — 남자, 여자, 그리고 아이들이 잡혀감에 따라 영국의 해적 행위는 큰 타격을 입었고, 이는 결국 영국 해적의 몰락으로 이어졌다.

그럼에도 불구하고 영국 해적들이 하룻밤 사이에 사라진 것은 아니었으며, 많은 해적들이 먼 바다에서 활동을 했다. 하지만 영국이 해적 활동의 근거지로 이용되는 경우는 17세기 중반에 급격히 감소했다. 한 세기가 지난 후의 영국 해군은 대규모의 강력한 상비군이었고, 영국 주변 해역 및 멀리 떨어져 있는 여러 지역의 바다를 관할했다. 19세기가 시작될 무렵 전시에 사략선을 승인해 활용하던 관행이 폐지되자 영국의 해적 행위와 사략 활동은 영원히 자취를 감추었다.

## Passage 3 • Psychology ——————— p.32

### 아동 발달에 있어서의 역할 놀이

대부분의 아이들은 노는 것을 좋아하며, 놀이는 사실상 모든 아이들의 학습 과정에서 중요한 요소이다. 아이들이 노는 방법은 다양하지만, 가장 중요한 놀이 중 하나가 역할 놀이이다. 이는 한 아이가 다른 사람인 척하는 활동에 참여하는 것이다. 역할 놀이는 아이의 상상력을 자극하고, 언어 능력 발달에 도움을 주며, 어떻게 계획을 세우고 어떻게 활동들을 순서대로 수행해야 하는지를 배울 수 있는 기회를 제공해 준다. 또한 무리를 지어 역할 놀이를 할 때 사회적 상호 작용을 경험한 아이들은, 이때 아이들은 다른 아이들을 도우면서 리더쉽, 협상, 타협, 그리고 공정함에 대해서도 배우게 되는데, 보다 정서적으로 발달을 하게 된다.

역할 놀이는 아이들의 상상력을 활용하기 때문에 여러 가지 형태를 취할 수 있다. 한 가지 흔한 형태의 역할 놀이에서 많은 아이들은 자신의 부모를 흉내 내려고 한다. 예를 들어 남자 아이들은 자신의 아버지처럼 면도하는 흉

내를 낼 수도 있고, 집 안팎에서 할 수 있는 다양한 집안일들을 할 수도 있다. (예를 들어 정원일을 하는 것을 흉내 낼 수도 있고, 집안에서 고장 난 무언가를 수리하는 일을 흉내 낼 수도 있을 것이다.) 반면 여자 아이들은, 특히 보다 어린 형제나 자매를 돌보는 경우, 일상적인 일을 하는 어머니를 흉내 내는 경우가 많다. 많은 여자 아이들이 아기 인형을 가지고 놀면서 어린이들을 돌보는 어머니 흉내를 내는 것을 좋아한다. 또 다른 유형의 역할 놀이로서 보다 복잡한 상황과 관련된 것도 있다. 아이들은 자신이 모험 중인 슈퍼히어로로 무리의 일원이라는 상상을 할 수도 있다. 이러한 놀이를 할 때 아이들은 특수한 의상을 입고 서로 다른 역할을 맡을 수도 있다. 때로는 실제 상황을 모방하기도 하는데, 예컨대 자신이 목장의 카우보이인 것처럼 행동하거나 혹은 범죄자를 체포하는 경찰관인 것처럼 행동하기도 한다. 아이들이 책에서 읽은 이야기를 재현하는 일 또한 흔해서 부모, 교사, 급우, 그리고 친구로 이루어진 관객들을 대상으로 공연이 이루어지기도 한다.

이러한 모든 활동들은 아이들의 학습을 돕는다. 아동 발달 전문가들은 역할 놀이가 학습을 가능하게 만드는 아이들의 뇌 연결성을 증진시킨다고 생각한다. 언어 능력은 학습에 있어서 가장 중요한 측면 중 하나이다. 다른 어린이들과 놀이를 함으로써 아이들은 구두 언어 능력을 향상시킬 수 있다. 그리고 다른 아이들을 조직화하고 지시를 내릴 수 있게 된다. 아이들은 또한 역할 놀이를 하면서 문제를 해결하는 능력을 키울 수도 있다. 때때로 어려운 문제를 해결하고, 임무를 완수하기 위해 필요한 조치를 취하고, 어떠한 모험담이나 이야기를 표현하기 위해 계획을 세워야 할 수도 있다. 이러한 활동을 하기 위해서는 아이들이 의상을 만들고, 재료를 모으고, 색깔과 장식을 결정하고, 모든 것을 어울리게 맞춰야 할 필요도 있을 것이다. 역할 놀이를 할 때 아이들은 종종 소품을 사용하기 때문에 이러한 소품들을 만들고 활용하는 방법을 생각해 낸다. 이러한 모든 활동들은 세상에 대한 아이들의 호기심을 자극하고 그들이 가능한 많은 것들을 배우고 싶도록 만든다.

역할 놀이의 또 다른 중요한 측면은 아이들의 사회적인 능력이 향상된다는 점이다. 그룹 활동에 참여할 때 아이들은 서로 다른 역할을 맡는다. 어떤 아이들은 지도자가 되는 반면, 추종자가 되는 아이들도 있다. 때때로 아이들의 의견이 일치하지 않는 경우도 있기 때문에, 아이들은 서로 협상하고 타협하는 법을 배워야만 하며, 심한 언쟁을 하거나 의견이 충돌한 경우 사과하는 법도 배워야만 한다. 더 나아가 아이들은 협동과 공유에 대해서 배우고, 다른 사람의 관점에서 상황을 이해하기 시작한다. 이러한 활동을 통해 아이들은 특정한 목표를 달성하기 위해 필요한 것이 무엇인지 알게 됨으로써 언어 능력을 더욱 발전시키게 된다. 어휘력을 향상시킬 수 있고, 문장 구성력을 발달시킬 수 있으며, 점차적으로 다른 구두 언어 능력도 향상시킬 수 있다.

역할 놀이의 이로운 점 중 마지막은 아이들이 감정적인 고통, 예컨대 학교에 처음 간 날 마주하게 되는 두려움이나 병원을 방문할 때 마주하게 되는 두려움을 일으키는 특정한 상황에 대처할 수 있도록 도움을 준다는 점이다. 아이들이 이러한 상황에 대해 미리 대본대로 역할 놀이를 하면, 현실에서 이러한 행동이 이루어 질 때 통상 겪게 되는 두려움은 감소하는 경우가 많다. 이러한 이유로 아동 발달 전문가들은 부모들로 하여금 아이들에게 역할 놀이를 허락할 것과, 두려움을 극복하는데 도움이 되는 이들 활동에 부모들도 참여할 것을 권장한다. 이렇게 하면 부모들은 부모와 자식 간의 유대감이 더 강해진다는 점도 알 수 있다. 아이와 부모 간의 상호 작용이 증가하고 이러한 시간이 보다 즐거워짐으로써 아이들과 부모 모두 살면서 겪게 되는 스트레스를 줄일 수 있다. 최종 결과로서 양쪽 모두가 역할 놀이의 혜택을 누릴 수 있다.

# Actual Test 02

## Passage 1 · Engineering ───────────── p.41

### 3D 프린팅을 이용한 수술

의료 분야에서의 획기적인 기술 혁신 중 하나는 수술에 3D 프린팅을 활용하는 것이다. 3D 프린팅은 3차원 드로잉으로 구체적 형태를 지닌 물체를 만드는 것을 가리킨다. 드로잉이 3D 프린트 기기로 스캔이 되면 3D 프린터가 재료를 — 보통은 플라스틱을 — 이용해 매우 얇은 층을 만들어 내는데, 이 층들이 겹겹이 쌓이면서 물체가 만들어진다. 3D 프린팅이 기존 제조 방식보다 이로운 점은 보다 까다로운 커스터마이징과 복잡한 물체의 제작을 가능하게 만든다는 점이다. 이러한 이점 때문에 3D 프린팅은 의료 분야에서 이상적인 도구가 되고 있다. 현재 3D 프린팅은 의료 산업에서 주로 두 가지의 목적으로 사용된다: 신체의 특정 기관을 제작하는 것과 향후 수술에서 도움이 될 수 있도록 의사가 이용할 수 있는 모델을 만드는 것이다.

의료계에서 3D 프린팅이 실제 적용되는 분야는 정형외과로, 주로 고관절 및 무릎 치환술에 사용되는 환자 맞춤형 임플란트 제작에 사용된다. 의사들은 MRI나 CAT로 문제가 되는 부위를 스캔한 후 치환이 필요한 신체 기관에 3차원 드로잉을 실시한다. 그 후 수술팀은 3D 프린터를 이용해 플라스틱으로 해당 기관을 만들고, 마지막으로 임플란트를 삽입하기 위한 수술을 실시한다. 환자 개개인에게 맞춤화된 기관을 만듦으로써 의사들은 수술 시간을 단축시킬 수 있으며, 수술 도중 및 수술 후에 나타나는 합병증도 감소시킬 수 있다. 과거에는 정형외과 의사들이 규격화된 대체물을 이용했으며, 수술 도중 새 기관을 환자 몸에 맞추기 위해 조악한 방법으로 뼈의 모양을 잡아야 했다. 최근에는 3D 프린터로 제작된 환자 맞춤형 임플란트가 사고로 턱뼈 및 두개골이 조각난 환자에게도 성공적으로 사용되고 있다.

3D 프린팅이 활용되고 있는 또 다른 분야는 실습용 장기 모형 제작이다. 모든 인간의 신체는 일반적인 장기 구조가 동일하지만, 환자에 따라 특이한 차이점이 존재하는 경우가 있다. (예컨대 심장 질환 및 암으로 인해 신체 내 특정 장기의 크기가 건강한 사람의 그것보다 훨씬 더 커질 수 있다.) 수술 시간을 감소시키고 수술의 성공 가능성을 높이기 위해 수술팀은 장기의 3D 모형을 만들어 실습을 한다. 어떤 환자에게 간 수술이 필요할 수도 있다. 수술팀은 이 환자의 간을 스캔한 후 3D 프린터로 정확한 간 모형을 만들 것이다. 이 모형은 형태가 뚜렷하고, 그 안에 있는 모든 혈관의 위치를 포함하여, 간의 내부 구조를 보여 줄 것이다. 간에 암 종양이 있는 경우라면 3D 프린터가 모형에 종양을 포함시킬 것이다. 실제 수술을 하기 전에 수술팀은 간 모형으로 실습을 함으로써 환자가 성공적인 수술을 받을 확률을 최대한 높일 수 있다. 현재 많은 의과 대학들이 3D 프린팅을 활용하여 예비 개원 의사들이 실습에 이용할 수 있는 모형을 만들고 있다.

3D 프린터로 만드는 대부분의 장기 모형들은 단단한 플라스틱으로 만들어진다. 현재 의사 및 의대생들이 실제 수술에서 사용할 수 있는 보다 유연한 모델에 대한 수요가 증가하고 있다. 보다 유연한 모형을 만들기 위해서는 3D 프린터의 재료로 실리콘이나 히드로겔을 사용해야 한다. 또한 많은 의사와 의과 대학들은 최대한 실제 상황과 비슷한 실습이 이루어질 수 있도록 피를 흘리는 장기 모형을 원하고 있다. 보다 유연한 재료는 탄력이 더 큰 특징을 나타내며, 이는 환자 장기의 실제 탄성과 비슷한데, 이를 통해 의사는 장기에 어느 정도 깊이까지 칼을 집어 넣어야 하는지에 대한 판단을 보다 쉽게 내릴 수 있다. 인간 장기의 특성을 그대로 나타낼 수 있도록 모형 제작자들은 환자의 몸에서 떼어낸 실제 장기의 특성을 조사한다. 3D 프린터로 장기 모

형을 만드는 기술이 발전하여 모형들이 보다 실제와 비슷하게 됨으로써 언젠가는 3D 프린터가 제 기능을 못하는 장기를 대체할 인공 장기를 만드는데 활용될 수 있을 것으로 기대된다.

3D 프린팅이 의학 분야에서 막대한 도움을 주고는 있지만, 그 사용을 둘러싼 몇 가지 문제들이 있다. 그러한 문제 중 하나는 비용이다. 최신 3D 프린터의 가격은 수만 달러에 이르기 때문에 병원 중에서도 가장 부유한 병원만이 한 대 가격을 감당할 수 있다. 또한 병원에서 프린터를 사용하기 위해서는 직원을 새로 고용하거나 직원을 교육시켜야 한다. 더구나 수술에 도움을 주는 모형뿐만 아니라 3D 프린터로 만드는 임플란트의 제작 비용에 항상 의료 보험이 적용되는 것은 아니다. 이는 금전적인 능력에 한계가 있는 사람들에게 두 가지 모두 현실적인 옵션이 되지 않는다는 점을 의미한다.

## Passage 2 · Art History ───────────── p.50

### 원시 동굴 미술

지난 150년 동안 유럽의 여러 지역, 특히 프랑스와 스페인의 동굴 내부에서 미술 작품들이 발견되었다. 이러한 미술 작품들은 세 가지 유형으로 구분된다: 부드러운 돌에 새긴 에칭, 단단한 돌에 새긴 에칭, 그리고 그림이다. 진흙 조각상이 발견되기도 했지만, 이들은 발굴된 다른 작품들에 비해서 비교적 그 수가 적다. 대부분의 미술 작품은 동굴 바닥이나 벽에 그려졌으며 동물의 형상들을 나타내는데, 이러한 동물의 일부는 현재 멸종된 것들이다. 처음에 누가, 왜 미술 작품을 만들었는지는 전문가들도 알아내지 못했던 미스터리였다. 하지만 시간이 흐르면서 고고학적인 방법과 과학적인 분석을 통해 여러 가지 해답들이 꾸준히 제시되었다.

1860년대 최초의 동굴 미술 작품이 발견되었을 때 그것이 무엇인지 아는 사람은 아무도 없었다. 어떤 사람들은 교묘한 속임수라고 확신한 반면, 가까운 과거에 살았던 실제 예술가들의 작품으로 간주한 사람들도 있었다. 답은 훨씬 더 복잡했다. 이 미술 작품에 사용된 재료와 동굴에서 발견된 유기 물질에 대한 방사성 탄소 연대 측정 결과, 그림이 그려진 시기는 기원전 40,000년에서 10,000년 사이라는 점이 확인되었다. 대다수의 그림들은 기원전 18,000년에서 10,000년 사이에 그려진 것으로 밝혀졌다. 이 시기에는 마그달레니안이라고 알려진 사람들이 서유럽에서 살고 있었다. 이들의 이름은 그들의 원시 사회 유적이 발견된 프랑스의 한 지역 이름에서 유래되었다. 마그달레니안이 그렸을 것으로 생각되는 동굴 미술 작품에는 프랑스의 유명한 라스코 동굴에서 발견된 작품들도 포함된다.

마그달레니안들은 손가락을 사용해서, 아마도 동물의 발톱 자국을 흉내 내어 부드러운 진흙에 최초의 그림을 그렸을 것이라고 생각된다. 때때로 이러한 진흙이 굳어져 손으로 그린 이미지들이 보존되었다. 이러한 경험을 바탕으로 고대인들은 다양한 석기로 무른 돌에 조각하는 법을 알게 되었다. 그 후

보다 단단한 부싯돌로 만든 도구가 만들어짐에 따라 그들은 보다 단단한 암석을 특정한 모양으로 만들 수 있었다. 몇몇 에칭 작업의 결과물들은, 암석 표면으로부터 수 센티미터 튀어나와 있다는 점에서 얕은 돋을새김 작품과 거의 비슷하다. 동굴 그림이 더 잘 알려져 있기는 하지만, 이러한 에칭 작품들의 수가 훨씬 더 많으며, 일부 장소에서는 그 수가 거의 그림의 세 배에 이르기도 한다. 미술사학자들은 그 수가 많은 한 가지 이유로 에칭이 채색이나 드로잉만큼 노동 집약적이지는 않다는 이론을 제시한다.

채색보다 조각이 더 쉬웠다는 점은 이상하게 들릴 수 있지만, 선사 시대에는 모든 물감을 손으로 만들어야 했고 이를 바위에 점착시키기 위해서는 추가적인 물질이 필요했다. 원시인들은 자신들의 작품에 몇 가지 색만을 — 주로 검정색, 빨간색, 하얀색, 노란색, 그리고 갈색을 사용했다. 이들 중 일부 물감의 원료들은 알려져 있다. 예를 들면, 빨간색은 산화철로 만들어졌고, 검정색은 이산화 마그네슘이나 불에 탄 소나무나 노간주나무로 만들어졌으며, 흰색은 운모로 만들어졌다. (일부 경우, 물감을 만들기 위해서 피가 사용되기도 했다.) 몇몇 장소에서 막자사발과 막자가 발견되었다는 사실은 선사 시대의 화가들이 이러한 도구들을 사용하여 광물 및 기타 재료들을 갈아서 고운 가루로 만들었다는 증거가 된다. 그 후 이들은 조개껍데기나 뼈로 만들어진 용기에 물을 넣어 물감과 섞었다. 그리고 나서 화가들은 물감이 바위 캔버스에 점착되도록 식물과 동물의 오일을 활용했다. 물감을 칠하기 위해 화가들이 식물이나 동물에서 나온 물질로 만든 붓을 사용했을 것으로 생각되지만, 이러한 도구들이 남아 있지 않기 때문에 고고학자들은 붓의 재료가 무엇인지에 대해 추측만 할 수 있을 뿐이다. 하지만 물감을 고운 입자 형태로 불어 암벽에 고르게 퍼지도록 할 수 있게 한, 속이 비어 있는 뼈로 만든 관 모양의 도구는 남아 있다.

많은 그림들이 동굴의 내부 깊숙한 곳에 있기 때문에 그림을 그리는 동안 틀림없이 빛을 비추기 위한 많은 노력들이 필요했을 것이다. 현대의 화가와 마찬가지로 선사 시대의 화가들은 동굴 벽의 높은 곳에 닿기 위해 발판 같은 것들을 사용했을 것이다. 몇몇 동굴의 벽에서 발견되는 구멍들이 아마도 그러한 목적을 위해 만들어졌을 것이며, 그 근처에 있는 그림의 높이가 이러한 이론에 신빙성을 부여한다. 이러한 모든 일은 노동 집약적인 것이었고 동굴 화가 혼자서 모든 일을 하지는 않았다는 점은 분명하다. 아마도 몇몇 공동체에는 물감과 붓의 재료를 모으고, 동굴에 빛을 비추기 위한 횃불을 만들고, 화가들이 높은 곳에 닿을 수 있도록 구조물을 만드는 팀이 있었을 것이다.

> **WORD REMINDER**
> baffle 당혹스럽게 하다  hoax 짓궂은 장난, 날조  deem 생각하다, 간주하다  attribute (말, 글, 그림 등을) ~의 것으로 여기다  flint 부싯돌  bas-relief 얕은 돋을새김 (작품)  protrude 튀어나오다  juniper 노간주나무  mica 운모  mortar 막자사발  pestle 막자  scaffolding 발판

## Passage 3 • Physiology ———————— p.58
### 인체 내부의 체온

인간은 내부 메커니즘에 의해 열을 만들어 내는 온혈 동물이다. 대부분의 포유류들과 마찬가지로 인간은 자신이 섭취한 음식을 에너지로 변환시킴으로써 열을 만들어 낸다. 인간은 외부 온도, 특히 극한의 더위와 추위에 영향을 받을 수도 있지만, 인간의 신체는 이러한 환경에 적응하여 생존 가능하게 만드는 수단을 가지고 있다. 게다가 인간은 다른 수단들, 예컨대 옷을 입

거나 추운 날씨에 불을 피우고 더운 날씨에는 수분을 섭취하는 것과 같은 수단을 통해 체온을 유지할 수도 있다. 이러한 내·외부적인 대처 수단이 없다면 인간은 혹독한 환경에서 살아남지 못할 것이다.

체온 조절은 인간의 신체가 내부 온도를 조절하는 능력을 설명하는 용어이다. 인간의 정상 체온은 섭씨 37도 정도지만, 신체의 다양한 부분은 서로 다른 온도를 유지한다. 신체 중심부의 머리, 가슴, 그리고 배의 온도는 사지, 즉 팔과 다리의 온도에 비해서 약간 높다. 그 이유는 사람의 대부분의 장기가 머리, 가슴, 배에 있기 때문이다. 인간의 생존에 있어서 가장 중요한 세 기관이 뇌, 심장, 그리고 간이기 때문에, 신체는 이들 기관이 최대한 기능을 발휘할 수 있도록 노력한다.

혈액은 온 몸을 흐르면서 동맥을 통해 열을 팔다리로 전달하며, 신체 내부로 되돌아올 때에는 정맥의 온도를 상승시킨다. 하지만 매우 추운 날씨에는 신체가 피부 근처의 혈관을 수축시켜 피부 근처에 도달하는 혈액의 양을 감소시킴으로써 주요 내부 장기로부터 가까운 곳에 있는 혈액을 따뜻하게 유지시킨다. 그 결과 피부의 수분과 외부의 살이 얼면서 사람의 피부는 창백해지고 동상에 걸리게 된다. 하지만 이러한 일이 일어나기 전에 신체는 두 가지 방어 기제를 활용할 수 있다. 첫째, 신체의 털 근처에 있는 근육들이 수축하여 털이 서고 사람의 피부에 닭살이 돋는다. 일어선 털은 열이 몸 밖으로 배출되지 않도록 하는데 도움을 준다. 둘째, 뇌는 다른 근육들에게 빠르게 수축하라는 신호를 보냄으로써 사람은 몸을 떨게 되는데, 이로써 체열이 높아지게 된다.

하지만 때때로 사람이 몹시 추운 날씨에 장시간 노출될 수도 있고, 뜨거운 음식이나 불과 같은 외부의 열을 구할 수 없는 경우도 있다. 열을 얻을 수 없으면 신체는 기능을 멈춘다. 신체는 최대한 많은 양의 혈액을 뇌, 심장, 그리고 간에 모음으로써 사람이 보다 오래 생존할 수 있는 기회를 만들어 준다. 하지만 결국 사람은 저체온증을 겪게 되는데, 그러면 말을 제대로 하지 못하고 제 기능을 못하게 된다. 체내의 열을 증가시킬 수 있는 극단적인 조치가 취해지지 않는 이상 그 사람은 죽게 될 것이다.

신체는 매우 더운 날씨에 대처할 수 있는 수단도 보유하고 있다. 어떤 사람이 운동을 하면 그 사람의 체온은 상승한다. 열이 가두어지지 않도록 몸의 털이 눕게 된다. 피부 표면으로 흐르는 혈액의 양은 증가하여 보다 많은 열이 체외로 발산된다. 또한 체온이 너무 많이 상승하지 않도록 신체는 땀을 발산시킨다. 땀은 땀 분비선에서 피부 표면으로 흘러나온 뒤 퍼진다. 이로써 체내의 열기가 보다 빠르게 사라지면서 냉각 효과가 일어난다. 하지만 몸에 땀이 많이 날수록 체내에서 수분 손실이 많아지는 부정적인 대가도 존재한다. 이러한 수분이 보충되지 않으면 체내 수분의 양이 너무 적어져서 탈수증이 발생한다. (주로 이러한 점 때문에 운동을 하는 사람들에게는 다량의 음료를 마실 것이 권장된다.) 사막과 같이 매우 더운 곳에서 신체는 피부에 미치는 태양열 복사 에너지의 영향으로 다량의 열에 노출된다. 어떠한 사람이 자신에게 노출된 열을 감소시키려는 시도를 적극적으로 하지 않는다면 내부 장기가 너무 뜨거워져서 장기들이 적절한 기능을 하지 못할 수도 있다.

사람의 체온은 높고 낮음에 한계가 있다. 사람의 신체 중심부 온도가 섭씨 32도 밑으로 떨어지면 의식을 잃게 된다. 섭씨 26도 정도에 이르면 거의 항상 사망에 이른다. 열에 대해 이야기하면, 체온이 섭씨 40도를 넘을 경우 중병이 발생하며, 체내의 온도가 섭씨 45도를 넘는 경우에는 살아남을 수 있는 사람이 거의 없다.

# Passage 4 • Art ——————————— p.65

## 조르조 바사리

미술사라는 학문은 이탈리아의 화가이자 건축가였던 조르조 바사리의 업적에서 그 기원을 찾을 수 있다. 그가 1550년에 쓴 *미술가 열전*이라는 책은 당시 화가들의 생애를 연대순으로 기록한 최초의 시도 중 하나라고 간주된다. 또한 바사리는 자신이 살던 당시에 존재했고 그 역시 선도하고 있었던 새로운 미술 양식을 지칭하기 위해 *르네상스*라는 용어를 처음 만든 것으로도 유명하다.

바사리는 1511년 이탈리아 투스카니 지방에 있는 아레초라는 도시에서 태어났다. 여섯 아이 중 첫째였고 미술과 오랜 관련을 맺어 온 집안에서 자랐다. 그는 라틴어에 중점을 둔 다양한 교육을 받았으며, 유명한 스테인드글라스 창 디자이너인 프랑스인으로부터 드로잉을 배웠다. 1524년에는 계속해서 미술 교육을 받기 위해 플로렌스로 갔다. 바사리의 가족은 유명한 은행업자 가문인 메디치 가문과 관계를 맺었다. (수 세기 동안 메디치 가의 몇몇 인물들은 플로렌스뿐만 아니라 이탈리아 전역에서 가장 강력하고 영향력이 컸던 사람들이었다.) 그는 새로운 집에서 메디치 가문의 아이들과 함께 공부를 했고, 짧은 기간이지만 미켈란젤로의 제자가 되기도 했다. 바사리가 16세 때 비극이 찾아와 그의 아버지가 전염병으로 사망하고 장남이던 바사리가 가정사를 떠맡게 되었다. 그 일 때문에 그는 자신과 가족을 위한 재정적인 안정성을 평생의 소원으로 삼았는데, 메디치 가문과의 우호 관계와 메디치 가문의 후원을 통해 그는 소원을 성취했다. 그는 성인 시절 대부분을 플로렌스에서 보냈으며, 이곳에서 메디치 가문은 그에게 종종 다양한 프로젝트를 맡겼다. 이후 1574년 그는 플로렌스에서 사망하게 된다.

화가로서 바사리는 후기 르네상스 매너리즘 시대의 일원으로 간주된다. 생전에는 화가로 유명했으며 그를 따르는 사람들도 많았는데, 이 중에는 이후에 유명해진 학생들도 많이 포함되어 있었다. 하지만 현재의 비평가들은 대체로 바사리의 스타일이 그보다 먼저 활동했던 대가들, 특히 친구인 미켈란젤로를 모방한 것이었다고 생각한다. 바사리는 또한 건축 작업으로도 잘 알려져 있으며, 여기에는 다수의 교회 리모델링 공사와 메디치 가문의 저택 설계 및 건설이 포함된다. 생애의 마지막 10년 동안 바사리는 바티칸에 의해 직접 고용되어 몇몇 교회들의 내부를 장식하는 일을 했다. 하지만 오늘날 그의 유산은 역사적인 저서인 *미술가 열전*에 주로 집중되어 있다.

바사리는 라틴어 및 고대 문학에 정통했기 때문에 화가들의 전기를 쓸 당시 플루타르크 및 비투루비우스와 같은 고대 로마의 작가들의 작품으로부터 영향을 받았을 것이다. 바사리는 이 책이 후대 화가들의 교육에 기초가 될 수 있기를 바란다고 주장했지만, 몇몇 사람들은 그가, 까다로운 성격 때문에 1540년대 후반 쇠퇴하고 있던, 자신의 명성을 되살리기 위한 시도로서 책을 쓰기 시작했다고 생각한다. 그는 또한 자신의 후원자였던 메디치 가문에 대해서도 걱정을 했는데, 그 이유는 오랫동안 그들과 관계를 유지했음에도 불구하고 그가 메디치 가문의 핵심 그룹에 들어가지 못했기 때문이었다. 마침

내 1554년 메디치 가의 수장이 바사리에게 가족의 일원이 될 것을 요청함으로써 그에 대한 메디치 가문의 후원은 공고해졌다.

*미술가 열전*은 13세기부터 16세기까지 300년이 넘는 기간에 걸쳐 화가들의 생애를 다루었다. 바사리는 레오나르도 다 빈치와 미켈란젤로와 같은 유명인들을 포함하여 수백 명 화가들의 생애에 대한 글을 썼다. 하지만 이들 대부분은 플로렌스 지방 출신이었고, 바사리는, 티티안과 같은 몇몇 베네치아 출신 화가들이 포함된, 1568년의 개정판이 나오기 전까지는 타 지역의 화가들에 대해 지면을 거의 할애하지 않았다. 이 책은 플로렌스에서 부유하고 힘 있는 사람이라면 누구나 읽는 책이 되었지만, 그가 살아 있던 당시에도 정확하지 못한 부분과 특정 사건을 미화한 점 때문에 바사리는 비판을 받았다. 때때로 그는 자기 자신을 역사의 한 가운데에 두기도 했다. 예를 들어 자신이 미켈란젤로의 조각상 *다비드*를 성난 군중으로부터 지켜냈다고 주장했다. 또한 자기 자신 및 자신의 가족에 대한 장문의 전기를 말미에 포함시킴으로써 책으로 자신을 홍보하기도 했다. 이러한 단점들에도 불구하고, 이 책은 바사리 사후 수 세기 동안 르네상스 화가들에 관한 정보의 출처 중 최고라는 찬사를 받았다.

# Actual Test 03

## Passage 1 · Meteorology ———————————— p.75

### 구름의 성분

구름은 전 세계에서 흔히 볼 수 있다. 비, 눈, 그리고 때때로 지면에 떨어지는 다양한 강수의 원인이 바로 구름이다. 구름 자체는 본래 수증기로 이루어져 있지만, 대기에서는 작은 입자에 붙어 있다. 이러한 입자들은 다양한 물질일 수 있다.

지구의 대기는 육안으로 보이지 않는 극도로 작은 물방울 형태의 수증기로 가득하다. 하지만 하늘에서 구름이 형성될 때 수증기가 눈에 보이게 된다. 그 이유는 수증기가 대기에 떠 다니는 입자에 달라붙기 때문이다. 이러한 입자는 주로 작은 먼지의 입자이다. 그런 다음 수증기의 물방울들이 모여 대기의 서로 다른 층에서 다양한 형태와 크기의 구름이 만들어진다. 시간이 흐르면서 점점 더 많은 수증기의 물방울들이 모이게 되면 구름이 너무 무거워져서 수분을 방출하게 되는 시점에 도달할 때까지 구름의 크기가 증가하는데, 이때 이 수분이 강수로서 지면으로 떨어지게 된다.

구름의 형성에 도움을 주는 대기 중의 입자는 주로 먼지이다. 대기에는 상당한 양의 먼지가 존재한다. 이는 눈에 보이지 않는 경우가 많지만, 가끔씩 안개, 스모그, 그리고 연무의 형태로 눈에 보이기도 한다. 태양이 뜨고 질 때의 붉은색은 태양빛이 이러한 먼지를 통과할 때 색깔이 있는 태양빛의 파장 중 일부가 차단된 결과로, 이로 인해 사람들은 대체로 붉은색의 파장을 볼 수가 있다. 이러한 먼지는 사람이나 자연에 의해 만들어진다. 사람이 원인인 경우에는, 농업, 임업, 광업, 그리고 제조업을 포함하여, 먼지를 대기로 유입시키는 모든 활동이 포함된다. (공장에서 배출되는 연기가 이러한 먼지의 주요한 원천이다.) 자연이 원인인 경우에는 산불, 화산 활동이 포함되며, 그 중에는 먼지를 공기 중에 퍼뜨리는 침식 현상도 있다. 게다가 대기에는 유기 물질이 포함되어 있다. 예를 들어, 산불이 발생하면 식물에서 비롯된 일부 유기 물질들이 대기로 유입된다. 마찬가지로 바람에 날린 식물의 꽃가루와 씨앗이 공기 중에서 발견되기도 하는데, 여기에 수증기가 달라붙어 대기 중으로 상승하면 이들이 구름의 일부가 되기도 한다.

일부 구름은 소금 입자와 얼음의 핵으로 형성될 수도 있다. 소금 입자는 주로 해양 인근의 대기에서 발견되는데, 육지에서 멀리 떨어진 바다에서 많은 구름을 형성시키며 대기 내 먼지 수준을 높이는 원인이 된다. 소금은 증발을 통해, 혹은 바닷물이 해안가에 부딪칠 때 생기는 물보라의 형태로 대기에 유입된다. 바다에서는 따뜻한 공기와 차가운 공기가 모임으로써 수증기와 소금 입자로 만들어진 짙은 안개가 형성된다. 얼음의 핵에 대해서 이야기하면, 이들은 먼지, 유기 물질, 혹은 박테리아의 주변에서 과냉각된 물방울들이다. 대기의 높은 곳에서 형성된 이러한 얼음의 핵은 눈이나 얼음으로 떨어지거나, 대기의 낮은 부분이 더 따뜻한 경우, 때때로 비로 떨어지는 얼음 결정체를 만들어 낸다. 또한 상당 부분 번개를 발생시키는, 구름 사이의 전기적 전이의 원인이 되기도 한다.

과학자들은 박테리아가 구름을 형성시키는 원인이 될 수도 있다는 점을 밝혀냈다. 25년 전, 박테리아가 얼음의 핵을 형성시키고 비나 눈과 함께 지면으로 떨어짐으로써 세계의 여러 지역으로 퍼져 나간다는 주장이 제기되었다. 초창기에 이 이론은 무시되었지만, 이러한 일이 실제로 발생한다는 증거가 많아지고 있다. 식물에서 일반적으로 볼 수 있는 다양한 박테리아가 서로 다른 여러 지역의, 심지어 식물이 존재하지 않는 극지방의 얼음 샘플에서 수집되었다. 박테리아가 대기에 유입되어 얼음의 핵을 형성한 후, 이들이 얼음

결정체가 되어 이후 비나 눈으로 새로운 지역에 떨어졌을 것으로 보인다. 어느 정도 믿기 힘들 수도 있겠지만, 많은 과학자들은 실제로 이러한 일이 일어나고 있다는 점에 동의한다. 사실 생명체들이 번식을 해서 새로운 지역으로 퍼져 나갈 수 있는 방법들을 종종 찾는다는 점을 고려하면, 박테리아가 구름을 이용해 다른 지역으로 이동한다는 것은 논리적으로 보인다. 그렇게 함으로써 이들은 하늘 높은 곳에 떠다니는 구름의 또 다른 성분으로서 — 여러 성분 중 하나로서 — 기능한다.

> **WORD REMINDER**
> precipitation 강우   mote 작은 입자   converge 모이다   haze 안개, 연무   nucleus 핵   super-cool (액체를) 응고시키지 않고 응고점 이하로 냉각하다, 과냉각하다   farfetched 빙 둘러서 말하는, 억지스러운

## Passage 2 · History ———————————— p.83

### 로마: 공화국에서 제국까지

로마는 기원전 500년경 티베르 강 유역의 이탈리아 반도에서 권력의 중심지로 부상했다. 초기의 군주제 시기 이후, 로마인들은 지도자를 몰아내고 민주주의적인 신념 체계가 반영된 문화를 설립했으며 로마 공화국으로 알려질 국가를 창설했다. 이들의 정치적 원칙은 중앙 권력을 다수의 행정관들에게 분배한 불문 헌법과, 이러한 권력을 제한하는 견제와 균형 시스템에 기반해 있었다. 이러한 시스템의 최상위에는 강력한 로마 원로원이 있었으나, 그 권한에도 제한이 있었다. 시간이 흐름에 따라 원로원은 로마에서 가장 강력한 가문들을 대표하는 대의 기관으로 변모했다. 원로원은 로마인들의 삶의 대부분을 통제했지만, 그 구성원과 기타 로마의 권세 가문 간의 정치적 음모와 내분은 결코 통제할 수 없었는데, 이는 원로원이 몰락하는 계기가 되었다. 기원전 1세기의 권력 투쟁으로 불안정한 시기가 이어지면서 결국 로마 공화국은 붕괴되고 로마 제국이 수립되었다.

이러한 갈등의 시기의 중심에는 율리우스 카이사르가 있었다. 로마에서 가장 위대한 군 지휘관 중 한 명이었던 카이사르는 여러 가지 정치적인 음모에 연루되어 원로원에 수많은 적을 두게 되었다. 기원전 49년 원로원이 카이사르의 로마 입성을 금지시키자 그는 경험이 풍부한 자신의 군대를 이끌고 가울에서 — 현재의 프랑스에서 — 이탈리아 반도로 이동한 후 로마로 진군했다. 카이사르의 베테랑 군인들을 물리칠 가망이 없는 신병으로 이루어진 허약한 군대만을 보유했던 원로원 및 군 지휘관들은 도시를 버리고 도망쳤다. 단기간의 내전이 끝난 후 카이사르는 적들을 물리치고 로마의 통치자가 되었다. 그는 여러 행정관의 권한을 자신에게 부여하고 5년 동안 사실상 독재자로서 통치를 했다. 카이사르의 조치로 원로원은 대부분의 권한을 박탈당했고 로마의 모든 권력이 한 사람에게 집중되는 과정이 시작되었다. 이에 대한 반응으로 원로원은 권력 및 위세의 박탈에 대해 격렬히 반응했는데, 원로원의 구성원 중 다수가 기원전 44년에 있었던 카이사르의 암살 사건에서 중요한 역할을 수행했다.

카이사르의 사망 후, 또 다시 불안정한 내전의 시기가 찾아왔다. 카이사르의 조카이자 그가 자신의 후계자로 입양했던 옥타비아누스는 카이사르의 측근이자 군 장교였던 마르쿠스 안토니우스와 동맹을 맺었다. 이 두 사람은 함께 카이사르의 암살에 책임이 있는 사람들을 물리쳤지만, 젊은 옥타비아누스 대신 자신이 카이사르의 후계자가 되기를 원했던 안토니우스는 자신의 질투심을 억누르고 있었다. 일이 성공하자 안토니우스는 이집트의 여왕 클레오파

트라의 군에 합류함으로써 옥타비아누스와 맞서게 되었는데, 클레오파트라는 카이사르가 사망하기 전 그와 연인 관계였다. 기원전 31년 악티움에서 벌어진 대규모 해전에서 옥타비아누스의 군대는 안토니우스와 클레오파트라를 물리쳤다. (그들은 전쟁에서 패배했을 뿐만 아니라 그 과정에서 목숨까지 잃었다.) 기원전 29년 무렵 내전은 종식되었고, 옥타비아누스가 카이사르의 업적을 완수할 것이라는 점이 명백해졌다. 그는 로마로 개선해서 스스로를 아우구스투스라 칭하고 로마의 초대 황제가 되었다.

서기 14년에 사망할 때까지 아우구스투스는 수십 년에 걸쳐 로마를 공화국에서 제국으로 바꾸어 놓았고, 권력을 황제의 수중에 집중시키는데 성공했다. 아우구스투스는 차후 로마 황제의 특징이 된 세 가지 선례를 만들어 냈다. 첫째, 옥타비아누스는 자신에게만 충성한 사람들을 제국의 요직에 앉혔다. 둘째, 그는 로마의 시민들을 존중했는데, 이로써 강력한 지지 기반을 확보할 수 있었다. 셋째, 그는 로마군의 충성심을 확보함으로써 이들을 이용해 원로원이 예전의 권력을 재탈환할 수 없도록 했다. 또한 아우구스투스는 카이사르의 전례를 따라 후계자를 입양해서 그를 미래의 황제로 만들기 위해 교육시켰다. 이렇게 함으로써 그는 자신이 사망한 후 권력이 순조롭게 이양되도록 할 수 있었다.

유능한 통치자들이 권좌에 있는 동안 로마 제국은 성공적이었다. 아우구스투스 직후의 황제들은 후계자를 입양하여 교육시켰던 그의 관행을 그대로 따랐다. 하지만 결국 황제의 지위는 세습되었고, 이후의 너무 많은 황제들이 약하고 제대로 된 교육을 받지 못했다. 그들은 권력을 유지하기 위해 로마 사람들과 로마군에 과도하게 의존했다. 하지만 로마 제국은 야만 종족들이 국경을 침범하여 로마를 멸망에 이르도록 만들기 전까지 거의 500년간 유지되었다.

**WORD REMINDER**

overthrow 전복시키다, 타도하다    unwritten constitution 불문 헌법    political office 행정 기관, 행정관    checks and balances 견제와 균형    representative body 대의 기구    power struggle 권력 투쟁    intrigue 음모    veteran 베테랑의, 노련한    seasoned 노련한    invest A in B A를 B에게 맡기다    set in motion 움직이게 하다, 추진하다    prestige 위세    hold ~ in check ~를 억제하다    come out against ~에 반대하고 나서다    power base 지지 기반, 세력 기반    competent 유능한    horde 유목민    overrun 침략하다

## Passage 3 • Botany ————————————————— p.91

### 식충 식물

식물은 다른 모든 생물들과 마찬가지로 영양분을 필요로 하며, 대부분의 식물들은 토양으로부터 질소와 같은 영양소를 흡수함으로써 영양분을 얻는다. 이들은 또한 광합성으로 알려진 과정을 통해 햇빛의 도움을 받아 잎에서 발견되는 엽록소를 포도당으로 전환시킨다. 하지만 식물 중 일부는 식충 식물인데, 이들은 곤충과 같은 작은 생물들을 잡아먹음으로써 생존에 필요한 영양분을 얻는다. 이러한 식충 식물들은 대부분 곤충을 유인하여 포획한 후 이를 소화시켜 양분을 흡수함으로써 그러한 목적을 달성한다.

현재 식물학자들은 600여종 이상의 식충 식물들을 발견하여 이름을 붙였다. 식충 식물로 분류되기 위해서는 그 식물이 먹이를 포획하여 붙잡을 수 있는 수단과 먹이를 소화시키는 수단, 그리고 먹이를 소화시켜 얻을 수 있는 양분을 흡수하는 수단을 가지고 있어야 한다. 이러한 특성들 전부가 아니라 일

부만 가지고 있는 몇몇 식물들은 식충 식물로 간주되지 않는다. 또한 식물학자들은 소화 메커니즘에 대해 서로 의견이 일치하지 않는다. 몇몇 학자들은 어떤 식물이 식충 식물로 간주되려면 그 식물이 효소를 활용하여 곤충을 소화시켜야 한다고 생각한다. 하지만 어떤 부류의 식물들은 곤충을 포획하여 먹이를 소화시킬 때 스스로 생산해 내지 않는 박테리아를 이용하기 때문에 일부 식물학자들은 이들이 사실상 식충 식물이 아니라고 주장한다. 식충 식물인지 아닌지를 판단하기가 어려운 식물들이 300여종 이상 존재하며, 이들은 유사 식충 식물로 분류되고 있다.

일반적으로 식충 식물은, 예컨대 늪지대 및 암석 지대와 같이, 열악한 토양 환경에서 자란다. 따라서 이들은 다른 공급원, 즉 곤충으로부터 영양분을 얻어 환경에 적응해 생존해 왔다. 곤충을 유혹하기 위한 방법은 식물마다 다르다. 일부 식물들은 달콤한 화밀을 이용하여 곤충을 포충엽으로 유인하는 반면, 독특한 냄새나 외형적 특성에 의존하여 지나가는 곤충의 관심을 끄는 식물들도 있다. 일단 식물 쪽으로 유인이 되면 곤충은 대개 식물의 포충엽 안으로 빠지게 된다.

식충 식물들이 가장 일반적으로 이용하는 포충엽은 다섯 가지이다: 함정식 포충엽, 올가미식 포충엽, 점착식 포충엽, 흡입식 포충엽, 그리고 통발식 포충엽이 그것이다. 일반적으로 함정식 포충엽은 낭상엽 식물과 같은 식충 식물들이 이용한다. 낭상엽 식물은 관처럼 생겼으며 어떤 식으로든 곤충을 유인하는 입구를 가지고 있다. 대부분의 경우, 곤충은 포충엽 밖으로 기어나가지 못한다. 파리지옥풀의 포충엽과 같은 올가미식 포충엽에는, 곤충이 도망치기 전에 재빠르게 닫혀 곤충을 가둘 수 있는, 잎과 같은 기관이 있다. 파리지옥풀이 비교적 잘 알려져 있는 식충 식물이기는 하지만, 이 식물은 사실 올가미식 포충엽 메커니즘을 활용하는 둘 밖에 없는 식물 중 하나이다.

대신 점착식 포충엽이 훨씬 더 흔하다. 점착식 포충엽을 활용하는 식물의 표면에는 곤충을 포획하여 도망치지 못하게 만드는 접착제와 같은 물질이 있다. 흡입식 포충엽은 불가에 있는 식물들이 활용하는 경우가 많다. 이들은 식물 내부의 공기 주머니가 수축될 때 진공 상태를 만든다. 지나가는 곤충들은 물과 함께 말 그대로 식물 안으로 빨려 들어가게 된다. 마지막으로 통발식 포충엽은 통발과 동일한 원리로 작동하는데, 이러한 이유로 그 이름이 붙여졌다. 곤충들은 식물 안으로 기어들어갈 수 있지만, 기어나올 수는 없다. 식물 표면에 있는 작은 선모들이 같은 곳을 향하고 있기 때문에, 곤충들이 들어갈 수는 있지만 다시 나오려고 할 때에는 이러한 선모 때문에 빠져나올 수가 없다. (나사골풀이 이러한 방법을 이용하는데, 기본적으로 선모가 곤충을 내부로 들어가게 만든 다음 소화가 이루어진다.) 올가미식 포충엽을 제외하면 식충 식물이 이용하는 포충엽은 매우 다양한 형태를 띤다.

식충 식물에 갇히면 식물 내부의 효소에 의해 곤충은 천천히 소화된다. 영양분은 세 가지 방법 중 하나로 식물에 흡수된다. 먼저 대부분의 식충 식물에는 상피라고 불리는 반질반질한 보호층이 있다. 하지만 일부 식충 식물들은 이처럼 반질반질한 내부의 층을 가지고 있지 않기 때문에 영양분이 식물에 직접 흡수되지 않는다. 영양분이 상피를 통과할 수 있도록 일시적으로 열리는 특별한 세포 구조를 지닌 식충 식물도 있다. 마지막으로 세 번째 유형의 식충 식물들의 경우 상피 내부에 영구적인 틈이 있어서 영양분이 통과할 수 있다. 어떤 경우이든 영양분은 결국 흡수되어 식물은 살아가는데 필요한 영양분을 얻는다.

# Actual Test 04

## Passage 1 • Paleoclimatology ———————— p.99

### 캄브리아기의 기후

　지구의 기후는 지구가 존재하기 시작한 오래 전부터 변해 왔다. 오늘날보다 훨씬 더 추운 때도 있었고, 기온이 훨씬 더 높았던 때도 있었다. 현재의 기후와 큰 차이를 보인 시기 중 하나는 캄브리아기였다. 캄브리아기는 5억 4,100만년 전부터 2억 8,500만년까지 지속되었으며, 이는 고생대라고 불리는 보다 긴 지질학적 시기의 일부였다. 캄브리아기는 기온이 훨씬 더 높았던 시대로, 이전 시기에 비해 새 생명체에게 보다 유리한 기후가 조성되었다. 이는 지구에 존재하는 생명체에게 중대한 변화를 가져 왔다. 주로 단세포 생물들이 최초의 갑각류 및 척추동물들을 포함한 복잡한 형태의 다세포 생물들로 바뀌었다. 생물의 개체수가 이처럼 폭발적으로 증가하게 되었기 때문에 과학자들은 이 사건을 캄브리아기 대폭발이라고 부른다.

　과학자들은 캄브리아기 지구의 평균 온도가 대략 섭씨 22도일 것이라는 이론을 제시한다. 이는 오늘날 평균 기온이 섭씨 14도라는 점과 비교된다. 오랜 기간 태양 열이 지구 표면 가까운 곳에 갇힘으로써 야기된 온실 효과 때문에 기온이 그처럼 높았을 것이라고 생각되었다. 이 이론은 최근 영국에서 이루어진 연구로 캄브리아기 기온을 측정하는 방법이 밝혀지기 전까지 수십 년 동안 입증되지 못했다. 과학자들이 과거의 기온 및 기후를 알아내기 위해 가장 흔히 사용하는 방법은 나무의 나이테와 얼음 핵을 조사하는 것이다. 하지만 당시의 나무는 존재하지 않았고, 과학자들은 수백 만년 이전의 얼음 핵을 찾아내야만 했다.

　캄브리아기의 기온을 알아내기 위해 영국의 과학자들은 화석 안의 산소 수치를 연구했다. 그들은 두 개의 산소 동위 원소, 즉 지구에서 매우 흔한 산소-16과 그보다 희귀한 산소 동위 원소인 산소-18을 조사했다. 캄브리아기의 생명체들은 주로 바다에서 살았으며, 바닷물로부터 산소를 흡수하여 이를 껍질과 뼈로 보냈다. 물의 증발률과 응축률은 산소 동위 원소의 존재 여부에 따라 약간 달라진다. 이들 화석 안에 있는 서로 다른 두 개의 동위 원소의 비율을 조사함으로써 과학자들은 캄브리아기의 기온에 대해 알 수 있었을 뿐만 아니라 그 결과로서 기후에 대해서도 알 수 있었다.

　산소를 흡수할 수 있는, 껍질과 뼈에 존재하는 탄산 칼슘 및 인산 칼슘의 특성 때문에 이러한 연구에는 화석이 필요했다. 하지만 초기에 학자들은 이러한 기술로 원하는 결과를 얻어낼 수 있는 화석을 단 한 세트만 찾아냈다. 코노돈트라고 불리는 초기 척추동물이었다. 안타깝게도 이 생물은 후기 캄브리아기에만 존재했기 때문에 이 화석은 초기 캄브리아기의 기온 및 기후 연구에는 유용하지 않았다. 최근 한 영국 연구팀이 완족류라고 불리는 갑각류의 화석을 이용할 수 있었는데, 이는 5억 1,000만년과 5억 2,000만년 전 사이에 영국의 석회석에 화석화된 것이었다. 이러한 방법으로 초기 캄브리아기 당시 지구 북쪽의 고위도 지방의 기온이 항시 섭씨 20도와 55도 사이였을 것이라는 데이터가 만들어졌다. 그리고 나서 이 데이터는 전 세계 평균 기온을 추정하는데 사용되었는데, 이는 또 다시 당시 지구에 온실 효과와 같은 현상이 있었을 것이라는 이론에 무게를 실어 주었다. 게다가 이 기온 데이터를 중생대와 신생대 때 온실 효과와 비슷한 현상이 있었던, 보다 더 잘 알려진 시기와 비교해서 이들이 서로 유사하다는 점이 밝혀지자 온실 효과 기후 이론은 더 많은 지지를 받게 되었다.

　캄브리아기에 이처럼 기온이 상승하자 한 가지 결과로서 새로운 생명체들이 대량으로 생겨났다. 이보다 앞선 시기에 살았던 대부분의 생명체들은 바다에서 살았고 단세포 생물이었다. 캄브리아기가 시작되기 수백 만년 전에도 이들 생명체들은 서서히 다세포 생물로 진화하기 시작했지만, 이는 매우 더딘 과정이었다. 하지만 전 지구적으로 기온이 상승하여 보다 우호적인 환경이 조성됨에 따라 캄브리아기에는 갑각류 및 척추동물을 포함하여 훨씬 더 많은 수의 다세포 생물들이 생겨났다. (캄브리아기 대폭발이라고 불리는 이 기간은, 오늘날의 수많은 생물들의 조상이 그때 등장했기 때문에, 지구 역사상 가장 중요한 시기 중 하나로서 간주된다.) 이러한 생명체의 껍질 및 뼈에 들어 있는 미네랄 성분으로 인해, 처음으로 의미 있는 생물 화석화 과정이 일어나기 시작했다. 캄브리아기를 시작으로 현재의 여러 생명체들의 조상이었던 생명체들의 화석 기록이 풍부해졌다. 이러한 화석은 또 다시 과학자들로 하여금 지구의 예전 기후에 대해 보다 잘 알 수 있게 해 준다.

---

**WORD REMINDER**

geological 지질학의   amenable to ～이 쉽게 받아들일 수 있는
vertebrate 척추동물   give way to ～에게 길을 내어 주다; ～으로 변하다
isotope 동위 원소   condensation 응축; 압축   calcium carbonate
탄산 칼슘   calcium phosphate 인산 칼슘   brachiopod 완족류
limestone 석회석   latitude 위도   extrapolate 추론하다, 추정하다
bolster 강화하다   fossilization 화석화   precursor 선구자; 전조

---

## Passage 2 · Physiology ———————— p.106

### 조기 노화

많은 사람들은 결국 나이가 들어서 죽는다. 하지만 아직 어린 나이임에도 불구하고 노화가 너무 빠르게 진행되어서 신체에 노화의 징후가 나타나는 아이들이 있다. 이는 조로증이라고 일려진 질병의 결과이다. 조로증을 앓는 사람들은 대다수의 아이들과 같은 방식으로 성장하지 않는다. 그 대신 이 병에 걸린 아이들은 노인들이 갖는 다양한 특징을 나타내며, 특히 심혈관 질환과 같이 노인들을 괴롭히는 질병에 취약하다. 조로증에 걸린 사람들 중 21세 이상까지 살아남은 사람은 거의 없고, 이 질병으로 사망한 사람들의 평균 연령은 13세이다. 불행하게도 극도로 희귀한 병이기 때문에, 이에 대한 치료법을 찾기 위해 사용되는 자금이 거의 없어서 치료법은 상당 기간 동안 발견되지 않을 가능성이 높다.

전 세계적으로 조로증 진단을 받은 경우는 50건도 되지 않는다. 이 질병은 사람 몸 속에 있는 라민A라는 단백질에 유전적인 정보가 결여되어 발생한다. 이 단백질은 세포핵을 보유하고 있지만, 그러한 결함 때문에 핵이 불안정해져서 사람이 빠르게 노화하게 된다. 이 질병을 앓는 사람이 거의 없기 때문에 의학 전문가들은 라민A 단백질에 결함이 생기는 과정과 원인에 대해 제대로 알지 못한다. 한 가정 내에 조로증에 걸린 아이가 한 명 이상 있었던 사례가 두 번이나 있었음에도 불구하고, 이 질병은 유전병으로 생각되지 않는다. 대신, 대부분의 케이스는 무작위적으로 발병한 것으로 보인다. 마찬가지로 이 질병이 다른 곳에 비해 더 많이 나타나는 인종이나 국가는 없다; 이는 다른 희귀 질환들과는 다른 점인데, 이들의 경우 다른 집단에 비해서 특정한 민족이나 인종에 영향을 미치는 경우가 많다. 그 결과 어떤 아이가 조로증에 걸릴 위험에 있는지를 알아내기 위한 조기 진단 검사를 만들어 내는 것이 불가능하다.

정상적으로 건강한 아이가 있는 가족은 그 아이가 조로증을 겪게 될 것인지 알 수 있는 방법이 없다. 그 이유는 조로증의 징후가 발현되려면 아이가 생후 10개월에서 24개월 이후가 되어야 하기 때문이다. 이 시기에 이르면

조기 노화의 몇몇 특징들이 눈에 보이게 된다. 이러한 특징에는 성장의 제한, 체지방의 감소 및 탈모, 관절 경화, 그리고 피부의 노화 현상이 포함된다. 또한 조로증에 걸린 아이들은 얼굴이 야윈 것처럼 보이고 작은 얼굴에 머리카락이 없는 둥근 머리의 외모를 갖게 되어 나이 든 사람처럼 보이게 된다. 조로증에 걸린 아이들의 공통적인 건강 문제로 골반 탈구, 심장병, 그리고 뇌졸중을 들 수 있는데, 이러한 문제들은 모두 전형적으로 노인들이 겪는 것이다. 의사들은 조로증 환자들의 노화 속도가 건강한 아이보다 10배 더 빠른 것으로 추정한다. (따라서 조로증에 걸린 10살 아이는 몇 가지 측면에서 몇십 년 더 나이가 많은 사람들과 비슷할 것이다.) 대부분의 환자들은 8세에서 11세 사이에 사망하며, 그보다 오래 생존한 환자들은 극소수이다.

아이가 조로증 증상을 보이기 시작하면 유전자 검사를 통해 그 아이가 실제로 조로증에 걸렸는지를 판단할 수 있다. 의사들은 조로증의 존재를 확인할 수는 있지만 치료는 할 수 없기 때문에 환자들은 모두 결국 사망에 이르게 된다. 최근, 치료법을 찾고 있는 학자들이 세포 핵에 영향을 미치는 기형을 바로잡는 일에 집중하고 있다. 고려되고 있는 방법 중 하나는 일부 암을 제거시키는데 도움을 주는 약물을 사용하는 것이다. 하지만 이러한 실험은 아직 초기 단계에 있기 때문에 실행 가능한 치료법이 존재하기까지 최소한 몇 년 더 있어야 할 가능성이 높다. 그 동안, 현재 조로증과 싸우고 있는 아이들은 식단을 조절하고 심장병을 치료하는 약물을 복용하면서 수명을 연장시키려는 시도를 하고 있다.

의학 연구원들이 조로증의 치료법을 발견하지 못하는 이유 중 하나는 이 질병이 매우 드물게 발생한다는 점에 있다. 조로증 사례가 드물기 때문에 전문 의학 연구원들과 자금 모두 그 원인에 대해 관심을 갖지 않는다. 대신 상당한 양의 전문 기술과 연구비는 훨씬 더 많은 사람들에게 기하급수적인 영향을 끼치는 암과 같은 질병에 투입되고 있다. 그럼에도 불구하고 최근에 조로증이 의학계의 일부 학자들의 관심을 끌고 있는데, 그 이유는 그에 대한 연구를 통해 사람들이 노화하는 이유의 단서를 찾을 수도 있기 때문이다. 몇몇 학자들은 연구원들이 조로증에 대한 치료법을 찾게 된다면 성인들의 노화 속도를 늦추는 법도 발견될 수 있을 것으로 기대한다.

---

**WORD REMINDER**

progeria 조로증   malady 병   susceptible to ～에 걸리기 쉬운,
～에 취약한   afflict 괴롭히다   cardiovascular 심혈관의   quite
some time 오랫동안   ethnicity 민족성   manifest 발현되
다   pinched 수척한   hip dislocation 골반 탈구   stroke 뇌졸
중   the lion's share 가장 큰 몫, 대부분   expertise 전문적인 기술
exponentially 기하급수적으로, 급격히

---

## Passage 3 · History of Technology ———— p.113

### 초창기의 시계들

오늘날 시계는 단순한 손목 시계부터 사람들이 정확한 시간을 맞추기 위해 사용하는 원자 시계에 이르기까지 어디에서든 찾아볼 수 있다. 하지만 시계가 항상 그처럼 흔했던 것은 아니며, 오래 전 사람들은 시간을 측정하기 위해 천체의 움직임과 계절 변화에 의존했던 경우가 많았다. 하지만 수 개월에서 수 년 정도 큰 단위의 시간을 측정하려면 별을 관찰하거나 계절의 변화를 지속적으로 추적해야 했다. 그러나 생활이 보다 복잡해지고 문명이 발생하면서 점차적으로 매일 시간을 측정하는 일이 필요해졌다. 따라서, 인류 역사 전반에 걸쳐, 수많은 종류의 시계가 사용되었다.

인류가 만든 최초의 시계 중 하나는 해시계였다. 해시계는 해가 지면 사용할 수 없고 해시계가 드리우는 그림자가 사람이 위치한 위도에 따라 달라진다는 점에서 한계가 있었다. 결국 해시계는 낮 시간의 현지 시각을 측정하는 데만 활용될 수 있었기 때문에 신뢰할 수 없었고, 상대적으로 비효율적이었다. 이러한 한계들로 인해 인류는 기계적 성질을 띠는 시계를 개발하려고 노력했다. 신뢰할 수 있는 최초의 기계식 시계는 물시계였다. 이 시계는 흐르는 물로 시간의 흐름을 측정하는 비교적 단순한 장치였다. 물시계는 물이 유입되거나 유출되는 유형 중 하나였다. 유입식 물시계에서는 표시가 새겨진 용기 안으로 물을 유입시켰는데, 이 표시는 얼마나 많은 시간이 지났는지를 보여 주기 위한 것으로 수위의 상승에 의해 결정되었다. 유출식 물시계는 용기의 수위가 낮아진다는 사실을 제외하면 동일한 개념을 사용했다. 물시계는 수천 년 전 고대 이집트인들에 의해 만들어졌으며, 기타 다수의 초기 사회들도 독자적으로 이를 개발하거나 다른 문명으로부터 물시계에 대해 배웠다. 고대에는 종교 의식, 특히 밤에 이루어지는 의식을 위해 천문학적인 현상들의 시간을 측정하는데 물시계가 가장 흔하게 사용되었다.

수 세기 동안 물시계는 인간이 제작한 것 중 가장 발전된 형태의 시간 측정 장치였다. 이는 1400년대까지 사실이었는데, 이때 새로운 종류의 시계인 태엽 시계가 발명되었다. (이때는 르네상스가 정점을 맞이했던 시기로, 당시 유럽인들은 여러 분야에서 커다란 발전을 이루고 있었다.) 단단하게 감겨 있다가 풀리는 태엽의 동력으로 시계 문자판에 있는 시계 바늘을 회전시키는 톱니가 작동되었다. 태엽 시계는 물시계를 뛰어넘는 몇 가지 장점을 가지고 있었다. 첫째, 태엽의 동력을 이용함으로써 보다 작은 시계가 — 심지어 사람들이 가지고 다닐 수 있는 정도의 시계들이 — 제작될 수 있었다. 또한 태엽 시계는 물을 채우고 빼낼 필요가 없었다. 하지만 두 가지 단점이 있었다. 첫째, 태엽 시계의 태엽이 풀리면 이를 다시 감아야만 했다. 둘째, 태엽이 풀리면서 동력이 계속해서 감소하기 때문에, 처음 풀리기 시작할 때와 비교했을 때 태엽의 힘이 약해진다. 이로 인해 태엽 시계는 부정확해졌다. 기술적인 해결 방법을 제시하기 위한 다양한 시도가 이루어졌지만, 태엽 시계는 1700년대 중반이 되기 전까지는 완벽하지 않았다.

1600년대 몇몇 시계 제작자들은 톱니를 움직이기 위해 진자 형태의 흔들리는 추를 사용하기 시작했다. 진자 시계의 추의 길이와 그 끝에 달려 있는 추의 무게는 정확한 수학 공식에 의해 정해졌다. 이러한 움직임을 통해 톱니가 작동하면서 시계에 시간이 기록되었다. 진자 시계는 상당히 정확한 것으로 입증되어 시계 문자판에 분침이 — 그리고 결국에는 시침도 — 추가되었다. 초기 태엽 시계에는 해당되지 않는 일이었다. 하지만 진자 시계는 커다란 시간 측정 장비에만 활용될 수 있었기 때문에 시계 제작자들은 보다 작은 탁상 시계와 손목 시계에 여전히 태엽을 사용했다.

태엽 시계는 1600년대와 1700년대에 인기를 끌었다. 처음에는 작은 시계처럼 보였지만 너무 큰 것으로 판명되자 시간이 흐르면서 평평하고 사람의 주머니에 들어갈 정도의 시계가 만들어졌다. 이러한 시계는 회중 시계로 불렸고, 남성들에게 유행한 반면 여성들에게는 유행하지 않았다. 결국 1800년대 후반, 여성들은 끈이 달린 작은 시계를 손목에 착용했지만 남성들은 이를 착용하지 않았다. 이후 1914년에서 1918년까지 지속된 1차 세계대전 당시 많은 군인들이 손목 시계가 전투 상황에서 실용적이라는 점을 깨닫게 되자 전쟁이 끝난 후 손목 시계의 인기는 급상승했다.

## 멕시코 시티의 아즈텍 사원

콜럼버스가 미대륙을 발견하기 이전에 세 개의 거대한 제국이 존재했다: 아즈텍, 마야, 그리고 잉카이다. 현재의 멕시코 시티 지역을 근거지로 삼았던 아즈텍 제국은 세 제국 중 가장 잔혹했다. 아즈텍 제국은 영토를 확장시켰고 정복을 통해 다른 부족들에게 영향을 미쳤다. 전투 도중 아즈텍의 군인들은 종종 적을 죽이는 대신 그들을 포로로 삼으려고 했다. 그 후 이 포로들은 인간을 제물로 바치는 아즈텍 사원의 의식에서 수천 명 단위로 학살되었다. 이러한 사원 중 가장 규모가 컸던 것은 템플로 마요르로, 이는 아즈텍의 수도인 테노치티틀란의 중심부에 위치해 있었다.

템플로 마요르는 대략 50미터 정도의 높이였고, 테노치티틀란의 넓은 광장의 중앙에 자리잡고 있었다. 가장 높은 위치에는 두 개의 신전이 있었는데, 하나는 아즈텍의 비의 신을 위한 것이었으며, 다른 하나는 아즈텍의 태양과 전쟁의 신을 위한 것이었다. 포로로 잡힌 적들은 두 개의 신전 앞에서 의식을 통해 두 신 모두의 노여움을 달래기 위해 희생되었다. 에르난 코르테스가 지휘하던 스페인 정복자들이 1521년 아즈텍을 정복했을 때 이 사원을 파괴했다. 시간이 흐르면서 사원 부지와 수많은 유물들이 묻히게 되었고, 결국 이곳에 멕시코 시티가 건설되었다. 500년 이상 잊혀졌던 사원의 유적은 1978년 마침내 발굴되었다. 불규칙적으로 뻗어 있는 대도시의 한 가운데에서 수많은 고된 작업과 마주해야 했지만, 발견 이후 고고학자들은 사원 유적지를 발굴하여 다수의 인상적인 아즈텍 유물과 유적들을 찾아냈다.

중요한 발견 중 하나는 템플로 마요르가 그곳에 지어진 유일한 사원이 아니었다는 점이었다. 실제로 일곱 개의 사원 유적지가 발굴되었고, 이 모든 사원들은 가파른 계단이 있는 피라미드 형태였다. 첫 번째 사원은 1325년경에 지어졌고, 이후 아즈텍의 통치자들은 템플로 마요르를 재건하고 확장시킴으로써 자신의 힘과 명성을 과시하고자 했다. 마지막으로 설계된 사원은 — 스페인인들이 파괴시켰는데 — 두 개의 사당을 갖추고 맨 위에 위치해 있던 본당과, 광장 내 존재했던 다수의 소규모 피라미드 및 외부 건물들로 구성되어 있었다.

현재까지 템플로 마요르 유적지에서 발견된 가장 중요한 것은 본당 하부에 위치한 실내 공간이다. 이곳은 아즈텍의 대지의 여신상이 새겨져 있는 거대한 석판으로 덮여 있었다. 석판 아래에는 다층의 실내 공간이 있었는데, 각 층에는 신에게 바치는 공물로 사용된 물품들이 놓여져 있었다. 이러한 물품에는 동물의 사체, 금과 비취로 만든 보석, 그리고 조개껍데기 등이 포함되어 있었다. 희생된 동물은 조류와 포유류, 특히 독수리와 개였다. 가장 낮은 층 중 한 곳에서 고고학자들이 호화로운 보석으로 치장된 개를 발견했는데, 고고학자들은 이를 귀족 견공이라고 명명했다. 처음에 고고학자들은 자신들이 왕의 무덤을 발견했으며 개는 사망한 주인이 사후 여행에서 길동무나 안내자로서의 역할을 시키기 위해 그곳에 있었을 것이라고 생각했다. 하지만 그곳에서 인간의 유골이 발견되지 않았기 때문에, 귀족 견공 유물의 목적은 미스터리로 남아 있다. (고고학자들이 그에 관한 몇 가지 이론을 제시했으나 아직까지 증명된 것은 없다.)

고고학자들에게 있어서, 수백만 명이 거주하는 멕시코 시티의 한 가운데에서 이루어지는 발굴 작업에는 자체적인 문제들이 있었다. 1978년 사원을 발굴하겠다는 결정이 내려졌을 때 해당 위치에는 13개의 현대식 건물들이 들어서 있었다. 멕시코 정부는 건물 소유주에게 보상금을 지급하고 건물을 철거했는데, 이로써 발굴 지점을 정리할 수 있었다. 하지만 발굴 인부들은 하수관, 가스관, 전기선, 그리고 과거 다른 건물들의 잔해 등으로 어려움을 겪어야만 했다. 지난 30년 동안 발굴 작업은 느리지만 꾸준히 진행되었고, 인근의 소규모 박물관을 가득 채울 수 있을 정도의 유물들이 발굴되었다.

멕시코 정부는 템플로 마요르를 발굴하기 위해 상당한 노력을 기울여 왔다. 그러한 이유 중 하나는 많은 멕시코인들이 아즈텍 조상들에 대해 가지고 있는 신비주의적인 애착심 때문이다. 그들에게, 아즈텍인들은 스페인인들이 도착하기 이전의 과거와의 연결성을 상징한다. 하지만 아즈텍인들을 존경해야 하는지, 혹은 심지어 사원을 발굴해야 하는지에 대해서 의문을 제기하는 사람들도 있다. 몇몇 사람들은 템플로 마요르가 악의적인 목적으로 사용되었고, 인신 공회는 도덕적으로 비난받아야 한다고 주장한다. 게다가 사원의 돌들을 화학적으로 분석한 결과, 그곳에 엄청난 양의 피가 뿌려졌다는 점이 입증되었다. 그럼에도 불구하고 다수의 멕시코인들은 아즈텍 사회가 현대인의 정서에 기반하여 판단되어서는 안 된다고 주장하며, 따라서 발굴 작업은 계속되어야 한다고 말한다.

# Actual Test 05

## Passage 1 • Environmental Science —— p.133

### 바하마 제도의 블루홀

플로리다 동부와 쿠바 북부의 여러 섬으로 이루어진 바하마 제도에는 블루홀이라고 알려진 매우 크고 독특한 동굴들이 있다. 블루홀들은 표면부터 너무나 아름다운데, 대부분이 짙은 파란색을 띠고 있다. 이 동굴들은 지표면에서 상당히 깊게 파여 있고 대부분이 바닷물로 채워져 있으나, 가장 윗부분에는 빗물로 이루어진 담수층이 존재한다. 이는 이들이 바다 근처에 위치해 있지만, 정확히 바다에 위치하고 있지는 않기 때문이다. 그 결과로 블루홀에는 독특한 생태계들이 발달해 있다. 이로써 전문가들은 다양한 과학 분야에서 통찰력을 얻을 수 있지만, 잠수부들은 어려움에 직면하게 되는데, 그 이유는 블루홀이 아름다운 동시에 위험하기 때문이다. 그럼에도 불구하고 잠수팀들은, 블루홀이 그다지 오랜 기간 존재하지 않을 수도 있기 때문에, 기꺼이 이러한 위험을 감수하고 블루홀의 깊은 곳을 탐험한다.

바하마의 블루홀은 육지에서 일어난 낙반 현상의 결과물이다. 이들은 일종의 싱크홀로, 입구는 하늘을 향해 있고 지하 통로는 바다와 연결되어 있다. 다수의 블루홀의 깊이는 30미터 정도이나, 깊이가 180미터에 이르는 것도 있는데, 이 블루홀은 세상에서 가장 깊은 수중 동굴 중 하나이다. 지금까지 2,000개 이상의 블루홀이 발견되었지만 단 200개에 대해서만 광범위한 탐사가 이루어졌다. 하늘에서 내리는 비와 아래쪽에 있는 바닷물에 노출되어 있는 블루홀은, 담수층과 해수층 모두를 가지고 있기 때문에, 그 성분이 독특하다. 전형적인 한 블루홀의 경우, 10미터 정도의 최상층이 담수로 구성되어 있다. 반면 10미터에서 30미터 정도의 중간층은 담수와 해수로 구성되어 있고, 그보다 아래에 있는 바닥층은 순전히 해수로만 구성되어 있다.

가장 윗부분에 담수가 있기 때문에 대기 중의 산소는 해수로 이루어진 바닥층까지 도달하지 못한다. 보다 아래쪽에는 생존을 위해 산소에 의존하지 않는 박테리아들이 많다. 이들은 담수층의 바로 아래층을 형성한다. 이들 박테리아는 햇빛을 필요로 하지만 산소는 견디지 못한다. 박테리아들은 자신들이 이용하는 광합성 형태의 부산물로서 황화 수소라는 유독 가스를 만들어 낸다. 극소량의 황화 수소도 인간에게는 치명적이기 때문에 이 가스는 블루홀을 탐사하는 잠수부들에게 가장 큰 위험 요소이다. 잠수부들은 황화 수소층을 빠르게 통과해야만 하는데, 만약 그들이 이곳에 너무 오랫동안 머무르면 황화 수소가 잠수복을 관통해 피부에 침투하고 결국 폐와 혈류에 도달하여 심각한 건강상의 문제가 발생함으로써 사망에 이를 수도 있다.

하지만 블루홀의 독특한 생태계를 통해 과학자들은 수십억 년 전 지구에서 생명체가 어떻게 태어났는지 알 수 있기 때문에 잠수부들은 블루홀 탐사를 계속하고 있다. 산소가 없는 이곳 환경은 지구가 형성될 때의 환경과 유사하다. 태고의 지구에는 독자적으로 존재하는 산소가 없었으며, 처음 10억년 동안 모든 생명체는 바다에 존재했고 이들은 산소를 들이마시지 않았다. 따라서 바하마의 박테리아를 연구함으로써 과학자들은 생명체가 산소를 호흡하지 않는 유기체로부터 생존을 위해 산소를 필요로 하는 유기체로 어떻게 진화했는지에 대해 보다 잘 알 수 있게 될 것으로 기대한다. 또한 블루홀의 생태계를 조사함으로써 과학자들은 산소가 존재하지 않는 행성에서 생명체가 어떻게 진화할 수 있을 것인지 알아낼 수도 있을 것이다. (이 때문에 천문학 분야에 종사하는 사람들도 블루홀에 대한 관심을 가지게 되었다.) 블루홀의 또 다른 장점은 산소가 없는 환경 때문에 화석이 특히 잘 보존된다는 점이다. 지금까지 과학자들은 3,000년 된 쿠바의 멸종 악어 화석, 멸종된 조류의 화석, 그리고 유럽인들이 신대륙에 도착했을 당시 자취를 감췄던 부족민의 유해도 발견했다.

하지만 과학자들은 블루홀에서 생명체가 더 이상 존재하지 않을 수도 있다는 두려움 때문에 서둘러 연구를 마치려고 한다. 해수면이 상승하면 블루홀의 윗부분으로 해수가 유입되기 쉽다. 많은 블루홀들이 바다 근처에 있기 때문에 이들은 곧 물에 잠기게 될 것이다. 이러한 일이 발생하면 블루홀의 생태계에 필요한 환경을 만들어 내는 담수와 해수의 섬세한 균형이 무너지게 될 것이다. 시간이 흐르면서 해수면이 계속 상승한다면 블루홀은 결국 완전한 해수 동굴이 될 것이다.

---

**WORD REMINDER**

deceptively 믿을 수 없이   perilous 위험한, 모험적인   cave-in 낙반, 함몰된 장소   sinkhole 싱크홀, 땅 꺼짐 현상   linger 남아 있다   free-standing 독립된   influx 유입

---

## Passage 2 • Archaeology ———————————— p.140

### 이집트학

이집트학은 고대 이집트 문명의 유적에 대한 연구를 의미한다. 사막 한 가운데에 위치한 이집트의 지리적 위치 때문에, 덥고 건조한 기후가 그곳을 모든 고대 문명 중에서 가장 보존이 잘 된 곳으로 만들어 놓았다. 그곳의 수많은 기념비, 사원, 피라미드, 그리고 무덤은 고대부터 탐험가, 보물 사냥꾼, 그리고 여행객들의 관심을 끌었다. 심지어 고대가 끝나기 전에도 이집트는 연구의 대상이었다. 기원전 484년부터 430년까지 생존했던 그리스 역사가 헤로도투스는 고대 이집트에 관한 글을 썼으며, 다른 무수히 많은 학자들이 수년 간 그를 따라 했다. 하지만 19세기 이후 전문적인 고고학자들이 고대 이집트의 오랜 비밀들을 다수 풀어내기 시작하면서 본격적인 이집트학이 시작되었다.

이집트는 파라오들의 고대 왕국이 쇠퇴한 후 2,000년이 넘는 기간 동안 정복의 대상이었고 여러 정복자들에 의해 점령되었다. 초기의 정복자들은 — 페르시아인, 마케도니아인, 로마인, 그리고 아랍인들은 — 모두 고대 이집트의 유적을 탐사하고 이용했다. 게다가 도굴꾼들은 유물의 보존이나 고대 이집트의 문화 및 역사에 대한 연구보다는 부자가 될 목적으로 보물을 찾으려고 했기 때문에 수 세기 동안, 심지어 현재까지도, 끊임없이 문제가 되어 왔다. 마침내 시간이 흐르면서 고대 이집트의 언어는 잊혀졌고, 다수의 유적들이 모래에 묻혔으며, 오래된 건물 위로 새로운 건물들이 세워지게 되었다.

그 결과, 이집트 역사의 상당 부분은 영원히 사라질 것처럼 보였다. 하지만 1798년 나폴레옹 보나파르트가 이끌었던 프랑스군의 침략으로 상황이 바뀌었다. 이집트 탐사만으로 목적으로 하는 과학팀이 나폴레옹 군대와 동행을 했다. 이 팀의 가장 위대한 발견은 로제타 스톤으로, 이 석판에는 세 개의 언어가 새겨져 있었다: 고대 그리스어, 콥트어, 그리고 상형 문자였다. 로제타 스톤에는 동일한 메시지가 세 가지 언어로 적혀 있었다. 이는 고대 이집트의 상형 문자를 해석하는데 열쇠가 되었다. 두 사람, 영국의 토마스 영과 프랑스의 장 프랑수아 샹폴리옹이 상형 문자의 비밀을 푸는데 중요한 역할을 했다. 그들은 상형 문자의 상징들과 그리스어 및 콥트어 원문을 비교하여 점차 고대의 언어를 읽는 법을 알게 되었다. 이들의 업적으로 이후 학자들은 이집트의 기념비와 사원에 새겨져 있는 수많은 상형 문자를 해독할 수 있게 되었다. 이로써 고대 이집트의 역사 뿐만 아니라 일반적인 고대 사회에 대해서

도 더 잘 알 수 있게 되었다.

1800년대에 많은 탐험가들이 — 주로 유럽과 미국의 탐험가들이 — 이집트의 전 지역을 탐사하면서 이집트학 연구가 활발해졌다. 안타깝게도 많은 이들이 자금이 부족한 아마추어들이었기 때문에 발굴 현장에서는 현지의 저임금의 미숙련 노동자들만을 고용해야만 했다. 그 결과 부주의와 조급함으로 인해 많은 유적지가 훼손되고 유물들이 소실되었다. 하지만 영국의 윌리엄 플린더즈 페트리라는 사람이 이집트학자들의 기준을 높여 놓았다. 비록 아마추어이기는 했지만 그는 탐험을 할 때 세심했으며 고고학에 과학적인 접근법을 적용시켰다. 그는 서두르지 않았고, 발굴 현장의 인부들에게 신중하게 발굴하는 법과 유물을 손상시키지 않고 발굴하는 법을 가르쳤다. (이로써 그는 자신이 발굴한 장소를 보존할 수 있었고, 이는 이집트학이 크게 발전하는데 도움이 되었다.) 플린더즈 페트리의 가장 위대한 업적은 1880년대 초반 기자의 대피라미드를 탐사하여 발굴한 것이었다. 그는 이집트에서 나머지 인생의 대부분을 보냈고, 하워드 카터의 스승이기도 했는데, 하워드 카터는 1922년 가장 유명한 이집트 유적지인 투탕카멘 왕의 무덤을 발굴했다. 플린더즈 페트리는 종종 현대 이집트학의 아버지이자 과학적인 고고학 조사법의 아버지로 간주된다. 그가 마련한 기준들은 자신이 적용하기 시작한 때부터 엄격하게 지켜졌고 개선되어 왔다.

대부분의 현대 이집트학자들은 이집트인이 아니라 프랑스인, 영국인, 그리고 미국인이기 때문에, 이들이 발굴한 많은 유물들은 각자의 고국에 있는 박물관에 전시되어 있다. 이집트가 외국에 점령되어 있지는 않으므로 이집트 사람들은 자신의 고대 조상들에 대한 권리를 재차 주장하기 시작했다. 외국인 고고학자들은 여전히 발굴을 허가 받고 있지만, 이집트 사람들은 해외에 있는 박물관들과 수집가들에게 수많은 유물들을 반환하라는 압력을 행사하고 있다. 일부 유물들이 반환되기는 했으나 다수의 유물들은 해외에 있다. 이집트 사람들은 이에 대응하여 이집트에서 발굴을 원하는 몇몇 외국인 고고학자들에게 허가를 내 주지 않고 있다. 이로써 최근 몇 년 동안 고고학적 발굴의 속도가 다소 느려지게 되었다.

---

**WORD REMINDER**

myriad 무수히 많은   emulate 모방하다   earnest 진지한   for the sake of ~을 위해서   hieroglyphics 상형 문자   negligence 부주의, 태만   meticulous 세심한   rigorously 엄격히, 엄밀하게   reassert 거듭 주장하다

---

## Passage 3 • Astronomy ———————————— p.148

### 외태양계

태양계 내부는 태양, 8개의 행성, 행성의 위성, 그리고 태양과 행성 사이를 도는 수없이 많은 기타 천체들로 구성된다. 또한 태양계 마지막 행성의 바깥쪽 공간에도 수많은 천체들이 존재하는데, 이곳은 외태양계라고 불린다. 이러한 천체에는 몇몇 왜행성 및 이들의 위성, 혜성, 그리고 크기가 너무 작아서 둘 중 어느 것으로도 분류할 수 없는, 얼음과 암석으로 이루어진 물체들이 포함된다.

태양의 중력이 미치는 모든 천체는 태양 주위를 돌기 때문에 태양계의 경계는 태양의 중력이 더 이상 미치지 않는 곳이다. 지금까지 가장 먼 곳에서 태양 주위를 도는 것으로 발견된 천체는 태양으로부터 대략 68천문단위(AU) 떨어진 곳에 있지만, 일부 천문학자들은 태양의 중력이 그보다 더 먼

곳까지 미칠 것이라고 생각한다. 1AU는 지구에서 태양까지의 거리로, 대략 1억 5천만 킬로미터이다. 천문학자들은 이처럼 멀리 떨어진 곳에서 태양 주위를 도는 천체들이 주로 존재하는 우주 공간을 카이퍼 벨트라고 부른다.

태양계의 일부이면서 눈에 보이는 천체 중 가장 멀리 떨어져 있는 것은 에리스로, 에리스는 가장 큰 왜행성이자 태양으로부터 63AU 떨어진 곳에 있다. 에리스는 태양으로부터 너무 멀리 떨어져 있기 때문에 이 행성이 태양 주위를 도는데 지구 시간으로 560년이 걸린다. 천문학자들은 지금까지 5개의 왜행성을 발견했는데, 이들은 실제 행성으로 간주되기 위한 기준에 부합되지 않는 커다란 천체이기 때문에 그러한 이름이 붙여졌다. 한때 아홉 번째 행성으로 불렸던 명왕성은 2006년 왜행성으로 분류 등급이 낮춰졌고, 현재는 외태양계에 속해 있다. 하지만 명왕성이 항상 태양으로부터 멀리 떨어진 곳에 있는 것은 아니며, 타원형인 궤도로 인해 명왕성은 때때로 태양에서 여덟 번째로 멀리 떨어져 있는 해왕성보다도 태양과 가까운 곳에 있게 된다. 명왕성과 에리스 이외의 왜행성으로는 세레스, 하우메아, 그리고 마케마케가 있다. 세레스는 화성과 목성의 사이에 있는 소행성대에 위치해 있다. 반면 하우메아는 태양으로부터 대략 43AU 떨어진 곳에 있고 공전 주기가 285년인 반면, 마케마케는 태양으로부터 약 46AU 떨어진 곳에 있으며 공전 주기가 310년이다. 멀리 떨어져 있는 왜행성들은 모두 크기가 작고 암석으로 이루어져 있으며 차갑고, 메탄으로 추정되는, 언 상태의 물질로 덮여 있다.

명왕성, 하우메아, 그리고 마케마케는 모두 카이퍼 벨트 내에 위치해 있다. 천문학자들은 카이퍼 벨트가 태양으로부터 30AU에서 50AU 거리에 떨어져 있는 도넛 모양의 영역이라는 이론을 제시한다. 이 벨트에는 대략 70,000개 정도의 천체가 포함되어 있으며, 이들 중 다수는 얼음 덩어리에 불과하다. 천문학자들은 이러한 천체들이 수십억 년 전 태양계가 탄생할 때 사용된 물질의 잔해일 것으로 생각한다. 혜성들은 태양의 주위를 돌면서 끊임없이 카이퍼 벨트에 진입했다가 빠져나간다. 혜성의 일부 궤도들은 길이가 매우 길고 불규칙하지만, 핼리 혜성과 같이 어느 정도의 규칙성을 예측할 수 있는 비교적 짧은 궤도를 가지고 있는 혜성들도 있다. (예컨데 핼리 혜성이 태양 주위를 한 바퀴 도는데 75년이 걸린다.)

에리스에 대해 말하면, 일부 천문학자들이 에리스가 카이퍼 벨트의 안쪽에 존재한다고 주장하기는 하지만, 에리스는 카이퍼 벨트의 약간 바깥쪽 부분에 위치해 있다. 하지만 에리스가 오트르 구름 내에 있다고 믿는 천문학자들도 있다. 오트르 구름은 이론상 태양으로부터 50,000AU 떨어진 곳까지 걸쳐 있는 영역이다. 네덜란드의 천문학자인 얀 오르트가 1950년대에 처음으로 이러한 지역이 존재한다는 이론을 제시했다. 오르트는 모든 혜성이 반드시 어딘가에서 생성된다고 믿었기 때문에 혜성이 생성되는 영역에 대한 이론을 세웠다. 그 후 혜성들은 중력에 의해 본래의 궤도에서 벗어나 태양계 내부로 들어오게 되었다. 오르트 구름에 존재할지도 모르는 천체들은 대부분 너무나 작고 멀리 떨어져 있어서 현재의 망원경으로는 볼 수가 없다.

사실 태양 주위를 공전하는 장주기 혜성들은 반드시 어딘가로부터 나오는 것이기 때문에 오르트 구름이 실제로 존재한다는 믿음은 주로 가설에 바탕을 둔 것이다. 오르트 구름 너머에는 광활하고도 공허한 우주가 놓여 있으며, 이 공간은 태양계로부터 수 광년 떨어져 있는 다른 항성들을 향해 뻗어 있다. 하지만 태양의 중력이 오르트 구름을 지나 얼마나 먼 곳까지 작용하는지는 확실하지 않다. 현대 과학이 기술적인 발전을 이루기 전까지는 그에 대한 답을 얻지 못할 것이다.

---

**WORD REMINDER**

celestial 천체의     innumerable 수없이 많은     realm 영역
moniker 이름, 별명     criterion 표준, 기준     asteroid 소행성
theoretically 이론적으로     divert 방향을 바꾸다, 전환하다

---

## Passage 1 · Zoology ———————————— p.157

### 흰꼬리사슴의 뿔

미 대륙에서 가장 크기가 큰 포유류 중 하나가 흰꼬리사슴이다. 주로 미국에 서식하지만 활동 영역은 캐나다, 멕시코, 중미, 그리고 남미의 일부 지역까지 걸쳐져 있다. 북미 지역에 서식하는 흰꼬리사슴의 개체수는 대략 2천 5백만에 이르는 반면, 다른 지역에서는 그 수가 더 적다. 수컷은 성장하면 몸무게가 120킬로그램까지, 그리고 어깨까지의 신장은 1.3미터까지 성장하는 경우가 많다. 흰꼬리사슴은 그 이름을 가져다 준 기다란 흰색 꼬리 외에도 머리에 달린 뿔로도 잘 알려져 있다.

흰꼬리사슴은 사슴과 동물에 속하는데, 사슴과에는 엘크, 무스, 그리고 카리부 등이 속해 있다. 사향노루와 고라니를 제외한 다른 모든 종의 사슴들과 마찬가지로 흰꼬리사슴에게도 뿔이 있다. 이들 뿔이 때때로 소, 양, 그리고 염소와 같은 동물들의 뿔과 같은 것으로 잘못 언급되는 경우도 있지만, 사슴뿔은 그러한 뿔들과 다르다. 사슴의 머리에서 자라는 뿔은 뼈로 이루어져 있으며 주로 칼슘과 인으로 구성되어 있다. 흥미롭게도 사슴뿔은 탈락성이기 때문에 봄과 여름에 자란 후 겨울에 빠지는데, 그 다음해의 봄과 여름에 뿔이 다시 자라기 전까지 사슴은 뿔이 없는 상태로 지낸다.

하지만 모든 흰꼬리사슴에게 뿔이 있는 것은 아니다. 예를 들면 암컷 흰꼬리사슴에게 뿔이 있는 경우는 극히 드물다. 뿔이 달려 있는 암컷 흰꼬리사슴에 대한 기록이 존재하기는 하나, 이들은 모두 변종이었다. 실제로 사슴과에 속하는 모든 동물들 중에서 오직 암컷 카리부에서만 정기적으로 뿔이 자란다. 암컷에게 뿔이 없는 이유는 본질적으로 진화 때문이라는 설명이 타당해 보인다. 수사슴은 주로 암컷을 유혹하기 위해, 그리고 짝짓기 경쟁 시 다른 수사슴들을 공격하기 위해 뿔을 사용한다. (또한 늑대, 코요테, 그리고 다른 포식자들로부터 스스로를 보호하기 위해 뿔을 사용할 수도 있다.) 두 경우 모두 암컷이 하는 행동과는 관련이 없는 것이어서 뿔에 대한 명백한 필요성이 없기 때문에 암컷 흰꼬리사슴에게는 사실상 뿔이 자라지 않는다.

일부 수컷 흰꼬리사슴들에게 뿔이 없는 경우도 있다. 일반적으로 수컷 흰꼬리사슴의 뿔은 생후 10개월이 되면 자라기 시작한다. 이후 매년마다 새로운 뿔이 자라며 이는 겨울에 빠진다. 하지만 때때로 사슴이 서식하는 지역에 먹이가 충분하지 않을 수도 있다. 이러한 경우, 사슴뿔은 매우 느리게 자라거나 전혀 자라지 않을 수도 있다. 4월부터 뿔이 매일 0.6센티미터씩 자라기 때문에 수사슴은 평소보다 많은 양의 양분을 필요로 한다. 한 달 후에는 뿔이 갈라져 각각의 가지가 독립적으로 자라게 된다. 대부분의 사슴의 경우, 뿔은 생기기 시작한지 4개월 이내에 완전히 자란다. 그럼에도 불구하고 가뭄, 기근, 혹은 먹이를 감소시키는 기타 문제들이 발생한 지역에서는 상당히 많은 수의 수사슴들에게 뿔이 자라지 않을 수도 있다.

사슴이 다리를 다치면 뿔의 성장 역시 영향을 받을 수 있다. 대부분의 수사슴의 경우, 한쪽 뒷다리를 다치면 반대쪽 뿔이 기형적인 형태로 자란다. 따라서 오른쪽 뒷다리를 다치면 왼쪽 뿔이 비정상적인 모습을 보이게 된다. 이러한 기형은 일반적으로 사슴의 상처가 치료된 후에도 매년 나타난다. 또한 머리에 상처를 입은 사슴의 경우 뿔의 성장이 저해되어 뿔의 길이가 건강한 사슴의 뿔보다 훨씬 더 짧아질 수도 있다. 마지막으로, 사슴의 뿔은 가끔씩 상처를 입기도 하는데, 예컨대 다른 사슴과 싸우는 도중 뿔이 부러질 수도 있다. 이러한 경우 사슴뿔은 거의 항상 이듬해에 다시 자란다.

마지막으로 모든 사슴들에게 뿔이 없는 기간이 있다. 암컷 사슴은 보통

11월쯤 새끼를 가질 수 있게 되며 그 후 몇 주간 짝짓기 시간이 이어진다. 짝짓기 시기가 끝나자마자 수사슴의 테스토스테론 수치가 감소하여 1월 중순에는 이들의 뿔이 빠지게 된다. 뿔이 빠지는데 걸리는 시간은 대략 2주에서 3주 정도이다. 그때부터 수사슴의 뿔이 다시 자라는 4월까지는, 수컷과 암컷 모두에게 뿔이 없기 때문에, 암수를 구분하는 일이 어려워진다.

## Passage 2 • History of Technology ───── p.165

### 헬리콥터

헬리콥터는 수직으로 이착륙이 가능하고 고정된 위치에서 공중에 떠 있을 수 있다는 점에서 대다수의 비행기와는 차이가 있다. 이러한 특징들 때문에 헬리콥터는 민간인 및 군인들의 삶에서 중요한 역할을 하고 있다. 헬리콥터는 무거운 무게를 들어올릴 수 있는 힘과 안정성이 요구되는 상황에서 사람과 사물을 비좁고 혼잡한 장소로 옮기는데 사용된다. 전시에는 무기를 장착한 장비가 되고, 군인들을 전장으로 신속히 보내고, 물자를 재보급하고, 부상당한 병사들을 후송한다. 또한 수색 구조 장비의 역할도 해서 험난한 지형과 화재가 난 건물, 그리고 침몰하는 선박에서 사람들의 생명을 구하기도 한다. 이 독특한 기기의 능력은, 완성되기까지 여러 해가 걸린, 설계 및 특성에서 비롯된다.

인간은 고대부터 하늘을 나는 꿈을 가지고 있었지만 현대가 되어서야 비로소 비행이 가능한 실용적인 기기가 발명되었다. 헬리콥터는 마지막으로 개발된 비행 장치 중 하나이다. 헬리콥터는 기구, 글라이더, 그리고 비행기가 발명된 후에 만들어졌는데, 그 이유는 수직으로 이착륙을 하고, 직선 비행을 하며, 공중에 떠 있을 수 있는 기기를 만드는 것이 어려웠기 때문이다. 20세기에 많은 발명가들이 — 주로 미국과 유럽의 발명가들이 — 실용적인 헬리콥터를 개발하기 위해 노력했다. 몇몇 모델들은 가까스로 이륙하여 몇 분 동안 비행할 수 있었으나, 대부분은 불안정해서 비행을 유지하는 경우보다 추락하는 경우가 더 많았다.

그럼에도 불구하고 1930년대 중반에 안정성의 문제가 해결되었다. 1936년 독일의 항공기술자 하인리히 포케가 최초의 실용적인 헬리콥터를 발명했는데, 이는 1940년대 제 2차 세계대전 중 제한적이지만 실전에 사용되었다. 하지만 최초의 대형 헬리콥터는 1942년 러시아계 미국인 항공기 설계사였던 이고르 시코르스키가 발명한 것으로 인정되고 있다. 그의 기기는 오늘날 대부분의 헬리콥터에서 흔히 볼 수 있는 메인 싱글 로터와 보다 작은 꼬리 회전 날개를 사용했다. 시코르스키는 미군을 위해 헬리콥터를 개발했기 때문에, 처음에는 대부분의 헬리콥터가 민간인 업무보다는 군사적인 임무를 위해 사용되었다.

헬리콥터는 1950년부터 1953년까지 계속된 한국 전쟁에서 처음으로 명성을 얻게 되었다. 한국에서 헬리콥터는 주로 정찰, 추락한 조종사의 수색 및 구조 활동, 그리고 부상병들을 전장에서 진료소로 신속하게 후송하는 일에 사용되었다. 부상병들이 적절한 치료를 받기까지 걸렸던 시간이 상당히 단축

되었기 때문에, 마지막으로 언급된 임무가 한국 전쟁 당시 헬리콥터의 가장 중요한 임무였다. 후송 시간은 1965년부터 1973년까지 더욱 감소했는데, 이 시기는 미국이 베트남 전쟁에 참전했던 시기였다. 이 기간 동안 부상자들은 종종 30분 이내에 전장에서 신속하게 구출되어 현대적인 병원으로 후송되었다.

베트남 전쟁 당시 헬리콥터는 다른 임무를 맡기도 했다. 헬리콥터는 주로 병력과 장비를 수송하는 수단으로 활용되어 인력, 무기, 그리고 장비를 필요로 하는 곳이 있으면 어디든지 이를 공수해 주었다. 하지만 헬리콥터는 소음이 심했기 때문에 보통 적들은 보기도 전에 그 소리를 들었고, 헬리콥터는 대공포에 취약했다. 미군은 베트남 전쟁 당시 수천 대의 헬리콥터를 잃었다. (실제로 연구에 따르면 베트남에서 사용된 대략 5,000대에서 12,000대 이상의 미군 헬리콥터가 파괴되었다.) 이러한 약점은 여전히 전쟁에 사용되는 헬리콥터의 중대한 문제이기는 하지만, 현대적인 헬리콥터일수록 보다 우수한 장갑으로 방어 체계를 갖추고 있으며 공중 및 지상의 적을 상대할 수 있는 보다 우수한 무기들을 보유하고 있다.

헬리콥터 산업의 초창기는 군용 헬리콥터가 지배했으나 민간 헬리콥터들도, 특히 미국의 벨 항공사를 비롯한 기업에 의해 서서히 개발되었다. 이 헬리콥터들은 대부분 두 개의 좌석을 갖추고 있었고 수송 능력이 제한적이었다. 초창기 대부분의 헬리콥터들은 — 군용과 민간용 모두 — 휘발유로 가동되는 내연 기관에 의존하고 있었다. 이후 1950년대에 엔지니어들이 내연 기관보다 가볍고 강력한 헬리콥터용 터빈 기관을 개발했다. 이로써 설계자들은 보다 크고 보다 강력한 헬리콥터를 제작할 수 있게 되었다.

시간이 지나면서, 상당히 많은 양의 물자를 수송할 수 있는 헬리콥터와 악천후에도 비행이 가능한 헬리콥터를 포함하여, 매우 다양한 다목적 헬리콥터들이 전 세계적으로 제작되기 시작했다. 오늘날 이러한 헬리콥터들은 민간 부문에서 수많은 목적으로 사용되고 있다. 일부 헬리콥터는 고층 건물의 건설, 산불 진화, 위험에 처한 사람들의 구조, 범죄자의 수색 및 체포, 그리고 교통 상황 및 뉴스를 보도하는데 사용된다. 현재 헬리콥터는 사람들의 삶에서 필수적인 부분이며, 헬리콥터가 발명되기 이전에는 사실상 불가능했던 일들을 수행하고 있다.

## Passage 3 • Biology ───── p.172

### 진화론의 경쟁 이론

1859년 찰스 다윈은 중대한 책인 *종의 기원*을 출판하여 생물이 점차적으로 어떻게 진화하는지에 대한 그의 이론을 자세히 밝혔다. 다윈은 자연학자로서 자신이 관찰한 점들 때문에 그가 쓴 내용이 옳다고 확신했지만, 종이 변화하는 실제 과정을 설명하는 것에는 어려움을 겪었다. 이러한 설명의 부족과 명확한 근거의 부재는, 점진적인 진화가 발생하는 대신, 하나의 종이 다른 종으로 즉각적으로 변화한다는 점을 암시했다. 다윈의 시대 이전에는 또 다른 진화론자였던 장 바티스트 라마르크가 종들은 자연 발생적으로 만들어지고 일련의 단계를 통해 진화한다고 주장했다. 결국 과학적인 연구 덕분에 진

화가 어떻게 일어나는지를 설명해 주는 유전의 과정이 밝혀지게 되었다.

다윈의 진화론은 자연 선택에 중점을 두고 있다. 모든 종들은 자손을 낳음으로써 살아남을 수 있도록 만들어졌다고 가정한다. 자원이 한정된 환경에서는 생존 능력이 있는 자손들만 살아 남아 이들이 다시 자손을 낳게 된다. 따라서, 이후의 각 세대에서, 생존 개체들은 종 내에서 가장 강한 구성원으로 자신의 능력을 다음 세대에게 물려 준다. 시간이 흐르면서 새로운 종이 ― 보다 잘 적응하고 생존할 수 있는 종이 ― 진화한다. 환경이 변화하는 경우에 특히 그러한데, 이는 새로운 환경에 적응할 수 있는 생물만이 살아남을 수 있기 때문이다. 더디지만 꾸준한 변화의 과정 때문에 이 자연 선택 이론은 때때로 점진론으로 불리기도 한다.

자연 선택이 어떻게 이루어지는지 설명해 주는 명백한 증거가 없었으므로 다윈의 자연 선택 이론은 관찰과 추론 모두에 바탕을 두고 있었다. 이 때문에 다윈은 공격을 받았다. 예를 들어 일부 비판가들은 두 종 사이의 연관성을 암시하는 화석이 없음에도 불구하고 화석 기록상 종 전체가 사라진 후 그와 유사한 ― 몇 가지 측면에서 차이가 있기는 하지만 ― 종이 등장했다는 점을 지적했다. 한 가지 예로 육상 동물과 고래를 연결시키는 화석은 존재하지 않았다. 다윈 자신은 고래가 육상 동물로부터 진화했다고 확신했지만, 화석 기록을 통해 이를 증명할 수는 없었다. (고래의 조상이 한때 육지를 걸어 다녔다는 점은 수십 년 후 과학적 방법이 발전함으로써 입증되었다.)

다윈이 자신의 점진론을 증명할 수 없게 되자 경쟁 이론에 힘이 실리게 되었는데, 이 이론은 모든 생명체가 자연 발생적이며 신비스러운 힘을 통해 지구의 원소들로 만들어진다고 주장한다. 이 이론의 기원은 수천 년 전 고대 그리스의 아리스토텔레스까지 거슬러 올라가며, 역사를 통틀어 지지자들을 갖고 있었다. 이 이론을 가장 열렬히 지지했던 사람 중 한 명이 1744년에 출생해서 1829년에 사망한 장 바티스트 라마르크였다.

라마르크는 자연 발생설을 믿었지만, 또한 종들은 일련의 계획된 단계를 거치면서 진화한다고 생각했다. 라마르크에 따르면, 종들은 자연 발생에 의해 단순한 생명체로 시작하지만 몸 속에 있는 자연적인, 생명 활동을 증진시키는 체액으로 인해 보다 복잡한 생물로 변화하게 된다. 이러한 체액들이 새로운 장기를 만들어냈고, 시간이 흐르면서 이들은 보다 복잡해졌는데, 이로써 생물의 진화가 한층 더 진행되었다. 또한 라마르크의 이론은 두 번째 힘이 살아 있는 종에 영향을 미친다고 주장한다. 이것은 적응력으로, 이로 인해 종들은 환경 변화에 적응하여 살아남을 수 있었다. 일부 종은 적응할 수 있었기 때문에 살아남았던 반면, 이러한 적응력이 없어서 ― 혹은 적응력은 있었지만 적절히 사용하지 못해서 ― 변화하지 못해 결국 멸종된 종들도 있었다.

라마르크가 생명을 창조시키는 힘으로 자연 발생을 지지했다는 점은 그의 이론의 중대한 약점이었다. 하지만 변화의 메커니즘에 관한 그의 생각에는 잘못된 부분이 많지 않기 때문에 그의 이론을 완전히 무시할 수는 없다. 그의 이론과 다윈의 이론 모두에서 생명체가 유전적 수준에서 어떻게 작동하는가에 대한 이해는 빠져 있다. 모든 생명체 내부에는 자신을 변화시킬 수 있는 생명력, 바로 유전자가 존재한다. 유전자는 생물체의 특성을 결정하며 부모로부터 자손에게 전달된다. 생물은 이러한 유전적 특성을 부모로부터 물려받고 다음 세대의 자손에게 물려 줌으로써 진화한다. 시간이 지나면서, 특히 새로운 환경에 적응해야만 하는 경우, 종의 특성은 변화할 것이다. 하지만 라마르크와 다윈 시대 이후에야 발견된 유전자에 대한 지식이 없었기 때문에 각각의 이론에는 모두 결함이 있었다.

**WORD REMINDER**

seminal 중요한, 독창적인    instantaneous 순간적인    postulate 가정하다, 주장하다    spontaneous generation 자연 발생    inquiry 연구, 탐구, 조사    posit 가정하다    lend weight to ～에 힘을 실어 주다, ～을 뒷받침하다    erroneous 잘못된, 틀린    outright 완전한    dismissal 묵살, 일축

## Passage 4 • Economics ——————————— p.179

### 동남아시아의 경제적 성공

세계에서 경제적으로 가장 활기찬 지역 중 하나는 홍콩, 마카오, 베트남, 캄보디아, 라오스, 미얀마, 싱가폴, 태국, 필리핀, 그리고 인도네시아를 포함하고 있는 동남아시아이다. 이 국가들은 한때 유럽의 식민 제국에 부를 제공해 주었지만, 이들 중 몇몇 국가들은 지난 50년 동안 탄탄한 경제를 구축했다. 저임금 노동, 풍부한 천연 자원, 그리고 세계 시장에 대한 접근성을 통해 이들은 향후 수십 년 동안 지속적인 성장을 누릴 준비가 되어 있다.

동남아시아는 16세기 유럽인들에 의해 처음 탐험되었고, 많은 사람들이 그곳에 남아 진귀한 향신료 및 기타 이국적인 제품들을 자신의 고국으로 수출하기 위해 무역항을 건설했다. 19세기 무렵 네덜란드인, 포르투갈인, 영국인, 스페인인, 그리고 프랑스인들 모두가 그곳에 식민지를 건설했다. 네덜란드인들은 인도네시아 제도를 차지했고, 포르투갈인들은 마카오에 무역항을 건설했으며, 영국인들은 싱가폴과 홍콩에 무역항을 건설했고, 스페인인들은 필리핀을 차지했으며, 프랑스인들은 오늘날의 베트남, 라오스, 그리고 캄보디아에 해당하는 지역에 광활한 식민지를 건설했다. 19세기 후반 미국의 식민지였던 필리핀을 제외하면 이 지역은 1945년에 끝난 제2차 세계 대전 이후가 될 때까지 유럽인들의 지배하에 있었다. 태국만이 유일하게 외세의 지배로부터 독립해 있었다. 하지만, 대부분의 다른 지역들과 마찬가지로, 태국 역시 제 2차 세계대전 중 일본군에게 점령되었다.

경제적으로 이러한 식민지들은 향신료, 고무, 그리고 석유와 같은 원자재들의 공급원이자 저임금 노동력의 원천이었기 때문에, 유럽 제국들에게 중요한 존재였다. 싱가폴과 홍콩은 동남아시아의 가장 큰 항구가 되었고, 전 세계의 상품들을 내륙으로 보낼 수 있는 진입점 역할을 담당했다. 대부분의 지역 경제는 농업에 기반했는데, 이는 대다수의 인구가 자급자족 상태에 있었기 때문이었다. 지배자에 따라 각 식민지들이 겪은 일은 서로 달랐지만, 외국의 식민지 개척자들이 가능한 많은 부를 얻기 위해 식민지를 착취했다는 점은 명백했다.

현지인들이 식민지 통치자들의 탄압을 폭넓게 인식하게 되자 그에 대한 한 가지 결과로서 거의 모든 지역에서 독립 운동이 일어났다. 대부분의 독립 운동은 성공을 거두었고, 2차 대전 후 식민지들은 하나씩 독립국이 되었다. 유일한 예외가 홍콩과 마카오로, 이들은 20세기 말 중국으로 반환되기 전까지 유럽의 식민지로 남아 있었다. 대부분의 지역에서 식민지 지배국으로부터 식민지로의 권력 이양은 평화적이었다. 이러한 신생 독립국들 중 베트남을 제외한 대부분의 지역에서 민주주의가 실행되었는데, 베트남은 오랜 유혈 투쟁 끝에 공산주의 국가가 되었다.

독립 후 모든 국가들이 빈곤 상태에 놓여 있었지만, 예전 식민지 지배자였던 국가들과는 무역 파트너로서 강력한 유대 관계를 유지했다. 동남아시아 국가들은 농업에 크게 의존했으나 다양한 산업에 진출함으로써 자국 경제를

발전시켰다. 그 결과 이들은 전자 제품, 섬유 제품, 그리고 자동차 제조의 중심지가 되었다. (가장 규모가 큰 몇몇 제조업체들은 세계적인 기업이 되기도 했다.) 또한 많은 국가들이 스스로를 관광지로 상품화하는데 성공해서 아름다운 풍경, 모래 사장이 있는 해변, 그리고 종교적이고 역사적인 유적지를 보러 오는 관광객들로부터 매년 수백만 혹은 수천만 달러를 벌어들였다.

몇몇 국가에서는 이러한 다양한 산업들이 서로 결합되어 강력한 경제가 만들어졌다. 경제력에 보다 자신이 있었던 다수의 동남아시아 국가들은 동남아시아 국가 연합(ASEAN)이라는 경제 블록을 조직했다. ASEAN의 주요 목표 중 하나는 지역 경제의 성장을 촉진시키는 것이다. 회원국 중 인도네시아의 경제 규모가 가장 크며, 인도네시아는 전 세계에서 가장 경제가 발전한 국가들의 모임인 G-20에 소속된 유일한 ASEAN 국가이기도 하다.

동남아시아 경제 성장에서 문제가 되는 측면 중 하나는 노동자들에 대한 처우와 관련된 것이다. 대부분의 고용인들은 유럽 및 북미 지역 국가들의 노동자들 보다 상당히 낮은 금액의 임금을 받는다. 예를 들어 미국 공장 노동자들은 보통 싱가폴 공장 노동자들보다 시간당 3배의 임금을 받고, 필리핀 공장 노동자들보다는 20배가 넘는 임금을 받는다. 따라서 수많은 해외 기업들이 생산 기지를 동남아시아로 이전시켰다. 이로써 제조 원가를 절감하고 이윤을 증대시킬 수 있다. 안타깝게도, 그곳에서 생산된 제품 중 일부는 아동 노동의 결과이다. 또한 다수의 노동자들이 열악한 작업 환경에서 장시간의 노동을 하고 있다. 하지만 많은 국가들이 이러한 부정적인 측면을 감소시키고, 자국민들에게 노동을 더욱 안전하고 많은 수익을 가져다 주는 것으로 만들기 위해 모든 노력을 다하고 있다.

# Actual Test 07

## Passage 1 • Environmental Science —————— p.189

### 대평원

북미 지역의 서쪽에는 파란 하늘과 이글대는 태양 아래에 광활한 대지가 펼쳐져 있다. 이곳이 대평원 지대로, 이곳은 세상에서 가장 넓은 평원 중 하나이다. 대평원은 캐나다의 북쪽에서 시작해 남쪽으로 미국을 가로지른 후 멕시코까지 뻗어 있다. 그리고 미시시피 강에서 시작되어 서쪽으로는 로키 산맥까지 뻗어 있다. 한때 수많은 아메리카 인디언 부족과 수백만 마리의 들소들의 고향이었던 대평원은 세계에서 가장 넓은 곡물 생산지이다. 하지만 이러한 농경으로 인해 대평원의 생태계는 매년 장기간 가뭄의 위협에 직면하면서 불안정한 상태에 놓이게 되었다.

수백만 년 전 대평원 지대는 거대한 내해의 바닥이었다. 시간이 흐르면서 바다는 사라지고 비옥한 토지가 남게 되었다. 하지만 대평원이 완전한 평지는 아니다. 대신 뚜렷한 구릉지, 고원, 드문드문 보이는 언덕, 그리고 나무로 이루어진 지역이 존재한다. 대평원의 대부분의 지역은 너무나 건조해서 넓은 숲이 자리잡을 수 없고, 추측하건대 과거에 산불이 발생해서 한때 존재했던 대규모의 삼림은 모두 파괴되었을 것이다. 강과 시내가 대평원을 통과하지만, 커다란 호수는 존재하지 않는다.

대평원에는 뚜렷이 구분되는 세 개의 지역이 존재한다. 강수량과 서식하는 야생 풀들의 높이에 따라 구분된다. 로키 산맥 가까이에 위치한 대평원 지대의 서쪽은 강수량이 적기 때문에 그 결과 풀이 낮게 자라며 흙이 푸석푸석하다. 이곳의 일부 지역은 강수량이 너무나 적어서 방목만 가능하고 경작은 불가능하다. 로키 산맥에서 동쪽으로 더 가면 나오는 중부 지역에서는 강수량이 증가하여 짧은 풀들과 긴 풀들이 같이 자란다. 마지막으로 대평원의 동쪽 지역은 가장 습한 곳으로, 이곳 풀들이 가장 길고 흙도 가장 단단하다.

대략 1만 2천년 전 인류가 도달하기 전까지 대평원 지대는 거대땅늘보, 매머드, 그리고 검치호랑이 등을 포함한 수많은 동물군의 서식지였다. 하지만 최초의 인류가 몸집이 큰 동물들을 대부분 멸종시켜서 이들의 뼈를 제외하고는 그 흔적이 남아 있지 않다. 수천 년 동안 이 아메리카 원주민들은 대평원에서 수렵채집민으로서 살면서, 그곳을 돌아다니던 방대한 들소 떼로부터 필요한 것들을 상당량 얻었다. 따라서 이들 아메리카 원주민들은 동부 및 남부의 부족들과 달리 농사를 짓지 않았다. 하지만 이후 유럽의 탐험가들과 미국인 사냥꾼, 목동, 그리고 농부들이 도착하자 대평원은 변화를 겪게 되었다. 사냥으로 인해 들소는 거의 멸종되었고 토지가 경작되기 시작했다.

1800년대에 수만 명의 이민자들이 미국의 서부와 캐나다로 이주하기 시작해 땅을 개간하고 새로운 삶을 살기 시작했다. 비가 자주 내리던 시기에는 번성했지만, 대평원에 비가 자주 내렸던 것은 아니다. 때때로 강우량이 부족했던 시기에는 흙이 굳어지고 건조해져서 바람에 날아갔다. 바람을 비껴가게 할 장애물이 거의 없기 때문에 대평원의 바람은 더 오래 지속되고 더 강한 경향이 있다. 최악의 가뭄이 1920년대에서 1930년대까지 지속되어 대평원의 남부 지역 중 상당 부분은 사실상 사막이 되었다. (이때는 또한 미국에서 대공황이 발생했던 시기로, 이 지역의 고통은 막대했다.) 거대한 모래 폭풍이 농장을 파괴했고, 많은 이들이 농사를 포기하고 떠나야만 했다. 서서히 복구되기는 했지만, 자연의 힘에 달린 일이기 때문에, 이 지역은 항상 위험에 취약한 상태에 놓여 있다.

'더스트볼'이라고 불리는 장기간의 가뭄 이후로 대평원에서 농사에 종사하는 사람의 수는 감소하고 있다. 그럼에도 불구하고 이곳에서 경작되는 밀,

옥수수, 보리, 귀리, 수수, 그리고 호밀의 양은 전 세계 생산량의 1/4을 차지하는 것으로 생각된다. 이는 현대적인 농법, 발달된 농기구, 그리고 광범위한 관개 시설 덕분이다. 이러한 관개 시설에 사용되는 대부분의 물은 지표면 아래에 위치한 지하수로부터 나온다. 하지만 이러한 점으로 인해 일부 사람들은 우려를 표하고 있는데, 그 이유는 지하수를 너무 많이 사용하면 다음 번 장기간의 가뭄이 '더스트볼'보다 더욱 심각해질 것이라고 두려워하기 때문이다.

> **WORD REMINDER**
> precarious 불안한   devoid ~이 없는   fauna 동물군   sloth 나무늘보   saber-toothed tiger 검치호랑이   deflect 비껴가게 하다   ravage 파괴하다   sorghum 수수   rye 호밀

## Passage 2 • Education —————————— p.196

### 교육의 경제학

전 세계 국가들 간의 경제 불균형은 심각하다. 가장 강력한 국가들, 예컨대 북미, 유럽, 그리고 아시아의 일부 지역에서 찾을 수 있는 국가에는 최고 수준의 교육을 받은 노동자들이 있다. 반면 경제가 다른 나라에 비해 뒤쳐져 있는 국가들의 교육 시스템에서는 대다수 시민들이 기초 수준 이상의 교육을 받지 못하고 있다. (이러한 국가 중 다수는 아프리카, 아시아 일부 지역, 그리고 중앙 아메리카에서 찾을 수 있다.) 국가 경제를 성공적으로 만드는 여러 가지 복합적인 요인들이 존재하지만, 그 중에서 교육 수준이 높은 노동자들을 보유하고 있다는 점이 가장 중요한 요인이라는 사실은 명백하다.

대부분의 경우 한 나라의 정부가 교육 정책을 결정하고 또한 교육에 투자한다. 최상부에서 내린 교육에 관한 결정은 사회의 최하층으로 내려가는데, 이들이 국민과 국가 경제에 명백한 영향을 미친다. 한 국가를 — 미국을 — 살펴보면, 이전 세기에 미국 전체에 이익을 가져다 주고 미국이 세계 최대의 경제 대국이 될 수 있도록 만든, 교육 정책 상의 몇 가지 요인들을 쉽게 확인할 수 있다. 이러한 요인 중에는 고등학교 교육의 확대, 제대군인 원호법의 시행, 그리고 20세기 후반에 이루어진 중등 교육의 폭발적인 확장 등을 들 수 있다.

20세기 초반에 미국은 이미 경제 대국이었지만, 당시의 교육 체계를 그대로 유지했더라면 결과적으로 미국의 성장은 제한적이었을 것이다. 1900년대 초반 대부분의 사람들은 농업에 종사하고 있었고, 그들의 아이들은 초등 교육만을 이수했다. 예컨대 1900년 5세에서 17세 사이의 아이들 중 71%가 학교에 다녔다. 대다수의 아이들은 초등학교 이상의 교육을 받지 못했다. 1900년에는 불과 62,000명의 학생들만이 미국 고등학교를 졸업했다. 20년 후인 1920년대에 미국 전역에 고등학교를 설립하여 아이들이 학교에 다닐 수 있도록 하자는 운동이 일어났다. 보다 많은 수의 고등학교를 설립하기 위한 이러한 노력은 주로 국가, 주, 그리고 지방 정부에서 비롯되었는데, 이들은 또한 자금을 마련하여 학교를 짓고 교사들을 교육시키고 교사들의 급여가 지급될 수 있도록 했다. 1940년 미국 아이들 중 26%가 고등학교에 등록했으며, 1980년대에는 그 수치가 32%까지 증가했다. 게다가 그러한 수치는 공립 학교에 다니는 아이들만 고려한 것이었으며, 사립 학교에 다니거나 홈스쿨링을 하는 수천 명의 다른 아이들은 여기에 포함되지 않았다.

대학 교육에서도 같은 경향이 나타났다. 20세기 초반에 대학을 다니는 미국인들은 거의 없었다. 1940년 미국의 대학교에 등록한 학생의 수는 200,000명이 채 되지 않았다. 하지만 1940년대에 제2차 세계 대전이 끝난 후 미국 정부는 제대군인 원호법을 시행했다. 이로써 군인과 여성들이 정부에서 지원해 주는 학비로 대학에 다닐 수 있었다. 1940년에는 순식간에 거의 400,000명에 이르는 학생들이 미국의 대학에 등록했다. 20세기 중반 이후, 그 수치는 2000년까지 지속적으로 상승하여, 해마다 백만 명 이상의 미국 학생들이 대학에 입학했다. 1900년대 중반 이후에는 전국에 건설 붐이 일어났다. 수백 개의 대학이 새로 건설되었고, 기존 대학들도 확장되었다. 오늘날 미국의 대학은 학생, 교수진, 그리고 시설의 측면에서 세계 최고라고 널리 간주되고 있으며, 매년 수만 명의 외국인들이 그곳에서 공부를 하기 위해 미국으로 오고 있다.

이러한 교육 확대의 경제적 영향은 여러 분야에서 찾을 수 있다. 첫째, 다수의 고등학교 및 대학 졸업자들이 관리자, 엔지니어, 교사, 의사, 그리고 기업가가 되었다. 이들이 세금을 납부했고, 늘어난 세수로 국가의 교육 시설을 더욱 확대시킬 수 있었다. 고등 교육을 받은 사람들의 수가 증가했다는 사실은 미국이 엔지니어링, 의학, 항공 우주 기술, 그리고 비즈니스를 포함한 여러 영역에서 글로벌 리더가 될 수 있었던 밑바탕이 되었다. 이처럼 교육을 받은 국민들이 없었더라면 미국의 경제는 그러한 수준까지 성장할 수 없었을 것이다. 고등 교육을 크게 강조했던 다른 국가들의 경우도 마찬가지이다. 이러한 국가들은, 특히 유럽과 동북아시아의 국가들은, 교육을 많이 받은 사람들을 보유하면 경제적 번영이 이루어진다는 점을 알고 있다. 반대의 경우, 아프리카의 여러 국가들과 같은 빈곤한 국가들은 어린이들에게 초등 교육을 제공하는 것에도 어려움을 겪고 있다. 그들 중 다수가 절망적인 경제적 상황에 직면해 있다는 점은 놀라운 일이 아니다.

> **WORD REMINDER**
> disparity 불균형   workforce 노동력   lag behind 뒤쳐지다   trickle down 아래로 이동하다   pronounced 뚜렷한, 두드러진   implementation 실행, 이행   GI Bill 제대군인 원호법   secondary education 중등 교육   powerhouse 유력 집단, 세력 집단   take ~ into account ~을 고려하다   serviceman 현역 군인   matriculate 입학하다   aerospace 항공 우주의   bleak 절망적인

## Passage 3 • Botany —————————— p.205

### 식물의 적응

지구에는 다양한 식물 종들이 존재하며, 사실상 이들 모두는 살아가기 위해 세 가지를 필요로 한다: 햇빛, 충분한 물, 그리고 양분을 지닌 토양이다. 안타깝게도 이러한 세 가지 필수 요소들을 — 특히 양분이 많은 토양을 — 모든 곳에서 구할 수 있는 것은 아니다. 예를 들어 토양에 수분이 너무 많거나, 돌이 많거나, 토양이 얼어 있는 경우에는 다수의 식물들이 자랄 수가 없다. 그럼에도 불구하고 일부 식물들은, 혹독하고 살기 힘든 지역에서 생존할 수 있게 해 주는 뿌리 체계를 발달시킴으로써, 그처럼 불리한 환경에 적응해 왔다.

모든 식물들은 관다발 식물이거나 무관다발 식물이다. 대부분의 식물들은 관다발 식물로, 이들은 물, 양분, 그리고 기타 필요한 성분들을 식물의 다양한 부분으로 운반시키는 내부 시스템을 갖추고 있다. 뿌리는 이러한 내부 시스템에 속해 있으며, 특히 예외적으로 습한 환경에서는 뿌리가 공기에 노출되어 있을 수 있지만, 일반적으로는 땅속에서 찾아볼 수 있다. 식물 뿌리의 크기 및 깊이는 식물과 토양의 상태에 따라 다르다. 건조한 지역에서 식물의

뿌리는 물과 양분을 찾아야 하기 때문에 땅속 깊은 곳까지 뻗어 있을 것이다. 몇몇 식물의 뿌리는 지표면에서 60미터 이상 아래로 뻗어있을 수도 있다. 하지만 토양의 윗부분만 얼어 있는 툰드라 지역에서는 식물의 뿌리가 지표면으로부터 겨우 몇 센티미터 정도 아래까지만 뻗어있을 수 있다. 얼음이 어는 상황 이외에도, 툰드라에서 자라는 식물의 뿌리는 지면 아래에 위치한 암석층 때문에 깊게 뻗어나가지 못할 수 있다.

식물은 다양하고 독특한 환경에 직면할 수 있기 때문에 많은 식물들이 특화된 뿌리 체계를 발달시켰다. 사막에서는 나무 뿌리가 지표면 아래 깊은 곳까지 자라는 경우가 많다. 예를 들어 메스커트 나무는 직근이라고 불리는 하나의 길고 곧은 뿌리를 가지고 있는데, 이 뿌리는 땅밑으로 약 30미터까지 뻗어나간다. 수많은 선인장 종을 포함하여 사막의 기타 식물들은, 가능한 넓은 지역에서 수분을 흡수할 수 있도록 수평으로 뻗어나 있는, 길이는 짧지만 넓게 퍼진 뿌리 체계를 갖추고 있다. 소택지, 늪지, 습지, 그리고 호수나 해안가를 포함하여 물이 있는 지역에서는 일부 식물들의 뿌리가 땅 위에서 자란다. 식물학자들은 이를 기근이라고 부른다. 맹그로브 나무와 사이프러스 나무와 같이 기근을 가지고 있는 몇몇 종의 식물들은 생존에 필요한 기체를 대기에서 직접 흡수할 수 있는 것으로 보인다. 마지막으로, 상층부에 양분이 몰려 있는 토양에서 식물들이 자라는 경우, 이들의 뿌리는 일반적으로 지표면을 따라서 자라거나 바로 그 아래에 뻗어있다. (사탕단풍, 은단풍, 그리고 기타 다른 단풍나무 종들은 모두 깊이가 얕은 뿌리 체계를 가지고 있는 나무들이다.) 비옥한 토양과 충분한 물이 존재하는 환경에서도 몇몇 식물들은 특이한 방법으로 적응해 왔다. 예를 들어 겨우살이풀은 수분과 양분을 흡수하기 위해 다른 식물에 달라붙는 뿌리 체계를 보유한 기생 식물이다.

식물이 자라는 가장 혹독한 지역 중 하나는 북극의 툰드라 지대이다. 툰드라 지역에서는 깊은 곳까지 땅이 완전히 얼어붙어 있는 경우가 많다. 해빙된 토양에도 양분은 거의 없는데, 그 이유는 토양에서 질소를 생성시키는 박테리아의 수가 적기 때문이다. 게다가 강한 바람 때문에 식물이 지면에 붙어 있기가 힘들다. 그 결과 툰드라 지역에서 자라는 식물들은 키가 작고, 땅에 붙어서 자라며, 뿌리의 깊이도 얕다. 그럼에도 불구하고 이들의 뿌리는 상당히 강해서 바람이 부는 상황에서도 식물을 고정시킬 수 있다. 또한 척박한 토양으로부터 수분과 양분을 끌어내는 능력이 탁월하다. 몇 개월의 여름 동안 지면으로부터 상당히 깊은 곳까지 대지가 해빙되는데, 이로 인해 식물의 뿌리가 보다 많은 양분에 접근할 수 있다. 이들의 뿌리 체계 덕분에 툰드라의 식물들은 날씨가 얼어붙는 상황에서도 생존할 수 있다.

때때로 몇몇 식물의 뿌리 체계는 환경을 변화시켜 다른 식물들에게 보다 적합한 환경을 만들어 주기도 한다. 하와이의 섬들이 처음 형성되었을 때 이 섬들은 주로 단단한 화산암으로 덮여 있었다. 그처럼 혹독한 환경에서는 식물이 거의 자랄 수 없었다. 하지만 강한 바람이 식물의 씨앗들을 바다 먼 곳으로 보내 이 섬들에 쌓이게 만들었다. 이러한 식물 중 하나인 오히아 레후아 나무는 독특한 뿌리 체계를 가지고 있어서 뿌리가 화산암 지대의 깊은 곳까지 뻗어나갈 수 있는데, 화산 폭발 당시 빠르게 흐르는 용암에 의해 만들어진 빈 공간인 이곳 용암 동굴에는 양분과 수분이 풍부하다. 이들 용암 동굴의 내부에 수분이 모임으로써 뿌리들은 이를 이용해 나무를 생존시킬 수 있었다. 시간이 흐르면서 이러한 뿌리들이 용암을 부수기 시작했다. 보다 많은 나무들이 자람에 따라 단단했던 용암은 비옥한 토양으로 변했고, 그 결과 하와이의 섬들은 오늘날 식물이 무성한 열대의 낙원이 되었다.

**WORD REMINDER**

vascular 관의   channel (물 등을) 나르다, 운반하다   mesquite 메스커트 나무   taproot 직근, 주근, 곧은 뿌리   bog 소택지, 늪지대   swamp 늪지   marsh 습지   aerating root 기근   mistletoe 겨우살이   parasitic 기생하는, 기생의   thaw 녹다   lava tube 용암 동굴   lush 풀이 많은, 무성한, 우거진

# MEMO

# MEMO

# MEMO

# TOEFL MAP

# ACTUAL TEST

New TOEFL Edition

Reading **1**